MACDONALD GUIDE TO
BUYING ANTIQUE FURNITURE

MACDONALD GUIDE TO

BUYING ANTIQUE FURNITURE

Rachael Feild

Macdonald

A Macdonald Book
© Brooks Stephenson Publishing Ltd, 1986

First published in Great Britain in 1984
by Macdonald & Co (Publishers) Ltd

This edition published in Great Britain in 1986 by
Macdonald & Co (Publishers) Ltd, London and Sydney

A member of BPCC plc

British Library Cataloguing in Publication Data

Feild, Rachel
 Macdonald guide to buying antique furniture — New ed.
 1. Furniture — Collectors and collecting
 2. Furniture — Prices
 I. Title II. Feild, Rachel. Buying antique furniture
 749′.1′0294   NK2240

 ISBN 0-356-12619-6

Filmset by MS Filmsetting Limited, Frome, Somerset

Printed and bound in Great Britain by Purnell
Book Production Ltd, Paulton, Bristol
A member of BPCC plc

Macdonald & Co (Publishers) Ltd
Greater London House
Hampstead Road
London NW1 7QX

Contents

Acknowledgments

Grateful thanks are due to the following for their considerable generosity in providing illustrations:

Sotheby Parke Bernet and Company, London.

Sotheby, Pulborough, West Sussex.

Sotheby, Chester.

Phillips, Son and Neale, London.

Lawrence Fine Art, Crewkerne, Somerset.

Reindeer Antiques, nr. Towcester, Northamptonshire.

Phillips and Harris, London.

The National Magazine Company and Church Street Galleries for the jacket illustrations.

The Consumers' Association for line illustrations taken from *The Which? Guide to Buying Antiques Furniture* (revised edition, 1983).

Nancy A. Smith for line illustrations inspired by *Old Furniture: Understanding the Craftsman's Art*, (Bobbs-Merrill, New York, 1975).

The Bridgeman Art Library for the main picture of the Victorian button-back chair.

The author's particular thanks are due to William Cook for his time, trouble, patient help and correction in the compiling of this book.

The History of English Furniture: an introduction

In about 1755, when the road from London to Oxford was at last wider than a single carriage and passable rather than navigable through axle-deep fords and potholes, a gentleman of means refurbished his old family manor house, added a neat Georgian wing to the old Jacobean stone building and completely refurnished it with the latest, most fashionable furniture from a London cabinet-maker by the name of Thomas Chippendale. His wife had tired of London life and wanted to bring up their three children in the peace and fresh air of Oxfordshire.

Most of the fine old panelling from the original house found a place in the fourteenth century private chapel, all that remained of the previous monastery which originally occupied the site. Some of the oak chests and coffers were useful to store vestments and altar furnishings, and several heavy, high-backed oak chairs also found a place in the chapel. The oak draw table, which once held pride of place in the parlour, was dismantled and laid across the beams in the granary. Once a year it was taken out and used for harvest suppers and occasionally it was brought out for al fresco meals on the stone terrace, when there was an occasion for celebration. The remainder of the furniture which could not be used in the servants' quarters was distributed among the tenant farmers, and some of it even found its way to the local inn.

Thirty years later his son, inheriting the comfortable estate, threw out all the old-fashioned furnishings and, at the wishes of his wife, sent for the very latest design books and pattern books published by Mr Hepplewhite and Mr Sheraton. He added a second wing to balance up the facade of the house and to accommodate his

Seventeenth-century oak refectory table.

growing family, had all his new furniture made by an excellent cabinet-maker in Oxford and filled the house with light and colour. A big dining table was installed in the new-fangled 'dining room' and the hotch-potch of smaller tables, at which guests had been accustomed to dine, were moved to suitable places about the house.

The seats of Mr Chippendale's fine ribband-back mahogany chairs were far too wide for the new dining table and for a while they were put to good use in the library in the new wing, and in various other rooms in the house. But eventually they too were replaced with pretty painted chairs. Not wanting to part with the old mahogany chairs completely, the head of the house sent for the estate carpenter, who cut down their legs and added narrow shelves to the top of their backs. Then they were removed to the private

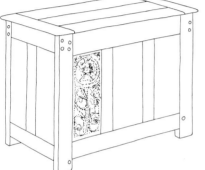

Frame and panel construction.

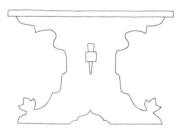

Trestle table showing the tusk tenon.

Panel-back chair with punch-hole decoration.

chapel where, with their backs to the altar they made excellent kneelers for the upper servants of the house, who until now had remained standing throughout morning prayers.

Those fine Chippendale ribband-backs are still in the chapel today, and people who see them exclaim with horror at the vandalism done to such fine antiques. In a way they are right, and in a way they are completely missing the point that antiques, when they were first made, were nothing more than pieces of furniture to be used, replaced and discarded with the changing tastes and fashions of succeeding generations.

The Reasons for Change

Taste and fashion alone, however, are not the only reasons for changing shapes and designs. Some understanding of the way people lived and how they used furniture helps to explain the difference in each period. A very basic knowledge of the materials available, the methods of construction, the tools available and the skills of the craftsmen who made the furniture is far more helpful than a study of the pieces in isolation. Furniture, however grand or humble, has a function as well as a design, and in its proper context is simply a reflection of the changing way of life down the centuries.

In England, the principal timber used for furniture-making, from earliest times until the end of the sixteenth century, was oak. It grew in abundance, and large tracts of countryside were covered in rich, impenetrable forests. As England's staple trade of wool increased, land was cleared to graze more flocks of sheep, and oak was cheap and plentiful. Houses were built with frames of oak beams and furniture was made from the smaller pieces of the felled forest giants.

Pieces of furniture which were anything else but plainly functional could be counted on the fingers of one hand: great beds, court cupboards, important chairs for feudal lords, and massive tables for communal eating. For the rest of their sparse furnishings, there were stools and benches, and caskets and coffers to hold treasured possessions. The Elizabethan love of colour was confined to painted furniture, and textiles: embroidery, Turkey work,

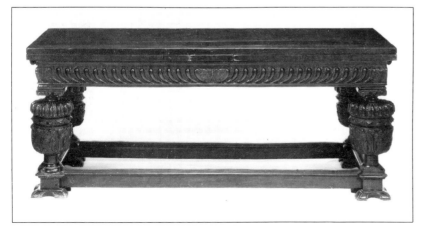

Tudor draw table with fine bolection moulding to the legs.

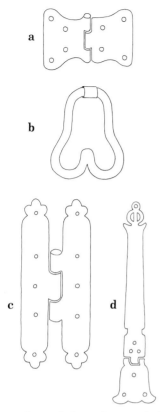

Iron or brass fittings characteristic of early oak pieces – (a) butterfly hinge, (b) loop handle, (c) cockshead hinge, (d) strap hinge.

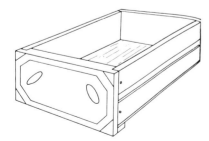

Hung drawer with side grooves for runners.

tapestries and stump work. The great bed stood in the centre of the house, draped with rich stuffs, covered in velvet, embroidered cushions and cloth. Most of the craftsmen, the stonemasons, carpenters, carvers and wood-workers, were centred on the monasteries, for the Church was the most important builder and the greatest influence in culture and design. Most elements of design were derived from the stonemasons' art, and their influence is plainly visible in the carved oak panelling which enriched both religious and secular buildings.

The Limitations of Oak

Oak had its limitations. It was coarse-grained and could only be joined by dowelling with pegs, and with mortise-and-tenon joints or, in the same way as panelling, with an outer frame into which an inner panel was slotted. England's carpenters, joiners and ship-wrights knew all there was to know about this native wood: its strengths and weaknesses, its tendency to move and shrink, the different ways of splitting and sawing it to make the most of its natural properties, and the importance of well-seasoned timber. Within these limitations, and the tools available, which were few and basic, the panel-backed chair and the joint stool were the least clumsy pieces of furniture that could be made. Lathe-turning, with the ancient pole-lathe used by bowl-makers, was used to a limited extent, but it was not very efficient for anything much larger than arm-supports and the front legs of chairs. In terms of design, England followed the rest of Europe, and most of her culture stemmed from Italy and France. The Reformation did more than isolate England politically. It broke up the communities of craftsmen centred on the monasteries and cut England's cultural ties with Europe.

By the end of the sixteenth century, England was running short of timber. Vast quantities of forest had been cleared and used up, great stands of timber had been cut down to make charcoal to smelt metals, make glass, and fire furnaces, as well as to build ships to drive the Spanish fleets out of the English Channel. Trading fleets were issued with instructions to return with timber for ship building and suitable woods for masts. The wool fleets returned from Flanders with bricks in ballast to build houses, for in some parts of the country there was no oak left to build houses with timber frames. Paradoxically, England's self-importance was growing and was reflected in more and more massive pieces of furniture. Great beds were even more extravagantly draped with velvets, embroidery and silks, and court cupboards displayed gold, silver, pewter and, a recent import from the Far East – porcelain.

Flemish craftsmen came to England and brickmaking, glass-making and metalworking at last began to flourish. Brick-built houses with glazed windows meant larger, lighter rooms, more space and a more civilized way of living. England, cut off from Catholic Europe, traded with the Baltic ports and merchant fleets returned with deal, softwood and 'wainscot oak'. The East India

Company's ships brought ebony and ivory inlaid panels to be incorporated into coffers and caskets; skilled craftsmen from the Protestant Netherlands brought new methods of furniture construction, lathe-turning with treadle-lathes, and new designs and shapes of furniture.

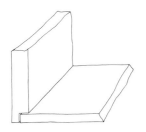

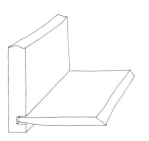

Left: *Simple rebate joins typical of early oak pieces.*
Below: *Mortise-and-tenon joint with dowel or peg.*
Right: *Seventeenth century drop handle and circular backplate.*

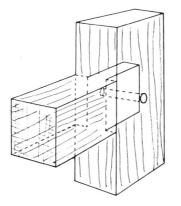

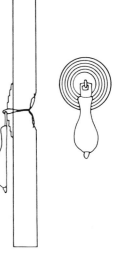

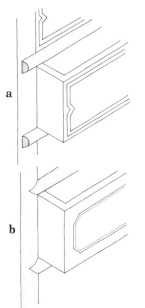

a

b

Left: *Characteristic seventeenth century drawer mouldings – (a) half-round moulding on drawer rails with a fielded panel, (b) mitred moulding with coffered panel.*

a

b

Left: *Some seventeenth-century leg styles – (a) turned and fluted, (b) turned and tapered.*
Below: *Tudor bolection moulding.*

Brief Baroque: a Prelude to the Civil War

There was more than a hint of Catholicism about the first two Stuart kings, with their ancient history of alliances with France. Taste, still greatly influenced by the Court, swung wholeheartedly towards the baroque at the beginning of the seventeenth century. It is a period largely ignored by the popular histories of English furniture because it was so out of line with anything that had gone

Commonwealth-style back-stool chairs.

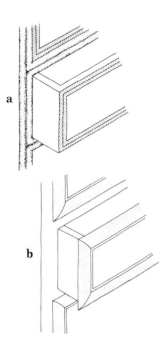

Late seventeenth-century drawer mouldings—(a) featherbanding (b) applied lip moulding.

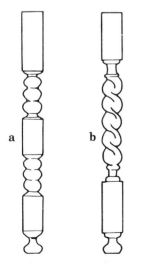

Common late seventeenth century leg styles – (a) bobbin-and-reel, (b) twist, or swash, turned.

before. Rich, ostentatious and lavish, the period falls between the so-called 'Age of Oak' and the 'Age of Walnut'. Chests were raised on ornate stands, gilded, silvered or even completely covered with beaten, repoussé sheets of silver. The chests or cabinets themselves were ornately made with black and gold lacquered panels. Scrolls, curves and carving were all gilded, beds were swagged in rich drapes, often with plumes like jousting pavilions. Angels and cherubs decorated ceilings, now heavy with decorative plasterwork and scenes of painted piety. Briefly, England followed the rich baroque taste of Catholic Europe before the glitter was enshrouded by the Civil War.

Accidents of History: the Great Fire of London

By the time Charles II returned to England in 1660 there were already many cabinet-makers and metal-workers from the Netherlands working in England, and a considerable number of Huguenots who had fled to safety from religious persecution. It only needed the impetus of Court fashion for the style which had lain dormant during the Commonwealth to become apparent. The change might have been slower if it had not been for the Great Fire of London of 1666 which destroyed all the old Tudor buildings in the city. In their place rose well-proportioned stone and brick-built town houses, designed by Sir Christopher Wren. Instead of dark, small-windowed houses with rooms roughly divided up with wooden partitions, these new houses each had entrance halls, staircases, and two or three separate rooms on each floor, all of them needing furniture. The houses were taller, too, rising three or four stories.

Even as late as this enlightened period, most furniture of any style was only to be found in a few large mansions owned by the aristocracy. Wren's houses had pine panelling instead of dark oak, and ceilings were decorated with plasterwork, but these were both part of the architect's design and had little to do with any overall concept of what the finished interior should look like. There was still little idea of designing furniture, other than adding decorative surfaces to flat-fronted cabinets and chests, and adding flat curves to the stretchers of small tables and to the stands for decorative cabinets.

These new houses needed a different type of furniture so far not made in England, except for the very rich. Chests with drawers were needed to store clothes and linen where old oak chests were no longer suitable. Small tables were necessary for the many different rooms, chairs were needed instead of stools, cupboards and dressers for storing and displaying porcelain and tableware, shelves for books, were all needed to replace the massive court cupboards of Tudor days. The Protectorate's Letter Office, originally for Government use only, had been extended to carry letters for the public, and there was a growing demand for writing furniture for an increasing number of literate households.

The social order had changed since the days before the Civil War. Whereas before whole households had lived together under one roof, sharing most things, certainly using rooms indiscriminately for all sorts of purposes, people began to separate off within those households. In towns, many servants lived out in appalling conditions, but 'free' from their masters. Women segregated

William and Mary period brass fittings – (a) S-hinge, (b) escutcheon.

William and Mary period brass drawer handle.

Early eighteenth century kneehole desk.

themselves in Wren's new town houses, using withdrawing rooms so that the men of the world could conduct their business undisturbed. The fashion in clothes meant that more care was taken with the daily 'toilette' of both sexes. Dressing tables, dressing glasses, indeed entire dressing rooms were needed, with separate clothes presses and chests of drawers for clothes which needed more care and attention.

The Beginning of the 'Age of Walnut'

Not all the changes in style and fashion were due solely to Charles II and his Continental tastes, or his retinue of Court painters, silversmiths and cabinet-makers. Some of the skills were already available in England. The new trade of 'cabinet-making' was already established, for English craftsmen had been incorporating into furniture fine inlaid lacquer panels imported from the East since the beginning of the century, and had discovered that the old frame-and-panel method of construction was not suitable for this purpose. England had already gone to war with the Dutch in 1652. No matter what the quarrels of the crowned heads of Europe were, the battle was now mercantile, with England contesting the sea lanes against the waning power of the Dutch.

Charles II reopened trade with Spain and France and, four years after the Restoration, the English were again fighting sea battles with the Dutch. Good timber was hard to come by and oak was reserved for ship building. Walnut, a native tree in France and Spain, began to filter into England's ports. The art of veneering, marquetry and parquetry had been demonstrated with great skill by Dutch craftsmen long before it was used in England. No doubt because their country was very short of indigenous timber and walnut was expensive to import, the Dutch had learned how to use it to maximum effect. Now that England was in a similar situation, with oak scarce and a growing demand for good furniture from the rising merchant class, it was almost inevitable that these new skills should be adopted, particularly once the Restoration had put an end to plain and simple Puritan ideas. The skills, the tools and the timber for swash-turning and twist-turning – used by the Spanish decades before – were now all available in England.

The style of post-Restoration English furniture was less flamboyant, the designs more muted than the previous period of baroque richness before the Civil War. Stands for chests were made of twist-turned walnut instead of heavy carved and gilded woods. Chairs were made with cane backs and cane seats of imported rattan, and walnut could be twist-turned and carved in far more detail than oak ever could be. The cherubs reappeared, particularly on cane-backed chairs where the 'boyes and crowne' was one of the most popular designs of the Restoration, celebrating the return of the monarchy and harking back to the angelic decoration so characteristic of early Stuart Baroque.

Much of the English furniture of this period is not very easy to identify or distinguish. The design looks foreign, the materials are

Flemish scroll on a chair arm.

Late seventeenth century oyster veneer: four pieces cut from the cross-sections of branches.

Opposite: *Chest-on-stand with fine oyster veneering.*

unfamiliar, and much of it was made by Dutch, Flemish and Huguenot craftsmen living and working in England. Only textiles and embroidery maintained a thread of continuity, and caskets, jewel boxes, upholstery, cushions and stumpwork caskets remained distinctly English. Chairs and stools with cane seats and panels, chests of drawers in marquetry, veneered cabinets and escritoires were all made on the Continent and, in particular, in the Netherlands during the same period. Inlaid floral panels and lacquer panels were popular in both countries, and both their trading fleets returned laden with silks and porcelain from the East Indies. Construction techniques were different: English chair-makers on the whole remained faithful to the traditional pegged and dowelled mortise-and-tenon joints, while on the Continent chairs were ornate but flimsily constructed with separate parts pegged together and extra stability provided by rather too many stretchers between the carved legs. Chests and cabinets were made with solid wood carcases with flat surfaces suitable for veneering, using stopped dovetails on drawer fronts. The English used close-grained yellow pine imported from the Baltic for carcases, while the Dutch used pine and softwoods with a coarser grain from more temperate European forests. Most of the softwood in the British Isles grew in Scotland, which was still feuding with England until 1707. Oak furniture of the period is much easier to identify, and has

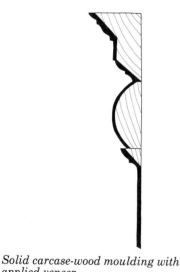

Solid carcase-wood moulding with applied veneer.

Flat-front chest of drawers with veneering and inlay.

a continuity which is lacking in grander pieces. The English also used oak with some success for twist-turned furniture, as well as elm and beech, which was usually painted.

The 'William and Mary' period is almost as difficult to identify. With a Dutch king on the throne, England's cultural influences were even more strongly reinforced by the Netherlands, not least because once again England was at war with France and all trade with that country was forbidden. English furniture-makers still lacked a style of their own – the serpentine-shaped stretchers, the cup and cover shape of table legs, arm supports and chair legs were all Dutch in origin, as were the chests of drawers and cabinets-on-stands decorated with inlaid panels of marquetry. Even the brass furniture mounts were imported from the Netherlands because England's brass industry was still not properly established.

English furniture was more restrained than the over-decorated Dutch pieces, and already there seemed to be a growing preference for using plain woods for veneer, relying on the figuring and grain alone with little embellishment or decoration. The style had been developing ever since the Restoration and coalesced in the dozen years from 1689 to 1702 when William of Orange ruled England – with Mary as his queen for the first six years, and alone for the next six. But it was the end of an era more than a beginning.

Walnut: First Signs of an English Style

Underneath the superficial dependence on foreign countries for its culture, a different England was slowly developing – an England of important provincial towns and ports, of growing industry and technical skills, and of an established middle class which did not necessarily take its lead from the Court. It could be argued that the 'English style' had its roots in the Civil War, with Royalist families toning down their extravagant tastes and the powerful new men from the Protectorate desiring an outward show of wealth and importance without ties to discredited kings or foreign countries.

The brass industry was at last established, centred on Birmingham, and England ceased to import furniture mounts from the Netherlands. The glass industry was independent of either Venetian or Netherlands influence, and Ravenscroft was making English glass with a whole new concept of baluster stems which were

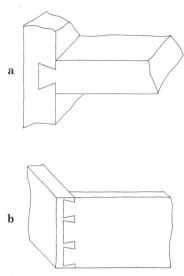

Stopped, or lapped, dovetail join for, (a) carcase construction, (b) drawer construction on veneered furniture.

Oyster veneer marquetry with inlaid holly wood stringing.

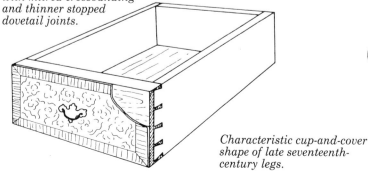

Early eighteenth-century construction with veneered drawer front with mitred crossbanding and thinner stopped dovetail joints.

Characteristic cup-and-cover shape of late seventeenth-century legs.

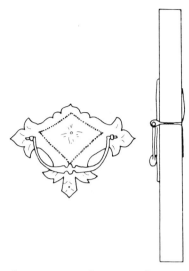

Late seventeenth century drawer handle secured by tangs through the backplate and drawer front.

instantly seized upon for adaptation by furniture-makers, and chair-makers in particular. Having turned out set upon set of cheap cane-backed chairs, they had reduced the construction to simply pegging the pieces together and relying entirely on increasing the height of chair backs in an attempt to improve the scale and make them suitable for higher, more spacious rooms. Window glass was being made in great quantities, so that fine large windows became the rule rather than the exception. Cabinet-makers incorporated chests of drawers instead of stands into the bases of display cabinets and writing furniture in order to raise them to a suitable height for the high-ceilinged, many-windowed rooms, with their elaborate decorative plasterwork.

From this period, a different air began to permeate the design of English houses and their contents. In their search for an architectural style which would be entirely individual, followers of Christopher Wren turned to classical Greek and Roman buildings for inspiration. William Kent (1686-1748), the great exponent of early Palladian architecture, designed some important furniture for great houses, but he reverted to the old practice of borrowing from the stonemasons for his designs, and the results were overpoweringly grand and monumental, quite unsuitable for any building other than those on the grand scale.

England's power as a trading nation was growing, just as that of the Dutch was declining. As a result, many things began to change. Roads and transport improved, the English gentry built new houses on their long-neglected country estates, communications between provincial cities and the capital became easier, and the number of people able to afford good furniture increased steadily. Display furniture, wall furniture, secretaires and bookcases were the first notable pieces to be designed with the interiors of houses specifically in mind. They are, in fact, simply indoor versions of the shapes of windows, with architraves and classical pediments, glazed doors and architecturally proportioned bases. Free-standing furniture was more difficult, and much of it was still based on traditional country designs, such as gate-legged folding tables, small side tables, and a more comfortable version of the high-backed oak settle – the wing chair. Settees were elongated chairs, and daybeds were based on the same idea. After sacrificing strength and stability to fashion, chair-makers emerged with one factor which was to govern their design for the next 50 years – the outward curve of the 'knees' of chair legs with Flemish scrolls.

As Inigo Jones incorporated the curved classical arch on exterior facades, so it was repeated indoors, and the rounded shape was incorporated into the pediments of secretaires, secretaire-bookcases and display cabinets. England had fallen in love with 'chinoiserie', and by the beginning of the eighteenth century japanned and lacquered furniture was immensely popular. Mirrored glass began to be made in England and tall pier glasses were added to the repertoire of wall furniture, designed to stand on the piers between windows.

The abrupt end to the fashion for lacquered Oriental panels at the beginning of the eighteenth century was due to jealous cabinet-makers finally putting a stop to imported inlaid work and taking over the entire field of veneer and inlay. Oriental lacquer was replaced with 'English lacquer' built up on pine carcases, sometimes on a layer of gesso, a pliable plaster-of-Paris substance. The tall Queen Anne secretaires in 'English lacquer' are essentially English, and the skill and artistry of their interior fittings show just how much English cabinet-makers had advanced in technique and craftsmanship in a bare two decades.

'William and Mary' to 'Queen Anne': Evolution not Revolution

It was a combination of many different factors which produced the apparently abrupt change from the end of the seventeenth century and the beginning of the eighteenth. The change did not occur overnight – it simply came together at a particular period when there was a need for curves to break up strictly classical, mathematical shapes and designs, coupled with an overriding desire for furniture to fill the elegant, empty spaces of Palladian-style houses. Add to these factors the happy coincidence that English furniture-makers now had tools and skills available and were wholly independent of any foreign workers other than those who had been settled for more than a generation in England, and change and innovation became inevitable.

For all but a few months of Queen Anne's reign (1702-14), England was at war, trying to prevent France and Spain from uniting. In this she failed, but she made it clear to the rest of the world that she was now a power to be reckoned with. The Duke of Marlborough was given Blenheim Palace as a battle honour, and the state of national pride can be gauged by its towering splendour. But there was still neither furniture to fill this marvellous palace, nor pattern books for cabinet-makers or chair-makers. England's craftsmen improvized, adding scrolls, curls and classical motifs in gilt gesso to furniture which was designed more for display than for use. The curving cabriole leg emerged in embryo on pier tables and chairs in an attempt to harmonize with the elaborate plasterwork ceilings, architectural mouldings, wall-furniture and mirrors. William Kent had used the hoofed foot of classical mythology on massive pier tables and, coupled with the rounded arches and broken pediments of exterior design, furniture-makers began to make furniture based on this classical 'cyma curve'.

The grander the house and the richer its furnishings, the more uncomfortable it was to live in. From the very beginning of their existence, these marvellous eighteenth century stately homes had a separate wing in which the family lived, while the rest of the state apartments and reception rooms were kept for occasional use, and as a conspicuous display of wealth. Whether the owners liked it or not, stately homes were open to the public who considered they had a right to share in the nation's pride and riches, and parties of

Queen Anne bureau-bookcase.

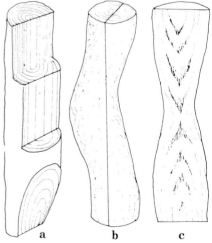

Wood cut at different angles produces differently figured veneers – (a) and (b) oyster veneer, (c) flame grain.

Early eighteenth-century gilt and gesso centre table.

Development of the cyma curve.

Right: *Cabriole leg, showing the different girth of timber for (a) the shallow carving more characteristic of Victorian and Edwardian reproductions, (b) the broader width needed for the deep carving of the eighteenth century.*

a   b

The cyma curve continued in the fiddle-back chair.

visitors knocked on the door at all hours, demanding to be shown the state apartments. They would have been surprised at the relatively humble furnishings of the private apartments, where the rooms were still full of a clutter of old-fashioned chairs and tables, old beds, practical chests of drawers, dressing tables, lowboys and tallboys, mostly made in plainly veneered woods or in solid walnut.

Extremely elegant but fragile gilt gesso chairs with curved legs inspired chair-makers to attempt the same curving line in solid wood, using the spring of the natural grain and dispensing with stretchers. At first they combined it with a type of hoofed foot, producing the first version of the 'cabriole' or 'capriole' leg, but

Typical construction of a Queen Anne spoonback with arms.

Side view of the cyma curve as expressed in the spoon back.

soon replaced it with the ball-and-claw foot. Remembering the fashionable craze for lacquer, japanning and chinoiserie, it is likely that the inspiration for this very typical feature of eighteenth-century English furniture came from the Chinese dragon's claw holding a pearl, rather than any of the other possible sources with which it has been associated.

The curving shape of chair legs demanded a corresponding curve to the back, and the bend-back or spoon-back chair, so typical of the Queen Anne period, at last emerged. The wide, comfortably upholstered seat and curving back conformed to the shape of the body and was eminently suitable for the spreading, stiffened skirts of gentlemen's coats and the ever-widening skirts of ladies' voluminous dresses. There was now a definite shape to which all furniture could conform, which was not only good-looking but practical and, above all, comfortable. It could stand up to any amount of use, it was beautifully made and finished, and at the same time it graced its surroundings. It was almost as if it suddenly dawned on cabinet-makers and furniture-makers that chairs and tables, display cabinets, secretaires and bookcases could be used as well as admired.

Old-fashioned gate-legged tables were slowly replaced with sleeker drop-leaf tables; there were wing chairs to draw up to the fire, comfortably upholstered wide-seated dining chairs, well-made writing desks and side tables. Meals were still taken at separate tables seating four or six. After the ladies and gentlemen left the room (not yet called a dining room), servants cleared away and ranged the chairs and tables·around the wall again, leaving the middle of the room empty except for a decorative centre table, on which stood a few chosen pieces of Oriental porcelain.

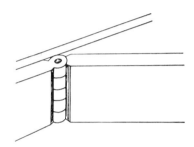

Wooden hinge with five knuckles for eighteenth-century drop-leaf table construction.

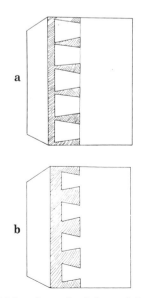

(a) hand-cut single-lapped dovetail, (b) machine-cut equivalent.

Queen Anne cabriole-legged arm chair.

The Georgians: Mahogany and Chippendale

The Court's sphere of influence diminished still further when the first of the Hanoverians succeeded to the throne in 1714. George I spoke very little, and then only in German. He and his Court kept themselves to themselves and the country more or less ran itself. For all that, the first Georgian contribution to the English way of life was a landmark in change, both for tradition and for furniture. Dining *à l'Allemande* or *à la Berline* meant dining at a long table, served by footmen, with matching sets of dining chairs, glasses, table services and cutlery, a civilized way of behaving which had so far escaped the English.

Attention was soon drawn to the North, and to Scotland, plotting with France to restore the Jacobites. French influence had diminished little since Scotland was united with England at the beginning of the century, but it was by no means the only important factor during this period. William Adam, architect and builder, was designing classical houses with well-planned interiors, for the Government and for the rich and influential families in Scotland and the North. It could be said that all the major influences on architecture and design which established the 'Georgian style' came from the North. The Duke of Northumberland, the Lascelles family, and many recently elevated families without titles but with a great deal of money, influence and culture, patronized William

Adam and his sons as well as another, younger architect – James Paine – who was working on Nostell Priory. Chippendale's father had already designed a suite of furniture for Nostell Priory with proper regard for the room in which it was to be used. There were chairs with a single wide vase splat, cabriole legs and ball-and-claw feet, adaptations of earlier designs for chairs, and daybeds with cane seats, scrolled legs and pad feet.

Thomas Chippendale the elder (1718-79) was the first person to grasp the necessity of designing a whole new range of furniture and interior designs suitable for the new, gracious Palladian-style houses, and for the additions and alterations to existing mansions. The Duke of Northumberland owned Syon House, on the Thames just outside London, and when William Adam's son Robert returned to England from his Grand Tour of Europe, the duke brought him together with Thomas Chippendale to work on the house.

Chippendale, meanwhile, had moved to London and opened his workshops in St Martin's Lane. In 1754 he published his famous *Director* or, to give it its full title, *The Gentleman and Cabinet Maker's Director,* the first comprehensive book of furniture designs ever to be produced. It was not confined to 'salon' furniture, nor was it solely for the rich. It encompassed the whole range of articles which was needed to furnish the houses of the middle classes as well as the mansions of the aristocracy. He supplied, from his workshops, furnishing materials, upholstered furniture, curtains, cottons, calicoes and even wallpaper, as well as a complete range of furniture. His designs furnished state apartments and middle-class parlours, and could be used by any furniture-maker who could interpret a drawing which gave constructional details.

Chippendale's whole enterprize was considerably advanced by what might have been a serious body blow to English furniture-makers. In about 1730 the French prohibited all further exports of walnut, the main wood for furniture-making in England. For a while, Virginia walnut was substituted for the fine French wood, but it was not good enough to use for veneering and new timber was urgently needed. Lacquered furniture and painted furniture could be made in beech and in pine, but the art of veneering depended on finely figured woods with a good, close grain. Baltic pine was still the principal carcase wood for walnut veneering, although English cabinet-makers used oak for drawers because they understood it better and could rely on its behaviour.

The first recorded use of mahogany for furniture was in 1584 when Phillip II of Spain had a suite of furniture made for the Escorial palace. At that time it would almost certainly have been brought back from South America, but trading fleets from England soon discovered that it was indigenous to Cuba, San Domingo and Honduras. The first mahogany used in England may have been imported from Colonial America where it had already been used for furniture-making, or direct from British possessions in the East and West Indies. There seems to have been a random selection of timber in the first cargoes, some good and with a beautiful grain, some less

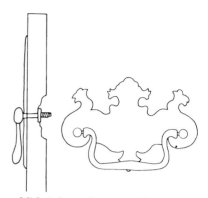

Mid-eighteenth century, brass, bat's wing backplate.

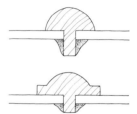

Astragal-moulded glazing bars; the upper profile is the outer part.

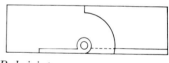

Rule joint.

Mid-eighteenth century drawer construction with cockbead moulding and thin dovetails.

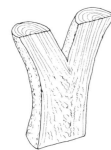

Flame-grain veneer cut from the fork of a branch.

The carcase construction of a mid-eighteenth century chest of drawers showing the veneering applied to the top, and the hidden dovetailing.

Right: 'Chinese Chippendale' folding card or tea table.

Detail of hidden, or mitred, dovetailing.

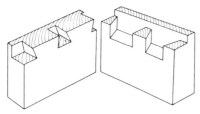

interesting for use as veneers, but still remarkably close-grained and of great girth and strength.

Although Thomas Chippendale is known to have made furniture in walnut, he clearly preferred mahogany, for it could be deeply carved, fretted, pierced, laminated, used in solid or as veneer, and with its great strength could be used for sweeps of unbroken polished surfaces for double-height furniture as well as for a whole range of new construction techniques. English furniture-makers quickly discovered which qualities produced the finest veneers and, once a regular supply began to be imported, used flame-grained and Cuban curl, as well as woods from San Domingo and Cuba for veneers and the duller varieties from Honduras for solid work and for carcase-wood. Carcase construction changed with such fine-grained amenable timber to work with: concealed dovetails and mitred dovetails could be cut safely without risk of splitting, and mahogany could be cut and sawn across the grain to produce undulating curves and serpentine shapes, either as carcases, or in solid wood.

Thomas Chippendale bridges the half-century between the first curving furniture and cabriole legs of the Queen Anne period and the last years of walnut, with its multiplicity of purpose-made small furniture for tea-drinking and card-playing, to the classical disciplines of the Adam brothers. It is interesting to note in passing that even as late as 1754 when the first edition of the *Director* was published, there were no designs for dining tables or dining-room

furniture, although, as the Georgians soon discovered, mahogany was perfect for great sweeps of gleaming polished wood. Separate rooms reserved solely for eating were still an innovation, and large dining tables and chair sets did not come into general use until as late as the 1780s.

Apart from his concept of decorating the entire interior of a house, or providing a complete scheme for a suite of rooms, and publishing his *Director* (to be used by furniture-makers all over England), there is one other special attribute which Chippendale possessed and which was lacking in all his successors. He worked closely with the architect James Paine and with the Adam brothers, and his knowledge of classical architecture was wide and sound. His designs were based on classical proportions, and the decoration was precise, never degenerating into meaningless embellishment.

From the publication of the *Director*, it can be said that English furniture depended more on the whim of fashion and less on techniques, timbers and methods of construction. From the mid-eighteenth century onwards, steam power was harnessed to machines, and many processes which had been difficult to achieve with limited tools and manpower alone were possible to produce for a far wider market. George Hepplewhite, (*d*.1786), for instance, began his career as an apprentice to a furniture-manufacturer, Gillows of Lancaster, rather than to a craftsman cabinet-maker. Gillows, incidentally, made considerable quantities of furniture from designs in Chippendale's *Director*, adapting them for production by new methods to reach a wider market, and simplifying them where they would be too costly to produce.

It is possible that George Hepplewhite was originally trained as a chair-maker, for it is here that his designs are original and show a sound understanding of construction and the mathematical principles of stress. Most of the rest of his furniture, while undoubtedly exhibiting great flair for the decorative, was not particularly original. But this was not the point of any of the books of furniture design from Chippendale onwards. Hepplewhite's *Cabinet Maker and Upholsterer's Guide* (1788), Thomas Shearer's *Cabinet Maker's London Book of Prices* (1794) and *Designs for Household Furniture*, Sheraton's *Cabinet Maker and Upholsterer's Drawing Book* (1791-94) were aimed at a specific market. Their object was to provide designs for the hundreds of cabinet-makers, furniture-makers and chair-makers who were working all over the British Isles, making furniture for the average home.

Fashion became the principal motive for change. Whereas Chippendale brought mahogany furniture to a peak of design, Hepplewhite chose to promote an altogether lighter style, riding on the back of Robert Adam and his followers, and interpreting strict classical motifs rather more loosely, so that Hepplewhite's swags, acanthus leaves and strings of husks were more romantic, more reminiscent of ribbons and flowers, of Fragonard and the pastoral. But then taste had become a far more feminine affair than in the early days of the Georgians. Mahogany, with its almost masculine

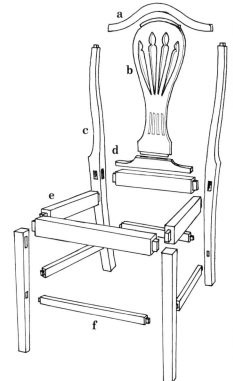

The construction of a typical mid-eighteenth-century chair – (a) crest rail, (b) splat, (c) side rail, (d) shoepiece, (e) seat rails, (f) stretchers.

Construction of a mid-eighteenth century drawer, with stamped brass backplate and brass bail handle.

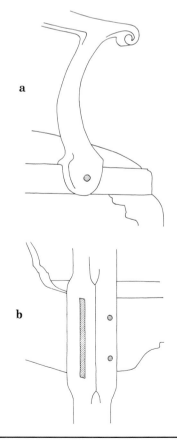

Details of eighteenth-century chair construction – (a) screw-holes plugged with wooden pegs; (b) tenon join continues through the chair frame and is secured with dowels.

solidity, was not entirely suited to the boudoirs of mid-eighteenth-century ladies, many of whom were dressing up as milkmaids and shepherdesses, a fashion set by the ill-fated Marie Antoinette.

Furniture designers of the last quarter of the eighteenth century had far more freedom than those who had gone before them, pioneering the use of cheaper grades of mahogany as a carcase wood and discovering how the timber behaved when it was cut and sawn to produce the undulating serpentine-fronted furniture of the mid-eighteenth century. It was much less necessary for these later designers to know many of the techniques of furniture-making at first hand. Once machinery improved and there was steam power to drive it, cutting, veneering, turning, shaping, inlay and ornament all became easier and more accurate. Some satinwood, for example, had been used during the first half of the eighteenth century, but it was much harder to work with, both to cut and to lay as veneer. By the end of the century it presented far less of a problem.

Metalworking had also changed beyond recognition. Screws and hinges were mass produced in all sizes, furniture mounts were cast or stamped out with mechanical precision. No pattern book of furniture contained designs which could not be made in any reasonably sized furniture-manufacturer's workshops, and if Hepplewhite and Sheraton designs are lighter and finer, their furniture owes as much to manufacturing techniques as it does to artistic inspiration.

The Continuity of Country Furniture

During all these swings of fashion, country furniture remained the mainstay of English traditional style. If a chair or a table or a cupboard fulfilled its function, there seemed little reason to change it as long as it successfully furnished the low-ceilinged traditional houses for which it had originally been made. The furniture which was still made and used for farmhouses and country dwellings was simply and stoutly made, using traditional construction techniques, because it was mostly made in oak, which was unsuitable for any other methods. Elm was also used to a great degree but, like walnut, it was fatally appetizing to woodworm and thus much of it has not survived.

Just as the gentry were inspired by the romantic ideal of the pastoral, so in the same spirit, did furniture-makers borrow woods, shapes and styles from country furniture. Hepplewhite used beech for many of his chairs, a wood which had been used by country chair-makers for centuries. The simplified shapes of Sheraton furniture certainly owed something to the plain, straight lines of country chests, chairs and tables. By the end of the eighteenth century, the interchange was quite considerable, with Windsor chairs epitomizing the extent of borrowing on both sides of the cultural divide.

The gap which remained to be filled was that of provincial furniture – made for the growing urban population, from the mid-eighteenth century onwards. It was to this potential market, for instance, that Hepplewhite addressed himself: 'To combine elegance and utility, and blend the useful with the agreeable', to design 'such articles only as are of general use and service'. Many of the designs in his pattern book were, in the eyes of fashionable society, old-fashioned, but the provinces were always behind the first wave of change, and the designs suited them very well.

Town Houses and the Feminine Influence

The proliferation of pattern books and design books which followed Chippendale's *Director* was a Pandora's box to many furniture-makers, eager to make their fortunes in growing provincial towns. So many possibilities were unleashed, so many designs were available, from Gothic to classical, Chinese, Japanese, French and Italian, that it was inevitable that some furniture-makers made pretentious efforts of their own to try and capture their local market. All the new crescents and streets full of Adam-style Georgian houses were there to be filled. Class was reflected by taste, and many a newcomer with a fortune made in trade was anxious to show his wealth and style in a proper manner. Provincial furniture tended to be heavier, more ponderous, and its lines were less pure, and more ornamented (the furniture-maker giving good value for money). It might even be said that some of George Hepplewhite's designs pandered a little to these new customers, curving the lovely straight lines of Pembroke tables *à la française* and adding perhaps a little too much inlay and ornament to the serpentine shapes of chests and cupboards. Adam's classical lines were severely geo-metrical – to soften the line and add a curve here and there appealed greatly to a less educated eye. But then, the whole way of life in the provinces lagged behind fashionable society. People still ate their meals at several separate tables rather than one. The provincial way of life used the parlour as a dining room, in much the same way as people had done 50 years before. To be sure, they no longer used oak gate-legged tables, but drop-leaf dining tables which were really quite elegant. Sets of dining chairs were pushed

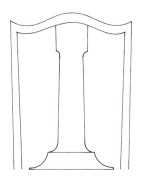

A classic mid-eighteenth century shape – the camel back.

Detail of a wooden knuckle hinge for fly-brackets.

Oak and elm dresser base, eighteenth century.

Construction of a typical Georgian flat-fronted chest of drawers in solid wood.

Georgian dumb waiter.

back against the wall when not being used.

In London and the provinces there was one common factor which increasingly dictated the choice of lighter woods and more ornamented furniture. The feminine influence was growing. Ladies now had at least four rooms which were more or less their domain – the drawing room, the boudoir, the dressing room and the bedroom – which required a whole new range of furniture. Dressing tables with mirrors, little tables for taking tea downstairs and breakfast upstairs, screens to protect them from the direct heat of the fire, sewing boxes, small writing furniture, comfortable chairs with upholstered backs, stools covered in needlework, storage furniture for their growing wardrobe of pretty clothes. Satinwood and painted furniture suited these suites of rooms far better than dark mahogany, which remained the favourite for libraries, dining rooms, parlours and gentlemen's dressing rooms.

George Seddon, who built up the largest furniture-making business in the country at the end of the eighteenth century, seems to have catered to a great extent to this new fashion for 'ladies' furniture'. He also provided mirrors and fabrics for curtains and bedcovers, and great quantities of 'straw-coloured' furniture as well as painted and japanned woods. Although his workshops were in London, he tended to gild the lily, perhaps for the slightly more ostentatious households. In his hands, George Hepplewhite's plain and simple shield-back chair was decorated with curving swags and painted with flowers and ribbons with great abandon. Severe, clean-tapered legs with squared, pegged feet were adapted in George Seddon's workshops to have rounded, turned legs – perhaps because they were cheaper to make, perhaps because in the provinces the old traditional turned legs were preferred.

Richard Gillow of Lancaster remained in the mainstream of Chippendale mahogany furniture, providing furniture that was always beautifully made, of solid appearance, and made mainly in glossy dark veneers. Thomas Shearer falls half way between these two extremes, specializing in multi-purpose pieces. His designs are based on straight lines rather than curves, and were made with ingenious flaps and fitted drawers, cramming as many functions as possible into into each piece of furniture.

Mathematics and Geometry: Thomas Hope and Thomas Sheraton

It was inevitable that what some would call a flowering and some a decadent trend would be halted – that the stern hand of classical discipline would be reimposed on 30 years or more of good design and of design run riot. Thomas Sheraton (1751-1806) was a man with a mission – and a considerable contempt for most of his predecessors, including Thomas Chippendale. Sheraton lived in the 'Age of Reason', and attempted to be its true exponent. He styled himself as a teacher of 'perspective, architecture and ornament', although from his earlier life as a journeyman cabinet-maker he clearly came from humble origins. But in those early days he must

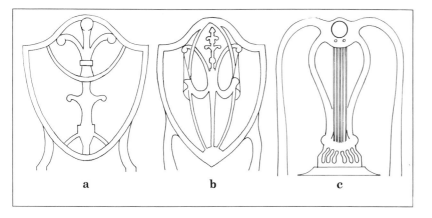

Characteristic late eighteenth century chair back patterns – (a) Prince of Wales' feathers, (b) shield back, (c) lyre back.

himself have felt a lack of guidance, and probably a great desire to improve the taste of those for whom he worked. Whatever the reason, when he published his *Cabinet Maker and Upholsterer's Drawing Book* (published in three parts 1791-94), it was directed at the trade rather than the customers, and intended to teach furniture-makers those basic rules which had been largely forgotten since the early days of furniture design when Thomas Chippendale was schooled in architecture by the Adam brothers. In almost the same way as Chippendale brought together a collection of random influences and styles to produce a distinct overall design for house interiors, Sheraton stylized many conflicting fashions into a disciplined, functional concept which epitomized late Georgian furniture.

It was a period of revolution. Across the Atlantic, America had fought and won her independence and, far closer to home, France had overthrown her monarchy. The Age of Enlightenment had dawned, with every man equal and every household with a right to the privileges hitherto denied them – in theory at least. England's power as a trading nation, in spite of her over-extended battle lines, continued to grow. War makes for technological advances. New trading ports brought exotic ideas and raw materials back to England to feed her growing industrial cities. The canal system expanded, taking raw and finished goods from the ports to the manufacturing towns and back again, to be sent abroad or sold in London. Thomas Sheraton's ideas and designs greatly appealed to furniture manufacturers, and in particular his dining-room furniture, purpose-built, in affordable designs, which appealed to everyone who desired to be *à la mode*. Whereas the Adam brothers had designed huge side tables flanked with urns on plinths for the houses of the great, Sheraton produced dining-room tables and sideboards to furnish middle class dining rooms. His furniture at last dispensed with the clutter of tables and chairs and followed the fashion for long, sleek dining tables with matching sets of chairs, a move which even Hepplewhite failed to encourage them to make.

In the workshops, new machines did what manpower could never do. Planing and sawing, machine-turning, grooving, reeding,

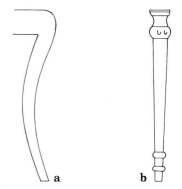

Characteristic leg shapes of the late eighteenth century – (a) sabre, (b) taper-turned.

fluting, moulding were all achieved with maximum accuracy. More and more exotic woods came into England and were used as veneers, machine-cut and thinner than before. They were used on their own to give an entirely new look to plain furniture, or were inlaid in panels and combined with Sheraton's neo-classical designs. But clearly the feminine style was still immensely popular, and Sheraton could not confine himself to strict geometric lines if his customers wanted curves, delicately painted panels and light-coloured woods.

Thomas Hope (1768-1831), however, was under no obligation either to earn a living or please his customers. He was rich, the son of a Dutch banking family, and indulged himself in collecting. Connoisseur and dilettante, he wanted rooms which would be a fitting background to his collection of antiquities, and when he could not find anyone to design them for him, designed them himself. It was he who restored aesthetics to the upper ranks of society and, in the grand manner, decorated the interiors of his many rooms with highly original taste.

A reasonable parallel could be drawn between the beginning of the nineteenth century and the beginning of the eighteenth, with Thomas Hope as the William Kent of the period. England was yet again victorious, celebrating Wellington and Nelson in effigy and symbol. Houses were spacious and uncluttered, with great sweeps of glistening dark mahogany reflecting the light from a thousand candles in Waterford glass chandeliers. Interiors reverted to well-designed, though more ornate, neo-classicism with a strong flavour of the Egyptian due to Napoleon's defeats, and a whiff of nautical symbolism, due to Nelson's victories. Of all the lavish yet restrained

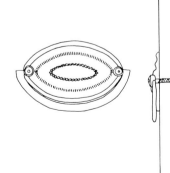

Late eighteenth century stamped brass backplate secured with a pommel pin.

designs of Thomas Hope's *Household Furniture and Interior Decoration from Designs by Thomas Hope* (1807), the most exemplary of its age is the flush-sided chair, built with mathematical precision and based on the principles of engineering stresses and strains.

By about 1820 brass inlay had developed from straight lines to curves, and from curves to Egyptian palmettes, lotus leaves and buds, used in conjunction with gilded sphinxes, hieroglyphics, Assyrian lions, on ebony or ebonized wood. And just as William Kent's monumental designs were adapted for more modest furniture, Thomas Hope had his own populist in George Smith, whose *Cabinet Maker and Upholsterer's Guide* (published in 1828) for the furniture-maker contained designs for solid middle-class homes. His earlier work, *A Collection of Designs for Household Furniture and Interior Decoration*, is a bible of Regency taste for the richer, more extravagant houses of the period.

Regency: Folie de Grandeur

The Court, so long out of fashion as a leader of taste, emerged once again with the Prince of Wales and his followers. Brighton Pavilion, a kind of English Versailles of its day – gilded, mirrored, unbelievably rich and ostentatious – is based on Prinny's revival of Louis XIV and Louis XV styles. It reflects not only his taste but also his lifestyle. Where brass inlay had been a delightful embellishment, it now led to a revival in heavily decorated Boulle – usually rosewood inset with brass or silver. Thomas Hope's Trafalgar chair with sabre legs, flush sides and rope-twist back was made in commemoration of Nelson's famous victory. So, too, was the riotous Dolphin Suite. The former incorporated all that was pure and disciplined, the latter was an overblown, gloriously lavish and decidedly decadent hint of what was yet to come.

The main collaborator in the overthrow of good taste at the beginning of the nineteenth century was the machine. The vicious circle had begun. Every household in the land could have plain, dark, glossy surfaces. Mahogany veneer, cut thin, on cheap carcase-wood, was French polished to make it even more glossy. Brass

A bureau-plat, late eighteenth century.

inlaid furniture was available to mass-producers of furniture at very little cost, once the molten metal could be poured directly into machine-cut grooves and channels. The leaders of fashion had to set themselves apart from the common man. There was a revival in Gothic, but an hysterical revival, although for the first time since the sixteenth century the designers of neo-Gothic furniture returned to oak, which required the revival of traditional crafts- manship and, therefore, emphasized its exclusiveness.

However, mass-produced furniture could play follow-my-leader, and it was not long before there was cheaply made oak furniture available to all, although it appealed less to the early Victorian citizen than grander-looking, decadent Regency with its bulbous, turned legs and lavish ornament and gilding. Machine-cut dovetails and joints needed no particular craftsmanship once the machines had been set. Cheaper veneers were used to imitate the pale 'ladies'

George III satinwood and rosewood secretaire.

furniture' in which Hepplewhite and his contemporaries excelled, and designs were modified and debased.

The William IV period (1830-37) was a transitional stage between Regency and Victorian, during which there was still some fine, well-proportioned furniture made by traditional furniture-manufacturers. But by the mid-nineteenth century, the design of furniture had burgeoned into so many derivatives of earlier, purer styles in a race to keep ahead of the mass-producers, that several movements grew up led by such people as J. C. Loudon, who attempted to reform and improve interior design and decoration. Loudon's *The Encyclopaedia of Cottage, Farm and Villa Architecture and Furniture* was full of excellent, plain, well-designed pieces, many of them in oak, many of them adaptations from earlier traditional shapes and forms of smaller furniture. It lead the public away from the over-stuffed, bulbous, ungainly lines of mass-produced furniture being turned out in London and the provinces for the new suburban dwellers.

Early nineteenth century drawer construction with machine-cut dovetails and a strengthening batten, or muntin, in the drawer bottom.

The Victorian Creed

While mainstream designers such as Gillows of Lancaster continued to produce the solid mahogany furniture so popular with Britain's solid middle classes, with reproductions of Chippendale designs as well as innovative shapes for chairs based on Thomas Hope's designs, others searched for ways to return to hand-crafted furniture based on traditional construction techniques. Simultaneously available to the bewildered buyer, there was Graeco-Roman, neo-classical, Regency revival, neo-Gothic, French Empire, 'Queen Anne', 'Jacobethan' or mock Tudor revival, with all versions of each style copied to a greater or lesser degree by the furniture-manufacturers. When Victoria became Queen Empress of India, there was added to this amazingly eclectic mixture the inlaid mother-of-pearl and japanned styles of Oriental and Indian culture. On the manufacturing side, sprung upholstery, patented in 1828, exaggerated the bulbously curvaceous shapes of seat furniture.

Small wonder, therefore, that William Morris, attempting to bring order out of chaos, began the Arts and Crafts Movement, or that other designers should find inspiration in the plain, clean lines of military campaign furniture in solid, brass-bound mahogany, teak, camphor wood and padouk. As if there were not enough fashion currents and contradictory trends, more were to come. Albert, Victoria's consort, was German, and medieval High Gothic style was a favourite with the royal couple, as well as the romantic Scotland of Sir Walter Scott. Coupled together, these two produced the 'Scottish baronial' style, so popular among the Victorian aristocracy and industrial elite.

Not all Victorian design was in bad taste by any means, and all high-quality furniture of the late nineteenth century was extremely comfortable, including many of the average run-of-the-mill chairs and sofas. Most enduring are the many variations on balloon-back and button-back chairs. Though the new pioneers of taste, such as

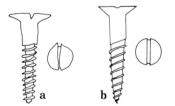

(a) hand-cut screw, (b) machine-cut screw.

The classic Victorian balloon back shape.

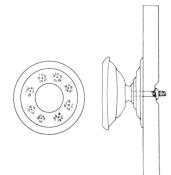

Early Victorian cast brass drawer pull.

Mackintosh, Gimson, Voysey, Godwin and many others, disdained curving shapes in favour of geometric designs, nevertheless the average British interior was fringed, tassled, draped with Oriental shawls and crammed with small pieces of furniture, nick-nacks and commemorative china.

Liberty's: the guiding light

All the efforts of the design reformers might have gone unnoticed had it not been for Arthur Lazenby Liberty, whose new premises in the rebuilt Regent Street were full of Oriental textiles, carpets, curtain fabrics and dress materials. Patronized by such influential artists as Whistler, Rossetti and Burne-Jones, he soon extended his range to include 'artistic furniture' as well as Oriental chinaware, glass and the now-famous Liberty light fittings. Liberty & Co. was opened in 1875 and was the first of the furnishing stores to offer a wide choice to the growing professional classes who, up to now, had only been able to buy 'sets' or 'suites' of furniture from manufacturers and retailers. It was a rapid education in taste, and Liberty's success proved that there was a great hunger for its distinctive 'house style', which included William Morris fabric designs, as well as furniture and furnishings designed by all the influential coterie of the Arts and Crafts Movement.

Other furnishing department stores opened in London and the provinces, some still confined to 'suites' of furniture, others offering more adventurous schemes to furnish avant garde middle-class homes. Inevitably there was a strong streak of conservatism, and 'Sheraton revival' and 'Hepplewhite revival' furniture still had a strong appeal, as well as the more fanciful Gothic furniture and good, solid mainstream mahogany. By the end of the nineteenth century it was often considered more desirable to have excellently made reproductions of classic designs than to continue to live with much-used originals. In this, Gillows of Lancaster continued to thrive, having opened an establishment in Oxford Street as early as 1760 to cater for the London 'carriage trade' and, 100 years later, was still making 'Chippendale' furniture adapted from the original pattern books.

Furniture-makers still styled themselves as 'cabinet-makers', though many of them had never come in contact with the tools of the craft. By the turn of the century there were workshops all over the country making excellent reproductions and variations of traditional styles and designs for rich and titled families. For example, Holland and Sons of Mount Street supplied most of the furniture for the Royal household, and by the end of the nineteenth century there were many excellent cabinet-making firms who specialized in copying fine furniture at considerable expense for the privileged few.

Edwardian: the good, the bad and the ugly

In the world of antiques, 'Edwardian' is still a perjorative word, partly because the period still falls outside the magic 100-year-old

Early Victorian table with fine decoration and brass inlay.

dateline of 'true' antiques, and partly because huge quantities of shoddily made furniture were made in poor representations of earlier, elegant styles, particularly in pale-coloured woods. There was a great deal of furniture with cheap carcase wood and thin, poor veneer, machine-cut inlay and painted decoration that has not stood the test of time. But, as befitted the last great golden age before the First World War, the best Edwardian hand-made furniture was of a far higher quality than many Victorian versions of traditional designs. Some classical designs lingered on, which it is as well to remember when it comes to buying Edwardian furniture. As with its antecedents 200 years before, much decorative furniture was made primarily to be admired and only occasionally to be used, and some extremely well-designed drawing-room furniture was never intended to stand up to the wear and tear of everyday use.

Already 'Sheraton revival' and 'Hepplewhite revival' furniture is increasing in value, and it is a fair guess that this period will soon be regarded on its own merit, which is often considerable. It is interesting to note that the first books on 'furnishing in the antique style' for the popular market were published at this time, one of the most influential being *How to Collect Old Furniture* by F. Litchfield, published in 1906. Advice was badly needed, for the first 'Wardour Street oak' had begun to appear in shops, which gave the burgeoning antique trade a very bad name. The only reassurance for a would-be buyer in those days were advertisements in the *Burlington* magazine and *The Connoisseur* which guaranteed that 'everything in this establishment is guaranteed old'. At the least, it is to be hoped that this guide will arm the potential antique furniture buyer with a little more substantial help.

Pine

Pine, fir-deal and softwood were first used in England in Christopher Wren's town houses for panelling, and for simple cupboards built into entrance halls and domestic service quarters. At the time it was mainly imported from the Baltic ports with 'wainscot oak'. During the Georgian period, built-in corner cupboards were incorporated into panelling even after it had ceased to reach the full height of the room and ran at dado level only. Once wallpaper took the place of panelling there was no place in the scheme of things for built-in furniture and most pine furniture, except for highly decorative lacquered pieces, was relegated to the servants' quarters where it formed part of the kitchen furniture, as dressers, tables, built-in cupboards and working surfaces.

However, when North American pine became available in bulk, it was used as carcase wood for cheaper grades of thinly veneered furniture for the mass-market, as well as being used by estate carpenters and country furniture-makers for simple 'cottage' furniture. Design was minimal, for the main object was to make cheap, functional pieces. Much of it is pleasingly plain and well-proportioned. Turned wooden knobs were usually all that graced the original chests of drawers and dressers, though later these were replaced with round, mass-produced porcelain drawer-pulls.

In the second half of the nineteenth century, in the huge Victorian mansions staffed by dozens of live-in servants, pine was used extensively for an increasing range of simple furniture, mainly chests of drawers, cupboards, washstands and strictly functional tables with turned legs. Most of the better pieces of simple furniture date from the nineteenth century, when pine was also used in rural dwellings for bookshelves, corner cupboards, hanging cupboards, spice racks, spice cupboards, knife boxes and a range of storage chests previously made in oak.

There are occasions when fashion does a disservice to antiques, and stripped pine is a case in point. During the craze for blond woods, more than a few early pieces were stripped of their original lacquered decoration, and literally hundreds of nineteenth-century pieces lost their veneer. In some cases this was not a tragedy, especially if it had originally been mass-produced and thinly veneered, but in many cases, where a proper knowledge of furniture was slight, good late Georgian furniture was subjected to the stripping tank, its detail irrevocably lost as acid dissolved applied gesso relief, the results are sad exposures of the basic carcase.

Woods: characteristics and uses

It is essential to be able to recognize the main woods used for furniture-making at different periods. No matter how well acquainted a person may be with the designs, the drawer construction, the brass fittings, mouldings and detail, if this knowledge is not accompanied by the ability to recognize the timber appropriate for the period and piece, it is almost useless. Anyone who cannot distinguish between a coarse-grained varnished oak bureau made around 1900 and its original, made in eighteenth-century oak, rich and dark with pale golden flecks and figuring, would do well to spend some time in a good antique dealer's shop getting the feel of different woods, and then trying out their knowledge on viewing day in their local saleroom, checking the descriptions and approximate dates in the catalogue.

A basic knowledge should encompass carcase wood, solid wood and veneers. Woods for inlays are less important, although the obvious difference between Edwardian 'satinwood' inlaid panels compared with eighteenth-century satinwood is important. The same applies to seventeenth-century walnut and its nineteenth-century counterpart, which looks and feels quite different. The list below will go some way to avoiding the worst mistakes, and should be read in conjunction with the descriptions of individual pieces under the heading of 'Construction and materials' and the general guide to the different ways woods were used in the historical introduction. Each wood is coded (S) (C) (V) and (I) for Solid, Carcase, Veneer and Inlay. Approximate periods of their most common use are also given.

Acacia: Blonde, yellowish colour with pale brown graining. Hardwood. Late eighteenth century. (I)

Alder: Pinkish brown with knotty figuring. Impervious to damp conditions. Good grain for turning. Country chairs, small table legs, eighteenth century. (S)

Amboyna: Light brown with chestnut-coloured flecks and curls, quite similar to burr walnut, eighteenth and nineteenth centuries. (I) and (V)

Apple: Pinkish brown, close-grained, good for turning. One of the fruitwoods used for country furniture, particularly in the eighteenth century. (S)

Ash: Whitish-brown, dense and heavy with good spring. Very suitable for chair legs and 'sticks' and legs of eighteenth century Windsor chairs. (S)

Baltic pine: see *Deal*

Baywood: see *Mahogany.*

Beech: Springy, dense, light-coloured with flecked grain. Excellent for turning. Painted for twist-turned chairs in seventeenth century.

Ebonized in the late eighteenth century. Underframes for over-stuffed seats and upholstered chairs in the eighteenth century. (s) and (c)

Birch: Light yellowish or pinkish wood with undulating grain. Used for country furniture, particularly chairs, late seventeenth and eighteenth centuries. Used as substitute for satinwood veneer and solid in the nineteenth century. Used for bentwood chairs in the nineteenth and twentieth centuries. (s) and (v)

Bog oak: Almost black, coarse-grained. Fashionable with Victorians for small furniture. (s)

Boxwood: Pale blonde to light brown with no figure, creamy texture, dense and solid. During the seventeenth and eighteenth centuries it was used for stringing on inlaid and veneered furniture. (I)

Cedar: Dark pinkish brown, moth and insect repellent, used for chests and coffers in the sixteenth and seventeenth century, also for drawer and chest linings and interior cabinet fittings in the eighteenth and nineteenth centuries. (s)

Chestnut: Light brown, maturing to chestnut brown. Used in country furniture, mainly for table legs and chairs from eighteenth century, but not as frequently as on the Continent, particularly France, where its use paralleled English oak. In the late eighteenth century it was a substitute veneer for satin wood. (s) and (v)

Coromandel (calamander): A hard wood sometimes known as 'Bombay ebony', it is blackish brown with a yellowish grain. Used in the late eighteenth century for crossbanding and for small boxes etc. in the nineteenth century. (v) and some (s)

Deal: In the seventeenth century Baltic pine was imported as planking, and 'deal' became the general English term for coniferous softwoods. In the eighteenth century, Scots close-grained pine and imported American pine with coarser grain were used. Deal was the principal carcase wood in the late eighteenth and nineteenth centuries. Used for cheap furniture of all sorts since the nineteenth century. (c) and (s)

Elm: Coarse-grained lightish brown, maturing to darker brown. Does not split or crack with changes in humidity but is susceptible to worm. Used in conjunction with oak for country furniture and as solid seats for Windsor chairs. (s)

Harewood: Dyed or stained sycamore with greenish-grey tint, fading in sunlight. Used as inlay mainly in the late seventeenth and the eighteenth centuries. (I) and some (v). See also *Maple.*

Holly: Almost white, dense hardwood. Used in conjunction with oak in alternate white and stained black as featherbanding from the sixteenth to eighteenth centuries. (I)

Kingwood: South American, almost purple reddish brown with black graining. Dense and fine-grained for crossbanding. Used for marquetry in the late seventeenth and early eighteenth centuries. (I) and (v)

Laburnum: Vivid ochre-yellow brown with dark-brown graining. A small-girthed timber, it was used as oyster inlay and for parquetry, as well as a showy veneer in the late eighteenth and nineteenth centuries. (I) and (V)

Lime: Pale greyish-yellow, close-grained and soft, used mostly as groundwood for giltwood and gilt gesso mirror frames of ornate carving. Late seventeenth, and eighteenth centuries. (S)

Mahogany: Used in many varieties from *c.*1730, it was prized for its great girth and strength, close grain and ability to take a high polish. Hispaniola or South American species were first imported *c.*1730. They were hard, close-grained and had little figure. San Domingo and Cuban was favoured from *c.*1750 with fine figuring and curl, excellent for crisp carving and detail. It was lighter-coloured than South American but darkened to a rich brown. Honduras mahogany was used from *c.*1750 and was commonly known as baywood. It was pinkish brown with little figure, and far cheaper than previous varieties. African mahogany in English furniture dates from *c.*1870. It is less dense and has poor figuring. Hispaniola (S) and some (V). San Domingo and Cuban (V) and some (S). Honduras mainly (C) some (V) and (S) in nineteenth century. African (S) and in nineteenth century (V).

Maple: Is the same species as sycamore, the name it is known by in England. It is honey-coloured, fine-grained and has curly figuring. It was stained to simulate harewood in the seventeenth century. Maple was used for underframes in upholstered and over-stuffed chairs, as well as for drop-in seat frames in the eighteenth century. American 'sugar maple' was used as 'bird's eye' veneer in the nineteenth century. (I) (V) (C) and occasionally (S) for small pieces.

Oak: Greyish-white to brown, hard and coarse-grained. English oak with silver grain was used to the seventeenth century but gave way to softer imported 'wainscot' oak from Germany from the seventeeth century onwards. English (S), wainscot oak (C) as drawers, drawer linings, interior cabinet fittings to the end of eighteenth century.

Olive: Hard, greenish-yellow with black graining. Used for oyster inlay, parquetry and cross-grain mouldings during the seventeenth and early eighteenth centuries. (I) and (V)

Padouk: From Burma and the Portuguese East Indies, it is a purplish-brown dense hardwood with black streaking. Used mainly for chest furniture and heavily carved work, often Dutch or Continental, from the mid-eighteenth century. Popular in England from early nineteenth, particularly for campaign furniture. (S)

Pine: Whitish-yellow to pinkish red characterizes Baltic, Scots and American pine. American 'pitch pine' is more yellow with black streaking. Red pine was used as a substitute for baywood. White pine was a cheap carcase wood used by the Dutch from *c.*1600, but in England seldom before the late eighteenth and nineteenth centuries. Used as a cheap solid timber from the nineteenth century. (S) and (C). See also *Deal*.

Plane: A whitish, close-grained and resilient wood, similar to beech. Used for plain and turned chair legs, underframes for upholstery, and fly-brackets for small tables. (S) and (C)

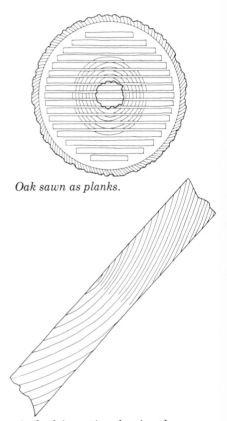

Oak sawn as planks.

A plank in section showing the curving grain – the cause of warping.

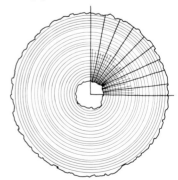

Oak showing natural lines of splitting along the medullary rays. Riven oak was split down these rays after the log had been sawn in quarters.

Plum: Deep reddish brown with yellowish sap rings. It is a hard, dense, fruitwood used for country furniture and, as inlay and veneer, up to the late seventeenth century. (s) (i) and (v)

Poplar: Greyish-yellow, close-textured softwood. Used for inlays in the seventeenth and eighteenth centuries and as a cheap substitute for beech and sycamore after the late nineteenth century when it was grown in quantity as 'matchwood'. (i) and (c)

Rosewood: From India and Brazil, it is heavy, red-brown with black streaks, fading to greyish brown with dark streaks. South American kingwood is very similar to Brazilian rosewood. In the eighteenth century it was used as a veneer, and in solid and veneer from the mid-nineteenth. (v) and (s)

Satinwood: Pale to dark golden with natural sheen. East Indies satinwood is a pale honey with dark streaks, while West Indies is more golden, with a richer grain. From *c.*1780 it was used as solid and veneer. In the late nineteenth century it was used mainly as a veneer, although there were many substitutes. (s) and (v)

Sycamore: See *Maple.*

Teak: Straight-grained and extremely dense, teak is oily and dark brown, maturing almost to black. It was used mainly for Oriental-style furniture, with some popularity in England from the nineteenth century. (s)

Tulipwood: South American species related to kingwood and rosewood. It is ochre-yellow brown with red-brown streaks. Used as crossbanding and, occasionally, as inlay, from *c.*1780. (v) and (i)

Walnut: The English and European species are a rich, golden brown with a darker brown figure. It was the main furniture-wood in the seventeenth century and early eighteenth century, both in solid and veneer. It was imported from France in large quantities until *c.*1720 when exports were banned by the French. Virginia walnut was imported in small quantities in the late seventeenth and early eighteenth centuries. In its unpolished state it was known as 'red walnut', but when polished became almost as dark as mahogany and was called 'black walnut'. It was used sparingly in the late seventeenth and early eighteenth centuries, but in quantity from *c.*1830 in solid. (s) and (v)

Yew: A red-brown, hard and resilient wood which takes a high natural polish. Used for country furniture from the sixteenth century in combination with other woods, particularly for chairs, and as parquetry in the seventeenth century and veneer in the eighteenth. Best-known as hoops on Windsor chairs. (s) and (v)

Zebrawood: African in origin, it is a showy yellow-brown with dark-brown strips. Used as crossbanding when it was scarce in the late eighteenth, and then as veneer from the late eighteenth century (particularly during the Regency). (v)

Cleaning and Care

Wood shrinks naturally as the sap dries out from the fibres, and even well-seasoned timber will shrink in width with time. With most antiques, this natural shrinkage has already occurred, a fact which made little difference to its condition in the mildly damp atmosphere of houses until the advent of central heating.

No piece of antique furniture can withstand the warm, dry atmosphere of a fully insulated, centrally heated house unless it has proper care. Polishing with a good wax polish is not just a house-proud practice – it is essential in order to seal the surface of the wood and keep as much of the wood's natural moisture from drying out, with the inevitable result of cracking and splitting. The fact that antique shops are centrally heated should mislead no one into thinking that this is the right atmosphere: antique dealers usually keep their stock in cold, unheated stores and their heated showrooms are well-equipped with humidifiers to protect fine furniture from damage.

Sudden changes in temperature and humidity do the most damage: antiques should be slowly acclimatized to central heating. Wherever possible, keep the radiators nearest to them turned off and make sure there is always fresh air circulating in the room. Small bowls of water on ledges over radiators will keep some moisture evaporating into the air, and if these look unsightly, make sure there is always at least one bowl of flowers in the room, summer and winter. In summer, keep the curtains drawn where the sunlight falls directly on any antique furniture, rug, tapestry or needlework. Sunlight will fade the natural pigment in wood and natural dyes and destroy the delicate colouring of inlays and veneers. Walnut veneer is particularly susceptible to sunlight which, apart from bleaching the colour, will cause the wood to pucker or crack as the animal-fat glues dehydrate beneath. Later mahongany veneers are not so susceptible, but satinwood and crossbanding are particularly vulnerable. Brass stringing and inlay are also damaged by a dry atmosphere, which will cause the metal to work upwards out of the surface.

Cleaning

Use cotton rags from old sheets or pillowcases for applying the polish, which should be used sparingly and lightly worked in with a circular motion. Shine up after polish has had time to sink into the wood. Use a soft cloth which will not catch or snag on veneered or inlaid surfaces. Sides of furniture, legs of tables, chairs and stands need feeding and protecting as much as the visible surfaces. Solid woods can stand any amount of elbow grease, but be gentle with inlaid and veneered surfaces.

Brass drawer handles, escutcheons and furniture mounts will need more than an occasional buffing up with a chamois leather where the atmosphere is smoky or where there is a coal or gas fire in the room. Rub wax polish into the surround before using a proprietory wadding cleaner wrapped in a thin cloth to prevent it from snagging round sharp edges. The spirits in most brass polishes will damage the surrounding wood if it is not protected with wax, and liquid polishes dry with a greenish-white deposit around the edges and detail.

Leather insets on writing furniture can be kept soft and supple by feeding occasionally with a neutral cream shoe polish. If the edges show signs of lifting, use a latex or rubber-based adhesive spread thinly and pressed down with a pile of books on a sheet of plain brown paper.

Glass panes and mirrors can be cleaned with a proprietory window cleaner and a soft cloth. Where there are fine glazing bars, a thin cotton rag lightly sprinkled with methylated spirits is simpler to use: window-cleaning preparations can dry and stick in inaccessible corners which may be damaged while trying to clean them off.

Giltwood furniture, picture frames and mirror frames also respond to gentle cleaning with methylated spirits and polishing with a chamois leather.

Marks and stains

One of the most common causes of marks on furniture are rings made by the bottoms of glasses. If the ring has been made by condensation from an iced drink, let the mark dry out completely, use turpentine and let it soak in, rubbing gently in small circles so that it penetrates the grain. Leave overnight and then polish. If the mark has been made by alcohol, treat in the same way. If the surface is varnished, the damage is more serious, since varnishes are soluble in spirits. Rub very lightly with the finest grade of glasspaper and then polish with a brown wax shoe polish of the nearest colour to the varnished surface. If this fails, then expert French polishing is necessary in order to build up the surface again.

Ink stains, if dealt with at once, need not be a calamity. Take up as much of the ink as possible with blotting paper, sponge immediately with fresh milk and then with clean water. If there is only pasteurized or treated milk available, use unsalted butter instead. Another treatment, to be used on solid woods only, never on veneers, is to mop the stain with clean water and then use lemon juice. Old ink stains are harder to deal with, but a weak solution of spirit of salts and warm water will often succeed.

Ivory inlay and escutcheons are often discoloured with age. If you prefer to see them white, rub gently with lemon juice. You may also use hydrogen peroxide (120 vols) on a piece of cotton wool, but the ivory needs to be rinsed well afterwards and this treatment, like soaking in milk (another well-tried method), is more suitable for small pieces of carved ivory.

Marble tops of side-tables and chiffoniers are very vulnerable to staining by spilt wine and rings from the bottoms of bottles and glasses. Marble absorbs marks and they are hard to remove. The best advice is to make sure the surface is protected with a good layer of colourless wax polish. If the stains are made by red wine, treatment with hydrogen peroxide (120 vols) may remove the mark completely but will still leave a matt ring in the surface of the marble itself. Repolishing by an expert is the only answer if this is the case, though sometimes a cloth dipped in a proprietory liquid metal polish may partly restore the damage.

Grease marks and spots can be removed by covering them with blotting paper and then applying a cool iron, which will melt the grease so that it can be absorbed by the blotting paper. Alternatively, use a thick dusting of unperfumed talcum powder or Fuller's earth, cover with a pad of tissue paper and apply a cool iron – the effect is much the same as using blotting paper.

Heat rings are far more serious: always use table mats under hot plates and never put any dish from the oven on a polished or marble surface unless it is protected by a solid mat of some sort, such as a heat-resistant glass mat or a wooden one with a plan cork-back. Cork mats, rush mats or heat-resistant cloth mats are not sufficient.

Make sure that flowers are removed before they start wilting, dropping or shedding pollen. Leaves of flowers can mark surfaces with water-stains, and many flower petals and pollen contain a natural dye which will mark wood. If this does happen, use the treatment suggested for ink stains.

Repairs and restorations: trade practices

There are three basic categories into which repairs and restorations fall:

1. Repairs carried out during the lifetime of a piece of furniture which has been damaged during use.
2. Restoration and rebuilding pieces of furniture too badly damaged to be sold or used, and 'improvements' which increase commercial value.
3. Deliberate alterations and pieces of furniture made up from old timbers and parts of genuine pieces solely for commercial gain.

1. It goes without saying that hardly any piece of furniture used regularly for 100 years or more can have escaped damage. Some repair on antique furniture is inevitable, unless it is a rare and perfect piece which has remained in the same place with virtually no use during its entire existence. Such pieces occasionally come on the market when a stately home is forced to shed some of its contents for tax reasons, and these naturally command extremely high prices.

Any furniture which is in constant use comes to grief sooner or later: legs of chairs are split or broken, arms work loose or break, flaps of tables split near the hinge, stretchers on chairs, tables and stands are weakened by worm and have to be replaced, and so on. Often the repairs carried out a long time ago were crude and roughly done in order to make the piece merely serviceable. Iron plates and brackets were nailed to the underframes of chairs or the undersides of tripod joints and the splitting curves of pillar-and-claw table legs. Veneer which lifted or chipped was replaced without much regard to detail, or glued roughly back into position with consequent bubbling and cracking. None of these repairs need necessarily detract from the value of a piece.

In some cases, these rough and ready repairs are removed by an experienced modern restorer and the piece is carefully repaired again until it is as near the original condition as possible – work which need not detract from the general value of the piece. The test of this sort of repair is whether the antique dealer points them out voluntarily or not. If he does, then the repair has been taken into consideration in the price, and the dealer is quite open about the fact that the piece has been restored.

Other work which may have been carried out perfectly legitimately includes the removal of Victorian French polishing and staining to a piece of an earlier period, and the stripping off of old oil-based paint from pieces which have fallen from grace and have been used in the servants' quarters or in the kitchen – a fate which has befallen quite a lot of furniture in its time. Black paint was considered fashionable during the early nineteenth century in imitation of expensive ebonized furniture, and it also covered a wealth of country pieces on the death of Queen Victoria's consort, Albert, as a tribute of national mourning.

2. This category is harder to define, and in many cases restoration has been carried out to increase the commercial value as well as to restore a piece to its approximate original condition. To this end, new tops are added to period underframes of tables when the veneer has lifted or the surface has been too badly marked to rescue. Broken block-fronted doors of cupboards and early bureau-bookcases may have mirrored glass or clear glass and glazing bars inset in their original wooden door-frames. Bulging Victorian tripod bases may be turned and reeded to resemble Regency pillar-and-claw supports and added to surviving period table-tops; rounded edges of Victorian table-tops may be reeded or carved with thumb moulding to match up to existing period supports. A highly carved cabriole leg missing from a good period chair may be made up from a plain leg carved up to match the remaining good one. While the finished piece, 'restored' to look original, merits a high price-tag in the showroom because of its good appearance, its value will be considerably lower when it comes to the question of resale.

The borderline between 'right' and 'wrong' restoration in this area is considerably blurred. One good chair may be made up from the best parts of two originals, both of the same period. Inlay and veneer may be replaced of an exact match with the original, or a central support may replace the damaged original cheval legs of a sofa table, taken from another of the same period. Pieces may be 'improved' by carving the original timber with period motifs: plain canted corners of double-heighted furniture or chests of drawers, squared knees of cabriole legs, plain bases and bracket feet, may all be embellished without in any way altering their structure or age.

The Victorians were responsible for a great quantity of 'oak restoration' and many chests and coffers were made up during the nineteenth century from bits and pieces, with panels and frames put together from old room panelling or church panelling, and carved panels inserted into plain panel-back chairs. Many 'Sheraton' and 'Hepplewhite' pieces emerged from Edwardian workshops with newly inlaid decorative panels on far later plain-veneered pieces, as well as additional carving and embellishment. In these days, the cost of labour for a skilled workman often outweighs the additional value, and this sort of work is less common.

Nearly all this 'twilight zone' restoration requires considerable skill and knowledge. In many cases it has been executed so convincingly that it has deceived dealers and collectors alike over several decades. Large numbers of 'enhanced' antiques were sold to America and have only recently begun to make their reappearance in England. Many more pieces were brought in good faith and have been part of the furnishings of houses for about 100 years –

particularly much Victorian oak in 'Renaissance', Tudor and Jacobean styles. The danger area here is that an inexperienced buyer may be told that these pieces are genuine antiques (which they are, being over 100 years old) but left in ignorance of their exact period which, of course, is not genuine at all.

3. The last category often gives itself away because the piece will have the wrong proportions, the wrong decorative motifs for the period, or be made from the wrong wood. The most common 'alterations' concern very large pieces of furniture cut down to make smaller, more valuable pieces. Chests of drawers, display cabinets, tallboys, secretaires, bureau-bookcases, D-ended dining-room tables, are some of the pieces which are reduced to make more commercially sized furniture

'Marriages' are also common: two halves of two pieces of approximately the same period and design are put together to make one single, expensive, piece. Table tops, underframes and legs are a case in point, while bureau-bookcases are another. Sometimes only the front legs of a period chair can be salvaged from a ruin, or the serpentine-shaped stretcher from a William and Mary table or stand. But they are the key parts which identify the final product, and may well deceive the inexperienced buyer into believing that the whole piece must be genuine – when in fact it has been put together with a hotch-potch of pieces which clearly do not belong together. It may be a fair imitation of what it ought to be, but as an antique it is virtually valueless. It is true that sometimes these odd-looking bits of furniture come up in the saleroom and are bought by dealers, but more often than not he or she is buying it for its parts, which are destined to restore a more valuable piece, and the price is only an indication of how much they are prepared to pay for the one bit of it they need – it is in no way the market value of the whole 'botched up' piece.

There is one other category of furniture which is found mixed up among antiques: the copy. These are usually encountered when sets or pairs are more valuable than singles, particularly with pairs of tables and sets of chairs. In the case of chairs, these may have been made up from parts, or simply copied outright to make up a set. A chair may have been broken, a not unlikely occurrence when one considers the amount of wear and tear that chairs can be subjected to, and a copy made quite innocently a considerable time ago, for purely practical reasons. But when a set is made up with deliberate intent to deceive, that is another matter. It may happen that five chairs of good provenance come on the market, are bought, and disappear for a considerable time. Some years later they reappear as a set of six plus two carvers. The remaining three have been made up from chairs of a similar design, doctored until they are a perfect match, or by taking the original five to pieces and reworking them with additional timbers so that every chair has some genuine and some replaced parts. When eventually this fact is discovered, as it surely will be, their market value drops like a stone.

Some examples of all three categories will be found listed under 'Likely restoration and repair' for each of the key pieces in this book, but even with these facts in mind, mistakes can still be made. It is perhaps stating the obvious to point out that if the correct drawer construction has been illustrated over and over again in books about antiques, then dealers and restorers must be keenly aware that this is a detail which must look right to the customer. Details like these should come last on the buyer's check list when considering a piece, reinforcing their opinion that the piece is genuine, and not the other way around. The points given under the heading 'Signs of authenticity' should only be referred to when other, equally important aspects have been examined.

Here, then, are a few helpful pointers about the way a piece of furniture should be examined before considering its purchase. First, stand well back. Do not get confused with details before being as sure as possible that the proportions seem right and that the wood and veneer is of the right period. If there is any difference in colour or patination of any part, ask whether it has been replaced or restored. If it has, and it is a bona fide restoration, the dealer should tell you so. Have the piece pulled out away from the wall so that the back and sides are clearly visible. Check the back edges of overhangs for recent work, and make sure that moulding is not a recent addition. If the piece has any drawers at all, pull them all out and check that both sides of all drawers have the same construction. Then check that they are right for the period. With tables with flaps or tilt tops, make sure the proportions are right when the flaps are down – far easier to see than when they are raised.

Wherever possible have a look at underframes and carcases where signs of restoration and repair are more likely to be visible. If pairs or sets are being considered, check that each one is right, and that the patination and signs of wear are not identical on any two – a give-away that one of them is a copy or has been heavily restored. Only when all this has been checked to your satisfaction should the finer points be taken into consideration: they should be the *confirmation* that in your opinion the piece is genuine, rather than the starting point. If there is something about the piece that you feel is not quite right, do not be afraid to ask. Remember to be practical: dining chairs should be the right height to sit at, dining tables should be high enough to fit your knees under comfortably, desks were made for writing and if the flap falls too low take another good look to see where it may have been cut down. 'Side' chairs and dining chairs are not the same height or size – the former were not made principally for use with tables and, apart from anything else, their seats are usually too wide and their backs too high to be used as proper dining chairs.

Finally, get the assurance of the dealer that he will take the piece of furniture back if your judgement proves faulty and it is the wrong size or shape to fit into your house. He may quite justifiably impose a time limit, which is fair enough. As an extra precaution, make sure that the full description of the piece is written on the invoice. If by any chance you revise your opinion about the piece of furniture and decide that it is not quite what its description says it is, return it within the dealer's time limit. There is little point in going out of your way to be unpleasant, since in the world of antiques judgements are finally no more than one person's opinion against another's and there is very little proof on either side. Wherever possible, buy from a dealer who is a member of an approved trade association.

Salerooms

Saleroom buying is a skill in itself, regardless of what you are buying, and strict conditions of sale govern all auction rooms. These are clearly printed in every catalogue and should be studied carefully before bidding. If you should decide to buy at auction, remember that you will be sacrificing your rights under the various laws of consumer protection, even if you ask a dealer to bid on your behalf. Salerooms are simply acting as agents between the seller and the buyer, a function they perform scrupulously fairly. Simply, it is not in the interest of salerooms to allow those much-publicized shady practices, since the goodwill of the public and the trade is essential to their commerical well-being. Private buyers often do very well when they buy at auction, as long as they impose an iron discipline on themselves and refuse to make a single bid above their own final price and do not get carried away by saleroom fever. But the atmosphere is heady, and seems to bring out a reckless gambling streak in the most sedate of people. When marking up catalogues with the top price to which you have limited yourself, remember the saleroom commission and the handling and transport charges which must be taken into account over and above the 'hammer price', otherwise you may find yourself paying a lot more than you intended.

Prices and price-guides

The prices paid at auction are not a true reflection of the market value of an antique, if indeed there is such a thing. Too many variables are involved, not least the current exchange rates, particularly between the pound sterling and the US dollar. Foreign buyers buy heavily, and not just in London, when the exchange rate is favourable, bringing quantities of oak, for example, on to the market for Continental dealers. Prices rise while there is a strong demand and then, almost overnight, as the exchange rate changes, the buyers have gone and the tempting oak is a glut on the market.

But those prices may already have been reflected in the shops, for British dealers have had to compete in order to maintain their stocks, and it is a while before the subsequent drop filters through to the general market. Just as prices on the stock market rise and fall for all sorts of reasons, so that it is impossible at any given moment for a stockbroker to state categorically the market value of any share he may deal in, so it is with antiques. There are rough guides, however, in both situations, which will give the buyer a general idea of what he may be expected to pay in an antique shop which normally deals in the items and the period in which he is interested. But antiques are no different from any other item on the market. Clothes in the West End of London cost more than they do in a provincial chain-store. Furnishing fabrics can be bought from a market stall at half the price a smart department store will be charging, and so on.

The prices quoted in the 'Price Bands' of each piece represent the average low and high for items in good condition, without over-restoration or excessive damage. They relate to prices in antique shops, and where there are large differences between, for example, mahogany pieces and rosewood pieces, a note will be found to that effect. But a 1920s tearoom chair is not the same thing as an original Michael Thonet bentwood rocker, nor is a piece of Victorian Tudor oak the same as an Elizabethan piece, which the price-bands make clear. The information given, it is to be hoped, will prevent such confusion from ever arising – the price bands will help the buyer to knew when a piece is over-priced or under-priced. If it is the latter, it is no bad thing to double-check that the piece is genuine before jumping to the conclusion that it is a bargain.

English Antique Furniture: the classic styles

Joint stool

Signs of authenticity

1. Grain of wood coarser than saw-cut timber, showing slight figure and rippling.
2. Thick timber for seats, curving slightly on the grain from shrinkage and age.
3. Stretchers, legs and feet worn with constant use.
4. Dowelling from tops of legs standing slightly proud of seat due to shrinkage and movement of timber.
5. Pegs on stretcher joints and frieze joints should not stand proud. Green timber was used and knocked in as it shrank.
6. Good width of overhang to seat.
7. Build-up of patination on underside of overhang which should feel almost polished with years of wear.
8. Legs and frieze tapering outward slightly on longer side of stool – neatly flush on short end for pushing together to make a bench.
9. Feet showing signs of 'frayed' end-grain damaged by damp and use and unevenly worn.

Likely restoration and repair

10. Legs replaced, usually below the square section, and concealed by turning.
11. Grain of wood ridged, artificially aged with wire brush, not worn smooth.
12. Grain running across width, not down length.
13. False dowelling in new seats where tops have been replaced. Regular shapes of dowels and holes drilled with mechanical drills.
14. Legs of wrong period baluster and turning – possibly replaced with old staircase balusters, quite old, but quite wrong.
15. Seat timber not thick enough. Genuine joint stools have seats at least an inch thick, tapering slightly where timber has been split, not sawn.
16. Pristine, glowing oak with good patination but not a sign of chip or crack is suspect: no genuine joint stool is likely to have survived so long without some damage or splitting.

Historical background

Seat furniture was very limited in range until the end of the sixteenth century. Built-in benches along walls and in window embrasures, and benches or formes which ran the length of trestle tables, were the most common.

Church stools were made by carpenters, who also made panelling and rood screens, choir stalls and pews. They were slab-ended with rough V-shapes cut to make rudimentary legs, and often the seats which slotted into the tops, contained a deep box with a hinged lid.

The joint stool or joined stool was made by the joiner, and its construction was the basis for all chair design until the eighteenth century. The legs were turned by hand in simple baluster and ring; the seats were tenoned to the tops of the legs, and a frieze was joined to the underframe with mortise-and-tenon joints. They had squared stretchers, set low, almost at ground level. Joint stools are sometimes known as 'coffin stools' and in varying heights and shapes they were made almost continuously until the end of the eighteenth century. There was a renewed fashion for these useful little stools during the Victorian Jacobethan revival, when they were made by the thousand.

Construction and materials

The joint stool was made of oak, quarter split and showing some figure in the grain on the seat. The legs were square-sectioned at the top and bottom, the tops forming the sides of the frieze and directly supporting the seat. The legs were slightly splayed for stability, from the top, so that the frieze slopes outwards very slightly, on the two longest sides of the seat only.

The grain of the wood always ran the length of the seat, and was usually finished with a simple edge moulding, and the timber was very thick. The dowelling which secured the seat ran the entire thickness, so that four irregular pegs and holes can be seen on the surface of the seat.

Detail

The frieze might have some simple arcaded or geometrical carving, and the legs were turned in simple baluster or reel-and-bobbin between the stout square sections into which the stretchers were fixed with mortise-and-tenon joints.

Variations

Before c.1500, no one other than people of importance had furniture of any kind, and at this time, virtually all furniture of any consequence was made of oak. It is probable that there were some stools made with elm tops, possibly some in yew wood and some in fruitwood, but a difference in material cannot constitute a dividing line between 'country furniture' and the rest. The joint stool itself became an essential part of country furniture at a later date, when there were chairs of all kinds for those who could afford them.

Variations, right: *seventeenth-century oak joint stool, with chip-carved decoration on the frieze, turned legs and block feet.*

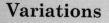

Reproductions

Victorian

The greatest number of reproduction joint stools were probably made during the Victorian Jacobethan revival, using the same construction methods, but making them of machine-cut timber with machine-drilled holes for dowels. On Victorian copies there are almost certainly lining-up marks on the tops of the legs indicating where the frieze should slot in, and above and below the stretchers. There are often patches of paler wood, mistaken for age, due to years of handling, wood which was originally stained. Victorian copies were made with saw-cut, relatively unseasoned timber of commercial thickness, with shallow machine-cut carving, sometimes also around the edge of the seat but almost certainly on the frieze.

Left: *sixteenth century, oak box-stool.* Above: *oak, with decorated frieze, cylindrical turned legs and block feet.*

Price bands

Seventeenth-century oak: £1,000–1,500.

Seventeenth-century yew wood: £1,250–1,750.

Restored original: £350–500.

Victorian reproduction: £100–150.

Panel-back chair

Historical background

These chairs were among the earliest pieces of furniture to be elaborately decorated and carved, as befitted the important seat of power they symbolized, whether ecclesiastical or temporal. There are many regional variations which are quite distinct and recognizable, for the feudal lords were still the equivalent of petty kings in their own territories.

Earlier versions have completely boxed-in seats, a design which lasted until the end of the sixteenth century and overlapped the more sophisticated design with turned legs, built more on the principle of the joint stool. Panelled backs persisted long after the base of the chair had lost its enclosed, coffered construction. Plain chairs without arms, which derived from this pattern, formed the basis of many country chairs for centuries, and the straight-backed, panelled chair continued to be made well into the eighteenth century.

Signs of authenticity

1. Well-worn oak, with no crisp edges. Carving should be worn and rounded with age and wear.
2. Panelled backs and seats of uneven thickness as wood was split and not sawn.
3. Same turning on front legs and arm supports.
4. Back legs slightly splayed, always square-sectioned, never decorated.
5. Panel grain vertical, not horizontal. Frame construction with chamfered panel to fit into grooves on the uprights, on the grain and not across it.
6. Dowelling and mortise-and-tenon joints to stretchers, frieze, seat and back frame. No nails used in construction.
7. Thick build up of patination under arms and arm scrolls where chair has been handled.
8. Some damage and distressing to vulnerable front legs, front stretcher, arms.

Likely restoration and repair

9. Back panel replaced with different panel, often Flemish, taken from coffer, church panelling, etc. Decoration will not accord with crest rail or other decoration on chair.
10. Completely replaced chair back, planed out to resemble framing. Grain will run on over the top and bottom frame.
11. Front legs broken and replaced. Grain of front leg will change, often on ring-turning, or below frieze where it has been joined.
12. Original plain back 'improved', usually by Victorians, often with early date added, in carving of wrong technique for the period, or with patriotic symbols: Scottish thistles, etc.

Construction and materials

Like all furniture of this early period, the panel-back chair was made of oak, quarter cut and split, with a ripple in the grain. The solid stretchers were often at ground level, reminiscent of its origins as a boxed-in chair. Where the stretchers are raised off the ground, legs always terminate in square block feet to take the width of the stretcher tenoned into it. Arm supports were a continuation of the front legs and the sides of the back panelling were a continuation of the back legs.

Detail
Arms were often scrolled, but square in section rather than rounded and often had carved decoration on the outer side. The top rail or crest rail was elaborately carved and often ended in scroll 'ears'.

Some chairs had plain backs, richly painted and gilded while others had carved backs with architectural elements – arches, architraves, columns, pillars and arcaded or geometrical strapwork – more reminiscent of the stonemason's, than the carpenter's craft. Stylized scrollwork and foliage is also to be found richly and deeply carved; rarely one might find carved heraldic devices or royalist symbols.

Variations

Variations are regional and quite distinct. The North country design is distinguishable by its over-running carved sides either side of the arms, and elaborately carved crest rail terminating in rounded scrolls. The East Anglian design frequently featured an arched panel in the back, which fanned out on a level with the arms and not below, as in the North country version.

Northern chairs are heavier, with more ornate scrolled carving incorporating leaves with column-turned or reel-turned legs, whereas southern counties followed more fashionable shapes, such as the baluster and a simple cup and cover or acorn shape for legs and arm supports. The straight-backed chair without arms also has distinct regional variations, notably the Yorkshire and the Lancashire, both of which derive from the armed chair, and have shaped crest rails and distinctive though simplified carved scrolled ends or 'ears'.

Reproductions

Nineteenth century
Whole sets of 'Lancashire' and 'Yorkshire' chairs were made to match up with the bulbous-legged 'medieval' tables made for dining in Victorian baronial halls, recognizable principally by the grain and colour of the oak, which is sawcut, stained and uniformly dark and lacklustre. Although the carving was shallow, these chairs were too ornamented, with frilled aprons and exaggeratedly curving, scrolling arms. The carved backs and crest rails were made in a single piece, with the grain running from top to bottom, with shallow carving in the wrong designs. The carved crest rail was made separately and pegged to the top rail.

Stretchers are too high off the ground and often the whole design has been 'modified' to what was considered to be better proportions and decoration. Single chairs were made to approximately the same design for public buildings, hotels, institutions and assembly halls, with plain panelled backs, or with leather backs studded to the sides, and overstuffed leather seats, also studded, a design that lasted well into the twentieth century.

Price bands

Plain backed, with 'ears': £1,250–2,000.

Genuine period carved back, rare: £3,500+.

Eighteenth-century country version, no arms: £150–300. Set of six: £800–1,000.

Nineteenth-century reproductions: £40–100.

Variations, far left: *James I, South Yorkshire or Derbyshire chair, with scrolled 'ears' and sophisticated turned and fluted arm supports and front legs.* Left: *Seventeenth-century panel-backed chair, with baluster-turned legs and high front stretcher.*

Carolean cane-back chair

Historical background

The art of twist turning and swash turning came to England from Spain and the Spanish Netherlands at the time of Charles II and revolutionized the shape of chairs, tables, stands and stools. Oak, which had previously been the dominating wood for furniture, was abandoned in favour of walnut which was ideal for turning and carving. Many of these chairs were, however, quite successfully made in oak, although the carving on the ornate crest rails was not as crisp and as detailed. The whole design reflected the Continental taste for greater ornament and elegance, so typical of the Restoration period.

Because the cane back and seat weakened the construction of chairs, additional H-shaped stretchers gave added strength, as did a central stretcher between the back legs set on a level with the elaborately carved front rail. Later, as backs became exaggeratedly high in the William and Mary period and scrolled legs were set at an angle, X-stretchers joined the legs, sometimes with a small central finial. These chairs were often known as 'periwig' chairs because the extreme height of their back seemed to mimic one of the fashionable hairstyles of the period.

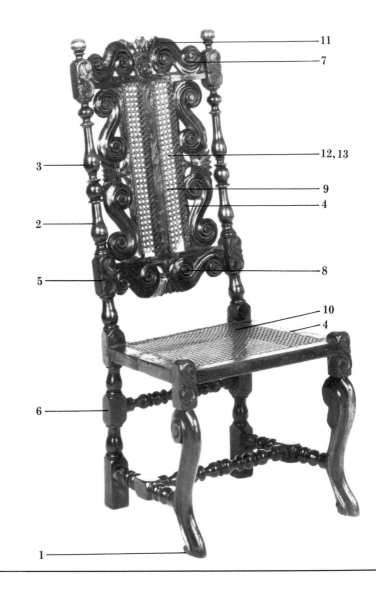

Construction and materials

The best examples of these chairs were made in solid English walnut which was close-grained and far less liable to split when heavily carved and decorated. They were also made in oak with less decoration owing to the coarser grain of the wood, and in beech, painted and gilded. The cane back to the seats was usually square in English chairs and oval in Dutch designs.

On chairs without arms, the front legs continue above the seat to form ornamental bosses designed to hold a loose cushion, and from *c*.1670 most chairs with arms were also made to have cushions on their seats, with the lower seat rail set correspondingly high so as to be seen above the level of the cushion.

From *c*.1690, the construction suffered in favour of ornament, and crest rails were often simply pegged to the tops of the chairs between the uprights. Front legs of single chairs were pegged into the undersides of seats – a construction which was hardly robust.

Detail

The crest rail, as its name implies, was originally heraldic and the carving varies from a fairly simple combination of 'S' and 'C' scrolls to the most intricate and ornate pierced work, of which the *amorati* – two little boys holding up a crown between them – is probably the best known. Carved and scrolled arms are also a common feature, but only the grandest chairs have scrolled feet. The majority of pieces have block feet, sometimes with a turned bobbin (usually worn or cut off) below. Reel-and-bobbin turning to stretchers, arm supports and even back supports is not unusual, though twist turning is commoner.

Reproductions

Nineteenth century

The most common are Victorian, in a mixture of early designs and later versions, with X-stretchers and a Flemish scroll on the crest rail. Another version has upholstered seat and back panel, often in Berlin woolwork, with twist-turned uprights, scrolled feet and twist-turned legs and stretchers. The over-sleek, slightly greenish-coloured copies of the periwig chair are a familiar sight, with a lower back, caned back panel and splayed back legs. They were first made in the Victorian period, and have been reproduced many times since.

Variations

Country versions were usually made in oak, but are sometimes to be found in mixtures of fruitwood and walnut, plane and sycamore, usually less ornately carved. They have wooden or rush seats and straight slatted backs, a raised bottom back rail for strength, and simple carving on the crest rail. The seats are often dished to take a cushion. They were also made with double stretchers on three sides, with a simple turned decorative stretcher in front. Another variation of later date has plain turned front legs, double side stretchers, a plain slatted back and a rush seat.

Left: *late seventeenth century, high-backed chair, with simple C-scrolled crest rail, bobbin and baluster turning and rush seat.*
Centre: *Carolean, with delicate 'boyes and crowne' crest rail. Oval cane panel may suggest Flemish origin.*
Right: *William and Mary stained beechwood armchair.*

Price bands

Walnut, *c*.1680: £1,800–2,500 pair.

Continental, *c*.1680: £700–1,000 pair.

Rush-seated country chairs: £300–500 each.

High-backed beechwood: £400–750 each.

Nineteenth-century reproduction: £120–200.

Queen Anne spoon-back chair

Historical background

The transitional shape of chairs at the end of the seventeenth century included the curved S-scrolling legs with pronounced 'knees' and a carved central splat. These two key features were swiftly followed by the cabriole leg and the single plain central splat so typical of Queen Anne chairs. The single innovation of the cabriole leg completely changed the construction of chairs, which no longer had stretchers and were made with deep aprons, solid underframes and curved backs. Drop-in seats, a feature of chairs from the 1690s, were soon adapted to the new seat-frame construction.

On arm chairs, the arm supports were no longer a continuation of the front legs and were set further back, attached to the outside of the seat frame and curved in modified Flemish scrolls, S-scrolls or shepherd's crooks, to the front of the back supports. Although stretchers continued to be an integral part of country chair construction, they were not used on high-quality chairs until Hepplewhite reintroduced them over half a century later.

Signs of authenticity

1. Back made up of five parts: two side supports (or 'stiles': continuation of back legs); a central curved, veneered splat; a shoe-piece attached to the bottom seat rail and a decorative crest rail.
2. Cabriole legs cut from thickness of timber, with generous spring.
3. Tops of cabriole legs form corners of front seat frame.
4. Underframe of oak or beech.
5. Walnut veneer on solid walnut for central back splat.
6. Made in walnut and walnut veneer to *c.*1735, then in mahogany.
7. Correct height of seat should be 1 ft 6 in.
8. All carved decoration integral, incised, including scallops, masks, etc. on aprons as well as carving on knees and crest rail.
9. Inner surfaces of drop-in seats and seat-frames unpolished, rough.
10. Shoe-piece made separately from back seat rail, not integrally.

Likely restoration and repair

11. New seat frames and back legs: underneath, the new wood can be clearly seen, as well as joints where legs have been attached to back seat rails not continuing in same grain all the way up.
12. Plain or squared cabriole legs decorated with later carving to add value: carving will be in line with silhouette, not standing proud.
13. Arms added to increase value, deceptively curving. Seats of chairs with arms should be at least 2–2½ in wider than singles.
14. Square corners to front of seat and integral shoe-piece suggests marriage between later base and original back.

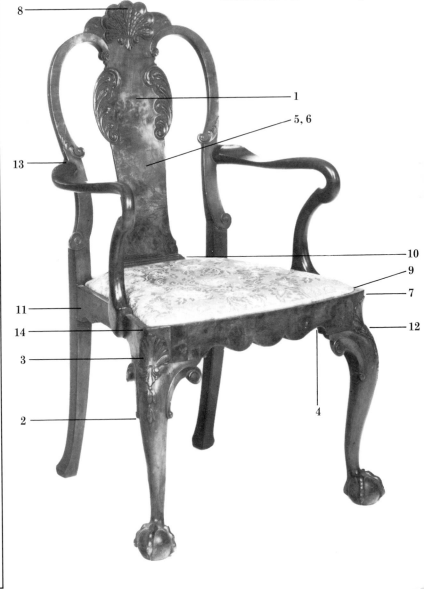

Construction and materials

The construction of the cabriole-legged chair differs so radically from its predecessors that it needs to be described in some detail. The cabriole leg was cut from a single piece of timber, using the natural spring of the wood for strength. The 'knee' was first cut in squared section, and then rounded and carved. Above the 'knee', the top of the leg formed the corner of the seat-frame, which had to be deep and was made with an apron to take the depth of the leg support. The back leg construction remained the same, with the legs continuing up to form the side rails of the curved back. The central splat was cut in serpentine shape, not steamed and bent. With some of the end grain showing where the shape cut into the wood, the splat had to be veneered, and great skill was required to fit the veneered splat into the short length of carved crest rail above it. Below, the splat fitted into a shoe-piece, made separately from the back seat frame.

On armed chairs, the chief difference was that the arms were no longer supported by a continuation of the front legs, the arm supports being set back and curved. The arms, instead of being fixed to the front of the back supports, curved outward and were fixed to the sides of the back rails.

From c.1715 the curve of the cabriole leg was taken up under the seat on either side with two decorative side pieces, glued or dowelled to the tops of the cabriole legs and the underframe. Up to that date, pad or club feet were usual, but after 1715 the heavier ball-and-claw foot became fashionable.

Detail
In many cases the apron was veneered – when it was cut in serpentine shape, for example, as with the central back splat.

The scallop shell was a favourite motif on the crest rail, knees and centre of the apron until c.1714, then leaf carving with eagle's heads on arms. From c.1720–35 the lion's mask appeared on the cabriole leg with lion's paw feet.

Variations

Period country copies were in oak or fruitwood and also in beech, with double stretchers on three sides and simply turned decorative front stretcher, still set high as in previous period. The front legs were often pinned into the underframe in a similar manner to the construction of later cane-backed and periwig chairs, which was simpler but not so enduring. Many had rush seats and the central splat rested on a cross-rail above the seat. Others had a shoe-piece and the splat was fiddle-shaped or vase-shaped, fitting into a slightly curved crest rail. Plain wooden seated versions were also made, with slightly dished seats to take a loose cushion.

Far left: *fine quality, c.1700, with shell-carved knee to the well-sprung cabriole leg. Positive cyma-curved side supports flow into crest.*
Left: *grand country version, with vase-shaped back splat, drop in seat, well-shaped cabriole legs on pad feet.*

Reproductions

Nineteenth century
Like all Queen Anne furniture, these chairs were copied in the Victorian period, but the cabriole leg looks bandy because the timber was skimped in the cutting. The back legs had an uneasy transition to the side rails of the back, often giving an ungainly line instead of a sweeping, raked curve. The shoe-piece was made as an integral part of the back seat rail, an easy sign to detect.

These chairs were too high-backed for dining chairs, having been made before the age of butlers and footmen, and of all chair designs, the Queen Anne spoonback is probably the least reproduced after the mid-nineteenth century.

Above: *nineteenth-century copy, with awkward side supports, heavy back legs and weak cabriole.*

Price bands

High-quality 'shepherd's crook' armchair, c.1700: £3,000–5,000.

c.1700 ball-and-claw with veneered back splat: £1,800–2,500 each.

Provincial, c.1700, with solid back splat: £500–1,000 each.

Nineteenth century, with veneered back splat: £300–500 each.
Set of six: £3,000–5,000.

Queen Anne wing chair

Historical background

The Palladian architecture of the early eighteenth century suited the English landscape beautifully, but the high ceilings and spaciousness of the interiors were more suited to warmer climates. Porters in draughty halls sat out their on-duty hours in deep, hooded chairs which almost entirely enclosed them. In drawing rooms, their masters and mistresses sat protected from draughts in high-backed wing chairs, elegantly upholstered in fine needlework. In libraries, wing chairs were leather-covered and edged with rows of brass studs.

The square shapes of earlier periods gave way to curving lines and hooped backs to seating furniture, which was designed for comfort as well as elegance. Over two and a half centuries have passed and the design of the winged chair has remained virtually unchanged.

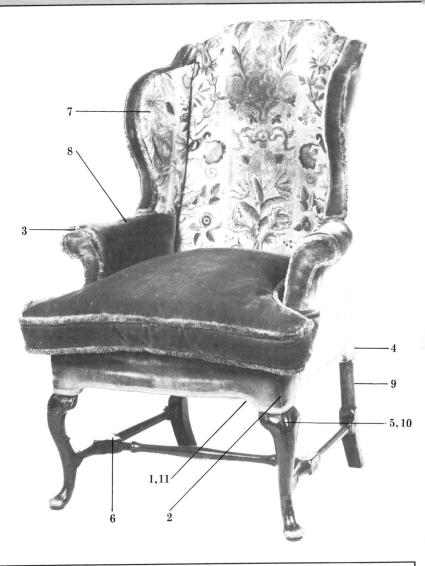

Signs of authenticity

1. Beech, plane or sycamore frame, with rust, dirt and embedded fabric where original upholstery was secured to the frame with square-headed iron nails.
2. Front legs continue up to form the corners of the seat frame.
3. Flowing S-curve of the arms, ending in rounded arm rests, curved and tapering down to the seat frame.
4. Back legs continue up above back seat level, raked inward before sloping gently outward to form shape of raked back.

5. Cabriole legs short, well-proportioned, with or without carving on the knee.
6. With pad feet and stretchers, the join is always into square-sectioned blocks, the stretchers usually H-shaped.

Likely restoration and repair
7. Almost certainly completely re-upholstered at least once in its lifetime.
8. Frames rebuilt, repaired, particularly on arms, which may have broken outwards and been pinned.
9. Back legs broken and replaced.
10. The whole built up from two good cabriole legs, perhaps from a stool or other piece of furniture.
11. No wing chair should be bought as genuine unless the underframe is visible at some part – particularly on the joins of the legs.

Construction and materials

The key shape of the eighteenth century wing chair is the curve, with the line carried down to the neat curve of the short cabriole legs in front and the splay of the back legs. For the first decade of the eighteenth century the seats were deep, and the arms set more or less square, but from c.1710 the seats flared out to accommodate the wide hooped skirts and full coat-tails of fashionable dress. The frames were made of beech, plane or sycamore – woods which could be close-nailed without splitting. Cabriole legs were of walnut until c.1720, and then of mahogany. They were upholstered with tow or horsehair, bound with webbing, and covered first with hessian and then with calico before the final upholstery in leather or needlework.

Detail

Early eighteenth-century wing chairs had little carved decoration on the front leg 'knee' (more elaborate carving became fashionable after c.1720 with the introduction into England of mahogany). They had shaped squab seats and frames were studded with small brass-headed nails around the outer sides of the wings and on the base above the legs, particularly when upholstered in leather.

In the early eighteenth century, front legs ended in plain pad feet and stretchers were slender. After c.1730, heavier ball-and-claw feet were preferred and stretchers were often omitted altogether.

Variations

Upholstered furniture of any kind was a luxury until the mid-Victorian period and was not made or used by any but the well-to-do.

The equivalent of the wing-back chair in country furniture is the high-backed, oak settle to seat three or four people near the fire, with wings to keep out the draught, and the high-backed, so-called 'lambing chair' which was simply a single version of the long settle. Later, Windsor chairs became the country equivalent of the upholstered wing chair.

Below: *wing chair with crisp outlines, c.1710.*
Right: *'porter's chair'.*

Reproductions

There has been virtually no break in the production of winged chairs of one sort of another since they were first made. Some later eighteenth century wing chairs have wide ribbed backs and are more curved, with shorter arms, but most originals are very hard to find in any good state. The only major change in construction came in 1828 with the invention of the coiled spring for upholstered furniture. In the mid-Victorian period some chairs were made with cast-iron frames, a short-lived idea because of their extreme weight.

Above: *nineteenth-century version, with bulging arm supports, drooping wings and insignificant legs.*

Price bands

Eighteenth century, with original upholstery: £5,000–7,000.

Eighteenth century, with later upholstery: £3,500–5,000.

Eighteenth century, with pad feet and stretchers: £4,000–6,000.

Nineteenth-century reproduction: £650–1,000.

Adam round-back chair

Historical background

By the end of the Chippendale period (Thomas Chippendale died in 1779), fashions had changed considerably, due to the influence of Robert and John Adam, whose classical interior designs and architecture were altogether lighter and less substantial than those of the early Georgian period. The emphasis laid on painted and applied decoration had a marked effect on furniture design, and the preference for lighter colours influenced the woods and finishes used for furniture. Although George Hepplewhite is better known for his famous shield-back chair, he designed many chairs for Adam interiors, among them the hoop- or round-back chair which was a transitional step towards the radical construction of the shield back.

This period of chair design is particularly associated with tapering legs, either square-sectioned and ending in neat spade feet, or round, taper-turned legs on small peg feet. Often the rounded central panel was upholstered, and the seats of Adam round-back chairs were nearly always overstuffed.

Fashions in clothes changed, too, and the more clinging lines of dress allowed arm supports to be set closer to the front of the seat and swoop back to join the sides of the rounded backs.

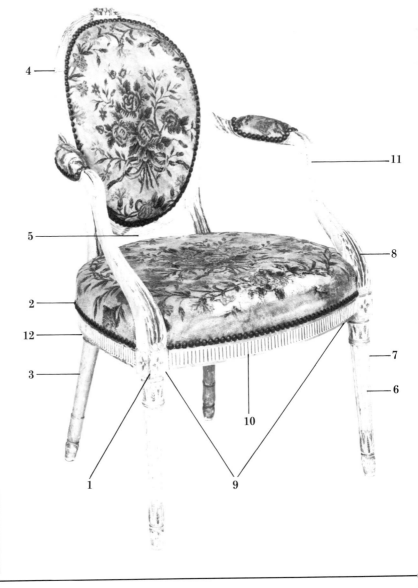

Construction and materials

These graceful chairs were made in mahogany, and in beech, ebonized with black japanning, as well as in satinwood and in satinwood and birch. The shape of the seat was nearly always curved or serpentine, and the back legs, while still continuing up to form the back supports, were slightly splayed. Legs were often tapered, and Hepplewhite reintroduced stretchers on many chairs to add strength to thinner tapering legs. Although the hoop of the back appears to be a continuous curved piece, it was still made with the same construction as earlier chairs, with the rounded crest rail meeting the top of the side rails almost seamlessly.

Detail
Often simple, tapering legs were lightened with fluting, or decorated with gadrooning or cabochon carving in low relief. On chairs with arms, the tops of the front legs were frequently decorated with classical motifs in accord with Adam designs. In earlier hooped-back versions of the Adam round back, the central splat was fretted and pierced, usually in vertical lines, and still fitted into a separate shoe-piece attached to the back rail – a design that came to be known as the wheatsheaf.

Variations

The classic country wheelback and the hooped-back Windsor chair are contemporary with Adam round-backed chairs, but form a special category of their own (see pp. 70–71). Most common country versions are the camel-backed wheatsheaf chairs, made in elm, or oak and elm with wooden seats and H-shaped stretchers and an additional back stretcher, still set high.

The construction and craftsmanship needed to produce a round back, other than the methods used for Windsor chairs, was beyond the country furniture-maker, who continued to make chairs with the traditional construction of separate crest rails attached either to the tops of the side rails, or fitting between them.

Reproductions

The more solid mahogany round back or hooped back has not been reproduced as often as its cheaper, more decorative counterpart, the painted beechwood chair of similar design. These were made in great quantities by the Victorians, with indefinably wrong proportions, as boudoir chairs and drawing-room chairs. The most favoured has an upholstered panel in the back and an overstuffed seat. To be fair, some nineteenth-century versions achieved a very pleasant look, though the Victorian tendency to make curved what should be straight often results in unattractive legs, bowed and serpentine, on an otherwise pleasing design.

There are some nineteenth-century florid 'spider's web' chairs, a variation on the plain wheelback, usually easy to recognize by the turning on the tapered legs which already shows a tendency to bulbousness.

The most popular design, reproduced incessantly since the late eighteenth century, is the 'wheatsheaf', often with a squared crest rail.

Price bands

Period painted beech or giltwood.
Pairs: £2,200–3,500.
Singles: £900–1,200.

Late eighteenth-century mahogany, with arms: £500–800 each.
Set of four: £3,000–4,500.

Nineteenth-century reproduction: £280–400 each.
Set of six: £1,200–2,000.

Variations, far left: *Provincial chair of Hepplewhite design.*
Left: *A late Hepplewhite-style armchair.*
Left, above: *Round-backed Adam-style chair, with raked back legs.*

Chippendale dining chair

Historical background

Designs for Thomas Chippendale's chairs were freely available once his pattern book, *The Gentleman and Cabinet Maker's Director* was published in 1754 and were made with modifications and variations by numerous furniture-makers throughout the period 1754–80.

The main shift in design from previous shapes was the squared, almost over-running shape of shoulder and crest rail, and the pierced and carved central splat. Mahogany was used almost exclusively for dining chairs of this period: its immense strength and density allowed pierced work of great elaboration. The beginning of the period maintained rounded corners to chair seats, but once Chippendale reintroduced plain squared legs, seat corners were also square.

Chippendale chairs were made in sets for dining rooms. Their backs were lower to allow the newly adopted custom of dining *à la Berline* – with footmen serving dishes individually, instead of the hitherto traditional English way of dining, from a side table heaped with food.

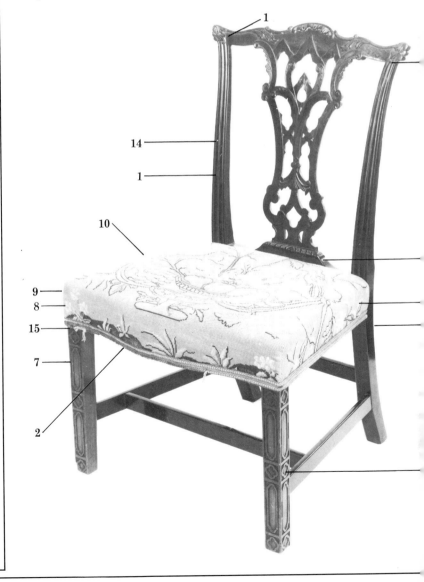

Construction and materials

Throughout the Chippendale period, dining chairs were made in solid mahogany, oiled and rubbed smooth with brick dust or sand to a glossy, silky finish. The backs of chairs were lower, with square shoulders often terminating in small upward-curling scrolls. There were two types of construction: the traditional, with the crest rail fitting between the two side rails which curved inward towards the centre, and the innovative, with the crest rail almost over-running the outward-curving side rails, like a cupid's bow. On chairs with arms, the supports were higher and the arms ran almost parallel with the seat, fixed to the sides of the seat frames almost half way back, to allow for fashionable full skirts.

Detail
Although the central splats, crest rail and legs were profusely decorated, the stiles were seldom carved, but left plain or fluted. Seats of chairs were sometimes overstuffed or had deep decorative aprons, often serpentine in shape.

It is surprising to learn that the technique of lamination was first used for the fretted backs and ornament of the Chippendale period. Layers of veneer of alternating grain were glued together and then cut with a fret saw into intricate shapes.

Variations

Simplified variations of Chippendale's designs were made by most country furniture-makers, usually in oak, but also in elm, beech, ash and fruitwoods. They had plain wooden seats made of planking nailed to the underframe, usually in more than one piece, with the grain going from side to side. Occasionally they are to be found with rush seats.

The designs of the back include the crudest cut-out work – most commonly a curving variation of four or five straight splats, either in a wheatsheaf shape or an open vase or violin shape. Most widespread and enduring are those made in a simplified ladderback design. Legs are square, sometimes slightly chamfered on the inner sides. The back stretcher is still set higher than the front, and the two side stretchers are parallel. The tops of the front legs form the sides of the seat frame, and there is usually a fairly deep apron.

Below left: *classic example of later Chippendale, c.1700, ladder-back.*
Centre: *a provincial vase splat.*
Right: *classic North country ladder-back.*
Far right: *nineteenth-century 'ribband-back'.*

Reproductions

Nineteenth century
Provincial furniture-makers were often as much as 50 years behind the most recent fashions, and 'Chippendale' chairs were still being made at the beginning of the nineteenth century. By the mid-nineteenth century they were being made by many furniture manufacturers, slightly modified, with rather meagre cabriole legs, or with the slimmer, scrolled leg and foot typical of the later period of Chippendale design. Often designs such as the ribband back and its variations had square legs and stretchers instead of cabriole legs.

Many Chippendale-style chairs were mass-produced for public rooms, assembly halls, hotels and board rooms, with machine-cut central splats, square, leather-covered seats, often dished, and with the shoe-piece made as an integral part of the back seat rail. Quality of materials and craftsmanship divide the mass-produced from good Victorian copies, which today are fetching extremely good prices.

Price bands

Late eighteenth-century mahogany: £400–550 each.
Set of six: £5,000–7,000.

Country versions: £280–350 each.
Set of six: £3,000–4,500.

Nineteenth-century walnut: £350–400 each.

Nineteenth-century mahogany. Set of six: £3,000–5,000.

Hepplewhite shield-back chair

Historical background

George Hepplewhite started his career as an apprentice to Gillows of Lancaster, and is the first recorded furniture designer to work for a large company of furniture manufacturers. His pattern book, *The Cabinet Maker and Upholsterer's Guide*, was not published until 1788, two years after his death. Its intention was 'to combine elegance and utility and blend the useful with the agreeable'. Although Hepplewhite died in relative obscurity, his designs continued to be made both in London and the provinces in large numbers well into the nineteenth century.

The shield back is probably his most famous design, which has been copied and reproduced in many variations, though seldom successfully. The remarkable point about the design is that the entire back is concave to take the sitter's back comfortably, yet seen from the front there is little or no distortion of proportion or shape. The shield-back design was a direct outcome of the round- or wheel-back chair and it marks another radical change in construction.

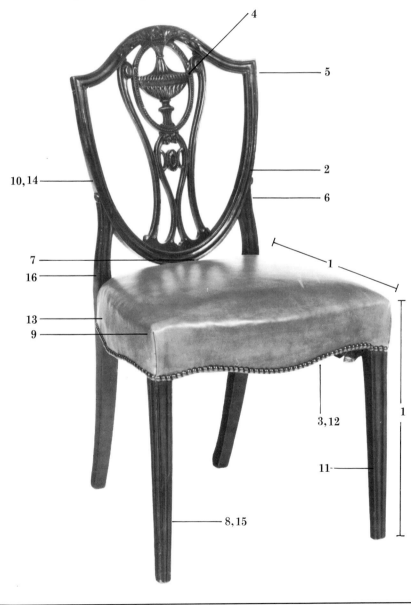

Signs of authenticity

1. Correct proportions laid down by Hepplewhite: height of seat frame 17 in, depth of seat 17 in, width of seat 20 in, overall height 37 in.
2. Legs and back of good quality, dense-grained mahogany.
3. Seat frames in beech.
4. All carving in low relief, softened with age and wear.
5. Top of shield construction still a crest rail, joined to the upward-curving sides of the shield.
6. Waisted join of back support to shield secured with hand-turned screws, concealed by plugs or dowels, now almost invisible.
7. Bottom of shield rounded, never pointed.
8. Tapered front legs fluted or carved with restrained motif.
9. On chairs with arms, arms set forward or directly over tops of legs.
10. Arms set into sides of shield, not spoiling the line.
11. Legs tapered on insides only.

Likely restoration and repair
12. Underframes of pinkish-tinged birch, used in the nineteenth century.
13. Seats upholstered within wooden frame indicate nineteenth century.
14. Arms set into sides of shield indicates possible replacement of original arm, or nineteenth-century copy, or a single chair with added arms to increase value.
15. Front legs tapered from the outsides indicating a replacement or a later copy.
16. Back legs square-sectioned to seat frame, then waisted (originals were shaped from the seat frame upwards in a graduated curve) indicates back supports replaced, or a later copy.

Construction and materials

The shield-shaped back was entirely supported by a short continuation of the back legs, shaped and waisted to flow into the outward curve of the shield. The base of the shield was rounded and the top crest rail was an exaggerated cupid's bow. Without the centre splat, the seat could be overstuffed at the back as well as the front, which was serpentine or curved with a much deeper apron than previous designs. As no part of the seat frame was visible, it could be made in beech, which was less expensive and did not split when close-nailed for upholstery. On chairs with arms, the arm support sprang from the tops of the front legs and curved up to meet the arms which were often set higher at the back to follow the natural line of the body.

Detail
A favourite motif for the central design of the shield back was the Prince of Wales' feathers and another was the Greek urn.

All the carving on the seat back was in low relief and, like the Adam round-back chair, the legs were tapered and fluted.

Occasionally, there was restrained decorative carving on the front legs and, on chairs with arms, on either side of the seat where the tops of the legs formed the corners.

Variations

The difference between a country version of a round back and a shield back is marginal, since both designs merged in the wheatsheaf, which could also be said to be a simplified Prince of Wales' feathers design. They were usually made in elm, beech and fruitwood, with square-sectioned legs and four stretchers (with the back one set slightly higher than the other three). The other variation of the Prince of Wales' feathers design is to be found in Windsor chairs (see pp. 70–73).

Reproductions

Nineteenth century
The shield back is one of the most copied and reproduced chair designs in the whole spectrum, yet it is seldom correctly achieved. Nineteenth-century copies were frequently made with stretchers to add strength to the construction. In spite of its apparent simplicity it was a difficult chair to make, and many of them were made with upholstered seats with solid mahogany frames and aprons instead of underframes and overstuffed seats.

Shields were made in three sections, tapering to a point at the base and mitred together, and the low-relief carving is mechanical and repetitive, adding little to the overall appearance.

Reproductions are quite easy to detect, since the shield looks flattened and too broad when seen from the front, although from the side the proportions seem right. Undeterred, manufacturers of reproduction furniture continued to make sets of 'shield backs' and its close relative, the 'lyre-backed' chair (with brass uprights to simulate harp strings), throughout the nineteenth and well into the twentieth century.

Price bands

Good quality, *c.*1780: £300–600 each.

Provincial camel back: £200–400 each.
Set of six: £2,000–3,500.

Nineteenth-century shield back, good quality: £250–500 each.
Set of six: £2,500–4,000.

Variations, far left: *Camel back, c.1790.*
Left, above: *Stubby, stretchered version, with the arms set into the front of the shield.*
Left: *Shield-back, c.1780.*

Sheraton chair

Historical background

Even at its most decorative and ornate, Sheraton furniture is made with very little integral ornament, and relies for its originality and sparkle on painting and gilding, inlay and japanning. Sheraton was puritan by conviction and by nature, favouring straight lines rather than curves, and multi-purpose space-saving furniture for the ranks of Georgian terraced houses which had recently been built. He came to London in 1790 from the North of England, and was designing during the Napoleonic Wars, when materials and money were short, and much of his furniture was made in cheaper beechwood and birch, rather than expensive mahogany, although he did favour satinwood which was costly. In construction, Sheraton was a traditionalist. He reverted to the old manner of making chairs with crest rails tenoned between the back supports, as opposed to overriding them or curving into them. On chairs with arms, he took the line even higher than Hepplewhite, so that the arm of the chair sweeps up to the crest rail in an abrupt curve, almost as though it is part of the back itself.

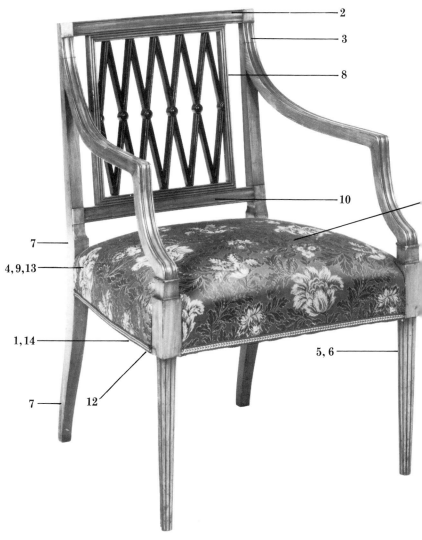

Signs of authenticity

1. Made of beech, with ash or birch underframes.
2. Crest rail tenoned into sides of back supports.
3. On chairs with arms, arms joined to fronts of back supports, high up and usually on a line with a horizontal back rail.
4. On chairs with upholstered seats, pronounced height of seat above frame.
5. Front legs taper-turned to the frame, then square-sectioned, forming the corners of seat frames on straight-fronted chairs.
6. On chairs with round seats, legs taper-turned to frame, then square-sectioned flush with curve to form solid underframe.
7. Back legs either square-sectioned or taper-turned, but always square-sectioned at seat level to form stout join of chair frame.
8. Crest rail, supports and arms all turned, reeded or fluted.

Likely restoration and repair
9. Original frames of seats overstuffed when re-upholstered – a frequent Victorian practice.
10. Stripped and repainted and gilded.
11. Recaned panels and seats.
12. New blocks on corners of drop-in seat frame.
13. Damaged cane seats overstuffed – signs of holes for original caning on underframe.
14. Made of cheaper birch entirely – probably a later copy.

Construction and materials

In spite of their air of fragility, Sheraton chairs were remarkably solidly constructed, often in beech, with a sound knowledge of timber and of stresses and strains. In their basic construction, they have more in common with the traditional framed construction than any chairs made from the beginning of the eighteenth century onwards. The back is supported by a top rail and lower rail set parallel and tenoned into the sides of the back supports. The back legs are raked back and square-sectioned in his early designs, though later they were less solid and usually tapered or taper-turned, like the front legs. On chairs with arms, the design exaggerates the line of continuity from front leg to arm support, carrying it up to elbow height, often without a curve at all. The back splats are arranged in geometrical patterns of parallel lines, lattice, or a mixture of both. Seats were often curved or round, upholstered and built up on a solid front apron. Drop-in seats were supported with four shaped brackets on the four corners of the seat frame. Front legs were taper-turned, and the use of beech allowed a slight splay since it is a pliable, springy wood, not rigid or liable to split.

Detail
Sheraton seats were often caned, sometimes also with caned panels in the rectangular backs. The back splats were characteristically arranged in geometrical patterns of parallel lines, lattice, or a mixture of both. Japanning, painting and gilding were also used. Crest rails, supports and arms were often turned, reeded or fluted to lighten the design.

Variations

The return to the square back suited many country chair-makers who were still making chairs with traditional construction, to which Sheraton had returned. Most typical of the country versions of his designs are the plain bar-back and rail-back chairs. The other two types of country chairs of the period could equally well have evolved naturally, without benefit of Thomas Sheraton's *The Cabinet Maker and Upholsterer's Drawing Book* (1791–94), and indeed could have been the inspiration for many of his rectangular chair designs. Both originated in the North of England – the spindle back and the bobbin back with their deep plain crest rails developed from the old box-construction.

The country tradition of setting the front and back stretcher slightly higher than the side stretchers continued, and the front stretcher was also often simply turned, again a country tradition. On country chairs of this period, wooden seats were often slightly dished. On chairs with arms, the construction was traditional, with the arm support being a continuation of the front leg, with the arm tenoned into it.

Top: *late eighteenth-century, cane-seated chair in simulated bamboo.*
Above: *Sheraton provincial chair, c.1810.*

Reproductions

Nineteenth century
Sheraton was very much a designer for the trade, and contemporary production of his chairs and other furniture was extremely large. During the early nineteenth century Gillows of Lancaster, the Seddons, Edwards and Roberts, Cooper and Holt, Wright and Mansfield, Jackson and Graham, Johnson and Jeans and many other large furniture manufacturers made quantities of Sheraton furniture.

The Victorians copied some of his more fantastic 'Egyptian' and classical designs, suitable for the increasing ostentation in taste, and many Sheraton-style chairs were made in mahogany to give them a more substantial appearance. Some of these nineteenth-century variations are pleasing, solid and well-constructed. Later versions are not so successful, having square-sectioned tapered legs and stretchers, or more bulbously turned front legs. The height of the bottom back rail was an integral part of the construction as well as the design, and on late versions chairs look oddly proportioned, as though the chair back has been compressed.

Twentieth century
During the Edwardian period, countless cheap copies of Sheraton's little cane-seated chairs, gold-painted and flimsy, were made for ballrooms and public functions. They should not be confused with Regency 'rout' chairs, which were elegantly proportioned and well-made, though few of them have survived intact.

Price bands

Simulated bamboo, *c.*1810: £210–350 each.

Square back, reeded, *c.*1810: £150–250.
Set of six with two arm chairs: £3,200–4,000.

Provincial reeded and plain: £150–250.
Set of six: £2,000–3,500.

Windsor chair

Historical background

Although these chairs are usually attributed to the end of the eighteenth century, their origins go back much further, and chairs of similar design are known to have been made as early as the end of the seventeenth century. Their construction is entirely different from any other type of country chair, and relates more closely to the joint stool than to any other early chair. It is probable that they evolved from the simplest form of seat furniture of all – the three-legged stool.

In the case of Windsor chairs, it is not the backs, arms or legs which are the most important feature. It is the seat, made of a single slab of wood, usually elm, and worked with an adze into a saddle shape. This single feature remains constant in all true Windsors, with or without arms.

The bending properties of yew wood had long been known, since it was the wood from which longbows were made. The first use of a yew-wood bow on Windsors was not the upright hoop but a circular back and arm support, parallel to the chair seat. Originally the legs were simply pegged into the

Signs of authenticity

1. Figuring of grain clearly visible on underside of seat as well as surface – timber was split, not sawn.
2. On chairs with arms, yew wood arm hoop until *c.*1790.
3. Back and front legs with matching turning.
4. No nails, joints of any description other than plain taper-turned tenons on all joins.
5. Saddle shape to seats, on versions with and without arms.
6. On chairs with arms without V-support and 'bob tail', grain running from side to side on seat.
7. On chairs with V-supports, and 'bob tail', grain running front to back.
8. Uneven thicknesses of 'sticks' on all hand-made chairs.
9. Back feet more worn from use than front feet.
10. Worn, rich patination on seat and all parts in contact with body.
11. On hooped backs, ends of hoops split and wedged under seat for added strength.

Likely restoration and repair
12. Legs replaced, so no wear on feet.
13. Sticks replaced and these not taper-turned.
14. Seats not saddle-shaped suggests recent reproductions.
15. Saw-marks on undersides of seats indicates recent manufacture. Seat timber was split not sawn.
16. Hoops not dowelled right through seat or split and wedged indicates recent manufacture.
17. Legs replaced with wrong timber, often elm, to match seat. Should be beech, birch or fruitwood.

Construction and materials

thick seat-timber without stretchers, and splayed to wedge them. A row of holes was dowelled round the seat, and straight taper-turned 'sticks' joined the arm-hoop to the seat, continuing up to form a curved back, held in place by a simple crest rail.

These early Windsors are often known as 'stick-backs' or 'comb backs' because the shaped crest rail resembles a comb. It was not a very solid construction, and sticks and legs became insecure and fell apart with use and as the timber shrank. But as long as the seat was intact, the pieces could easily be replaced, since they were extremely simply made. This rudimentary design seems to have been made independently by foresters and wood-turners all over the country, with regional differences in woods and detail, wherever there were good supplies of suitable timber. They are found in the West Country, and the Midlands, and notably in Buckinghamshire, in and around High Wycombe, which later became the heart of English chair-making, and has continued to be the centre of the industry until the present.

Improvements in the rudimentary design were soon apparent: a thicker central splat, often only below the arm-hoop, appears on many chairs before the full-length decorative central splat. Stretchers were inevitable to make the construction more solid. They were either very simple, joining the front and back legs on either side, or H-shaped, taper-tenoned and swelling in the centre. Extra support was given to stick-backs with a short extension to the back of the seat, with two extra stays in a V-shape behind the back.

It is hard to determine precisely when the hoop back first became a feature of Windsor chairs, but certainly it was contemporary with Hepplewhite's round-back chairs. Up to this period, the arm hoop was still a relatively open curve, but with improved techniques of steaming and bending wood, introduced

continued overleaf

Variations

Invariably the saddle seat was made from well-seasoned elm, a wood which did not warp with damp and was less likely to shrink or split than oak. Ash is also sometimes found in some districts. Legs were often of straight-grained beech, easy to work and turn, and less liable to wear. Arm hoops were almost always of yew wood until the beginning of the nineteenth century. The 'sticks' were of ash, beech, birch or fruitwood – pliant woods with spring, rather than solid woods like oak and elm which are more rigid and liable to split. All four legs were turned to the same pattern and pegged or tenoned into holes in the seat, often with the dowels continuing right through the seat, as on joint stools. Stretchers were plain H-shaped on most straightforward Windsors, taper-turned and tenoned into the legs. In the mid-eighteenth century the 'cow's horn' or crinoline stretcher was a feature of Windsors with arms, curving back from the two front legs and joined to the back legs with two angled, taper-turned stretchers. On these chairs, legs and arm supports were of a simplified baluster shape with ring turning. The hooped back on armed chairs is pegged right through the arm hoop – on chairs without arms, right through the seat. The back 'sticks' are the full height of the chair, running through the arm hoop from seat to crest.

Reproductions

Victorian
Windsor chairs have been in continuous production quite authentically until the end of the nineteenth century, with small differences in methods of manufacture. As is to be expected, those made during Victorian times, such as the smoker's bow, have rather more bulbous turning than earlier periods, but not enough to detract from their obviously traditional pattern.

Twentieth century
Everyone should be familiar with the innumerable mass-produced versions – usually singles – made by furniture-makers with well-known names. Their chief difference lies in the materials: machine-sawn woods for seats, with no figured grain on the underside and very little on the seat surface, steamed hoops, straight 'sticks' without taper turning, machine cut and fretted centre splats and identical machine-turned legs.

Recently, smoker's bows have been made in blonde woods, and in cheap pale woods, stained and ebonized. Some are of excellent quality but will not endure one quarter the length of time as an original Windsor. Most of them are not cheap, and with diligent hunting it is still possible to find genuine Windsors in twos and threes, and even sixes, for the same price, though they are more likely to be of the less attractive 'kitchen chair' type than hooped backs, which are now extremely scarce.

Genuine Windsor chairs dating from the eighteenth century are extremely expensive and sought after. Even late nineteenth century Windsor chairs with hooped backs can cost as much as their dining-room counterparts. Good Windsor chairs with arms are very much in demand.

continued over

Windsor chair

towards the end of the eighteenth century, woods other than yew could be used. It was steamed and bent, then clamped and cooled in the shape of a horse-shoe or hoop. By this time there had already been many refinements in the basic design: legs were bobbin-turned, front and back, as were the arm supports. Cabriole legs were used in the mid-eighteenth century, in most cases not very successfully as far as design was concerned. During the 'Chippendale period' many chair-makers attempted variations on the 'Gothic' with some curious results.

The two best-known designs for the central splat of the hoop back are the 'wheelback' and the 'Prince of Wales' feathers', both contemporary with Hepplewhite. It was probably around this period that these essentially country chairs were dignified with the name 'Windsor', by which they have been known ever since.

Child's high chair, early nineteenth century, in elm, ash and yew, with cow's horn or crinoline stretcher. The footrest is missing.

Highly-prized late eighteenth-century Windsor, with cabriole legs, crinoline stretcher, well-designed pierced back splat and curving arm supports.

Price bands

Elm and yew smoker's bow: £320–450.

Comb back in yew, ash and elm: £500–800.

Child's high chair: £600–850.

Cabriole leg, eighteenth century: £850–1,200.

Nineteenth-century 'kitchen' chair: £85–160.

Yew wood always more.

From the beginning of the nineteenth century the hoop back armchair was made in a design known as a 'smoker's bow'. This was a squat version of an arm chair, with a flat bow cut from a single piece of wood, with a dumpy little crest rail dowelled on to the back. The 'sticks' were far stouter, and were usually bobbin-turned, splaying out from the seat and dowelled into the underside of the flat armpiece. Hooped-back armchairs, wheelbacks and Prince of Wales' feathers designs have rather eclipsed all other varieties of the Windsor chair such as the rail back, the lathe back and the spindle back. The two factors which characterize a Windsor remain constant however: a solid seat into which the legs are pegged or tenoned, and a separate back structure, pegged or tenoned into the seat. No Windsor chair has back legs which continue up to form the supports of the back.

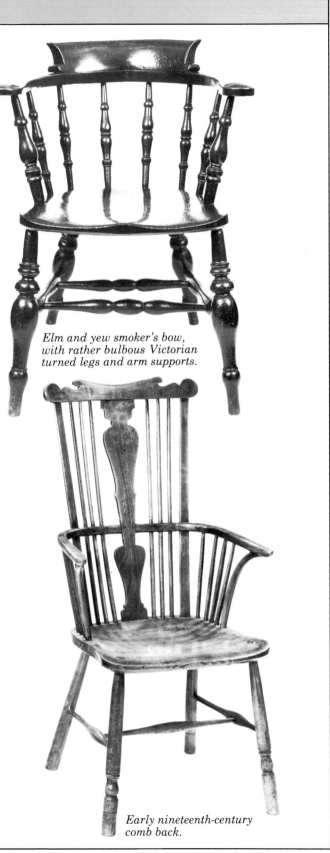

Elm and yew smoker's bow, with rather bulbous Victorian turned legs and arm supports.

ate nineteenth-century rsion of classic Windsor, with avy arms, crest rail and thick ck splats.

Early nineteenth-century comb back.

73

Sabre-leg chair

Historical background

Thomas Hope, connoisseur and dilettante, is credited with the original concept of this radical design, but it was George Smith, cabinet-maker and furniture-maker who simplified the neo-classical shape and made the flush-sided chair a practical commercial proposition. Its lines derive from Ancient Greek and Egyptian rather than the Adam 'classical' and it represented the height of the Regency taste for unbroken lines and severe curves. Probably the most well-known design – certainly the most copied and reproduced – is the 'Trafalgar' chair, with a rope-twist incorporated into the crest rail or back rail, made to commemorate Nelson's victory.

There had been many technical advances in furniture-making by the end of the eighteenth century. Steam-driven machinery, bonding, laminating and veneer-cutting all had a considerable influence on furniture design. There was also a far greater scientific understanding of weight and stress. The flush-sided chair is a remarkably modern construction, with the timbers cut scientifically across the grain so that the leg and side-frame were made in a single piece, bonded to the curving back and back leg in a single continuous line.

Signs of authenticity

1. In solid wood, cut across the grain on the side frames so that at no point is the grain running at an angle of more than 45°.
2. Back rail and crest rail tenoned inside back frame supports.
3. Seat frame flowing in continuous line from crest rail to legs.
4. Upholstered seat contained within seat frame, not overstuffed.
5. Decoration, stringing, brass inlay, flush with surface and silhouette.
6. On chairs with arms, arm supports in counter-curve to front legs, often with scrolling at armrest.
7. Arms follow precise curve of seat and back frame, finishing flush into front of back support.
8. On chairs with arms, upholstered seat contained within seat frame and arms.
9. Front legs with more pronounced forward curve than back curve of back legs.
10. All legs square-sectioned, unstretchered.

Likely restoration and repair

11. Caned seats replaced with upholstery, covering front seat rail.
12. Legs broken, split and pinned – most vulnerable point just below knees of front legs. Examine grain closely for repairs.
13. Back supports broken and repaired. Both these points may not detract from appearance but considerably weaken structure.
14. Decorative brass rosettes on sides of knees, seat frame junction with back legs – may conceal pinning or repair.
15. Attractive if incongruous carving on front legs other than reeding. Probably conceals a partly replaced leg.

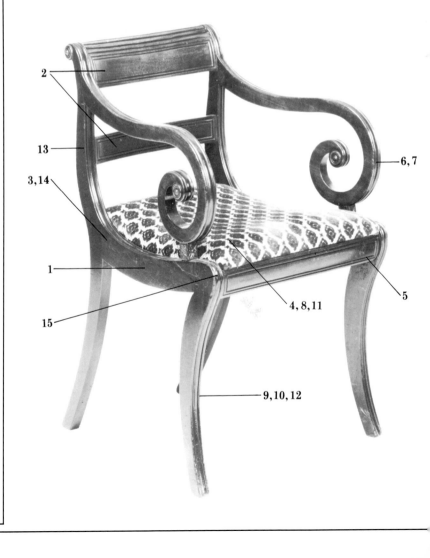

Construction and materials

This radical design was made in solid mahogany, rosewood, simulated rosewood, ebonized beech, real and simulated calamander, and, in some less costly versions, with side frames and seat rails of solid dark woods with a beech underframe. The test of a genuine flush-sided chair is that it can be laid completely flat on its side on the floor. Legs are always unstretchered, the front legs frequently have a more pronounced curve than the back legs – hence its name 'sabre leg'. The crest rail, often several inches deep, is tenoned to the inside of the back supports and does not overrun the seat frame. Chairs with flush sides and crest rails over-running the side are of later date. Seats were upholstered and curved with the side-frame. They were never overstuffed at the front, where there was always a straight seat rail joining the two high-curving knees.

In line with the fashions of the day, the sabre-legged chair was also made in a lighter construction, with a dark wood, or ebonized beech for the frame, and caned seat and back panel.

Detail

Frequently there was continuous reeding which carried from the side of the crest rail, down the top of the seat frame, over the knees and down the front of the slightly tapered square-sectioned legs. Brass inlay, stringing and decoration were flush with the surface. On arms, there is often scrolling at the end of the armrest.

Variations

These chairs required a considerable amount of technical knowledge and equipment to make, and consequently there are no country versions of this design.

The simple shape of the traditional slat back with a deep, plain crest rail and plain wooden or rush seat could probably be related to the sabre-legged chair, but it would be stretching the point. The most commonly reproduced design is the over-curving S-armed chair with matching dining chairs, often with caned seats, and most frequently found in beechwood, ebonized or painted and gilded. Strictly speaking, these are not true flush-sided chairs, since their arms are round-sectioned and their wide crest rails usually overrun the sides.
Below left: *flush-framed, c.1830.*
Right: *cane-seated, flush-framed, c.1820. The rope-twist crest rail has been broken by a stylized decorative design.*

Reproductions

Victorian
From the beginning of the Victorian period, the pure shape of the flush-sided chair became spoiled by turned front legs instead of the strict curve of the sabre leg. This was probably because the flush-sided chair was by nature expensive to make and used a considerable amount of timber to achieve the right spring and strength to the legs.

Twentieth century
Few of the myriad variations begin to match the elegance and simplicity of the original. About 30 years ago the lyre back was very much in fashion, and a variation of the flush-sided chair was made commercially by some high-quality manufacturers, usually in ebonized beech. They proved to be far less durable than the originals, mainly because the difficult cross-cutting of the timber was skimped, and the sabre legs split where the grain ran at too acute an angle.

Modern versions of a cane-seated flush-sided chair are to be found in some high-quality department stores, made with modern techniques, probably in High Wycombe, centre of the chair-making industry in England, where many of the originals were also made.

Price bands

Late Regency, with over-running crest rail:
£200–400 each.
Set of six: £2,200–3,500.

Cane seat, simulated rosewood, beech frame, set of six: £1,800–2,200.

S-arm chair: £320–450.

Plain mahogany, set of six: £2,200–3,200.

(Rosewood more expensive than mahogany; brass inlay also more expensive.)

William IV turned leg.
Set of six: £1,280–2,100.

Balloon-back chair

Historical background

The voluminous skirts of the mid-nineteenth-century woman needed wider, broader seats to chairs, and so the severe curves of Regency furniture swelled and rounded. There were several conflicting currents which influenced the Victorian furniture designers: the slim silhouettes of Sheraton furniture, the more angular shapes of the sabre-legged and the flush-sided chair, and a nostalgic hankering for the 'romantic' shapes of Queen Anne and early eighteenth-century designs. Added to these, the technical advances in mass-production and the cheapness of labour lured designers into a tangle of unhappy liaisons. The cabriole leg reappeared, but with a thin scrolled or pad foot, all heavily carved and decorated. The fine lines of Sheraton's taper-turning became bulbous, the reeding thickened, and even in such designers as Gillows of Lancaster, chairs seemed the least successful pieces of furniture as far as the eye was concerned.

In the balloon back, however, there was a mixture which, if not immediately appealing to the stricter rules of design, was extremely successful as far as its function was concerned. It was, and still is, one of the most comfortable chairs ever made. Its waisted back reflects the shape of fashion, and though in many mass-produced chairs the front legs seem ill-assorted with the plain square-sectioned back legs, in many the results are well-balanced in a peculiarly Victorian way.

Balloon backs were made for a variety of purposes and differ slightly in shape, depending on whether they were intended for the parlour, dining room, bedroom and drawing room, or for occasional use as side chairs.

Signs of authenticity

1. Good quality solid woods with good graining.
2. Well-made frames with good thickness of wood for legs, back and seat frame.
3. Deep, incisive carving and shaping of back and seat rails.
4. Crest-rail join to tops of side supports should be seamless, virtually invisible with well-matched woods.
5. Solid, high-quality upholstery in curled horsehair – white for the very top quality.
6. No stretchers to legs – cheap mass-produced 'period' balloon backs were made with stretchers but they are neither durable nor particularly attractive.
7. Grain of front legs running up to corners of seat frame.
8. Grain of back legs continuing well above seat level to terminate at crest rail or design feature.

Likely restoration and repair

9. New upholstery covering whole of seat frame. This may indicate seat frames are split or broken, repaired and covered up.
10. Front legs replaced – either broken or 'married' from a better-designed chair.
11. Backs broken and repaired. Vulnerable points on inward curve of waist, and where crest rail joins back supports. Plugs will probably be clearly visible.
12. Strengthening blocks or metal braces added to corners of underframe.
13. Original drop-in frames filled, upholstered over front and side seat rails.

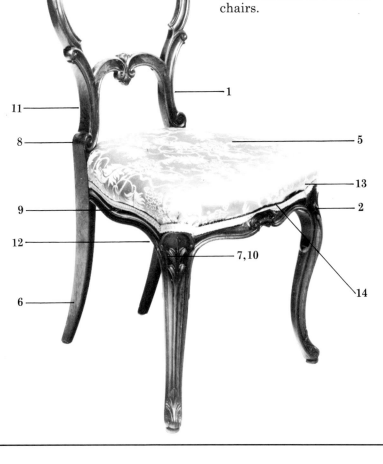

Construction and materials

Balloon backs were made in solid wood, in mahogany, rosewood, walnut, and simulated rosewood. Their construction reverts to the traditional one of front legs tenoned into the sides of the seat-frame and back legs continuing up to form the side supports of the back. Frames were usually of beech or birch with seats upholstered in cloth, needlepoint or leather with brass studs.

Many lighter balloon backs were made entirely in beech, stained or ebonized, and mass-produced with machine-cut timber and shallow mechanical carved decoration. With these chairs, it is quality rather than date which determines price – good and bad designs were made simultaneously during their entire production period which spans nearly 100 years.

Detail
The most characteristic balloon-backs have a waisted back and a single seat rail, usually set low, carved and decorated. There were some designs made with a vertical back splat, carved and decorated, reaching only to the seat rail, and these were known as crown back.

The most familiar shape, with a crest rail which dips in the centre, is usually associated with rectangular, square-fronted upholstered or drop-in seats and a straight seat rail. This design usually has heavily turned front legs, or stout, bulbous reeded front legs. On oval-back chairs, the seat is rounded and the legs are frequently an emasculated version of the cabriole leg, terminating in little scrolls, outward curving and somewhat bandy, sometimes with small tapered feet. Heavier salon chairs were often set on castors. Some of the more pleasing designs have upholstered back panels.

Variations

Period country designs were not made by individual country chair-makers, involving as it did many mass-production methods. Cheaper versions made in very reputable furniture-making centres were certainly destined for Victorian cottages, and were usually made in beech, painted or stained, with cheap-quality upholstery materials and little or no carved decoration. Many people find these simple shapes preferable to the more ornate provincial chairs, so they are by no means always less expensive.

Below left: *nineteenth-century Adam revival chair with upholstered back, carved crest rail and apron, and curving, 'French style', legs.*
Below right: *early balloon-back, c.1845, with curved crest rail, waisted back, neatly turned front legs and upholstered seat.*

Reproductions

It is doubtful whether any manufacturer has yet found it a commercial proposition to reproduce balloon-back chairs. They were made in such enormous quantities that there are still plentiful supplies of genuine period chairs available which, with restoration, stripping, reupholstery and general repair, find a ready market.

Mixing and matching is carried out on quite a large scale; for example, a bulbously unattractive front leg replaced by a better-looking design, either newly made or taken from other chairs in poor condition. The only pitfall occurs when mahogany front legs have been added to a chair otherwise made entirely of beech, or vice versa. It does not enhance the value, since, although the ultimate product may look better, it is clearly a marriage and therefore not worth as much even as the original cheaper chair made entirely of beech.

No doubt there will come a time when these extremely comfortable, typically Victorian chairs are reproduced, then it will be a question of becoming aware of modern methods of construction and the use of woods which were definitely not part of the Victorian chair-maker's repertoire.

Price bands

Upholstered back: £350–500.

Standard plain: £30–70.
Set of six: £600–800.

Rosewood, mid-Victorian: £50–80.
Set of six: £650–900.

Carved, mid-Victorian.
Set of six: £800–1,000.

(Rosewood-framed chairs are the most expensive, followed by walnut, then mahogany.)

Victorian button-back chair

Historical background

The relative austerity of Regency furniture and the soft clinging clothes worn by the ladies of the period were ousted during William IV's reign by the new 'Naturalistic' line. Furniture became more curvaceous, seats of chairs wider to accommodate the increasing volume of ladies' skirts and gentlemen's frock coats, both of which were smartly nipped in at the waist.

This hour-glass shape was echoed in seat furniture, and when Samuel Pratt took out a patent for sprung upholstery in 1828 it was in answer to a demand for even more comfortable chairs and sofas.

Even as late as the early Victorian period, it was considered strange for the centre of rooms to be cluttered with furniture except when in use, and seat furniture was always on castors so that it could be moved back into a tidy arrangement round the room when not in use. Once the rounded, curving lines of upholstered furniture began to be exploited, all kinds of central seat furniture made its appearance, notably the back-to-back sofa and the circular sofa, deeply sprung, tasselled and curving.

Arm chairs at first had sprung seats and button backs, developing from the lines of the Adam round-backed chair into one of the most familiar pieces of Victorian furniture. Later, seats as well as backs were buttoned, and there were high-backed 'grandmother's chairs', more dumpy, rotund 'grandfather's chairs' and their counterparts without arms, as well as tub chairs, bedroom chairs, nursery chairs and parlour chairs, all made with carved mahogany, Virginia walnut or rosewood frames and beech underframes. Some of the most successful designs incorporate a cabriole-type leg with a scrolled 'French foot', far more elegant than the later, bulbously turned legs of mass-produced and provincial chairs.

Signs of authenticity

1. Solid 'black' Virginia walnut, rosewood or solid mahogany frame, carved and decorated.
2. Front arm supports and front legs in one continuous piece with decorative motif integral to the shape and design.
3. Deep, crisp carving with scrolling or floral and foliate motifs.
4. Original upholstery in worsted damask, cotton-and-worsted, or silk-and-worsted, machine-woven, or in heavy velvet. Floral, stripes and imitation tapestry or dark plain colours.
5. Deep buttoning to backs and inside arms, plain sprung seats until c.1890.
6. Backs curved in spoon shape to fit the body – buttoning to 'waist' of back only.

Likely restoration and repair

7. Back legs broken and replaced. Replacements may be simple and slightly raked, looking well but less solidly balanced.
8. New upholstery – almost inevitable, but buttoning should not continue below the line of the 'waist' of the back.
9. Front legs and/or feet repaired where broken or split. Change in patination is always on a diagonal line with repair and runs into the leg grain.
10. Original, bulbously turned legs, replaced with a 'marriage' of legs from another, similar chair. Line of front seat rail will carry through between arm and leg, whereas on genuine carved cabriole-type legs there is no break at seat level.

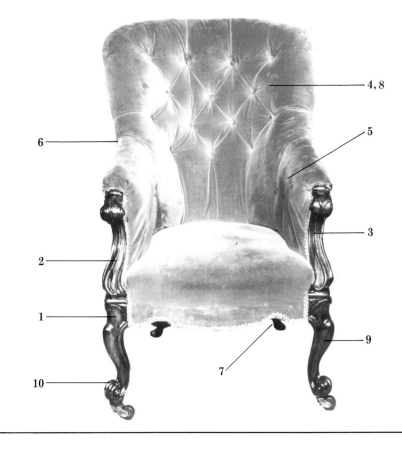

Construction and materials

Early versions of Victorian upholstered chairs from c.1830–50 were usually open-armed, with small upholstered elbow pads and ornate curving scrolls to arms and back, with a solid Virginia walnut frame and a curved, plain seat back. Underframes were of beech, ash or birch, and the construction was still similar to earlier armed chairs. From c.1850 the arms were filled and upholstered, and the backs, shaped with two low scrolls like a judge's wig, had small decoratively carved features rising above the curved back frame. The back legs, until now plain and slightly raked, developed a bowed curve and there was often a decorative carved apron across the front seat rail below the upholstered sprung seat. At the same period low chairs with hourglass or balloon-shaped upholstered backs were made without arms, their seats wide and generous, their curved cabriole-type legs set wider than the back legs. These were known as 'ladies' chairs' and their high-backed, armed equivalents as 'grandmother's chairs'.

Detail

After the introduction of machine-carving around 1850, upholstered chairs of all shapes and sizes were made with less detail, shallow carving, and generally with turned front legs. Early upholstery tended to be unyielding because it was a mixture of linen waste and horsehair, but this was soon replaced with American cotton and wool waste mixed with horsehair, a combination that was much softer and more comfortable.

Variations

Suites of drawing room balloon-back chairs with high backed 'grandmother's chairs' with buttoned backs and open arms were made in great quantities, some of them very decorative, others of poorer quality, for they were mass-produced from inferior materials. As with much Victorian furniture, quality and craftsmanship distinguish between early, well-made and well-designed button back chairs and later versions. This type of chair continued to be made well into the early Edwardian period, although in the main it was relegated from drawing rooms and parlours to bedrooms and the servant's upstairs quarters.

Right: *a low button back, sometimes called a nursing chair.*

Reproductions

The revival in popularity of Victoriana in recent years has led to many furniture-manufacturers producing copies of the smaller tub chair with button back and low rounded seat. On the whole these look perfectly adequate, but fillings for upholstery are more often than not a polystyrene-type foam chip which goes flat and loses its spring after some use. In terms of value it is better to seek out one of the many varieties of original on the market than spend money on short-lived modern reproductions.

Price bands

Open-armed, well-carved, solid walnut frame and apron, c.1850: £450–650.

Spoonback, no arms, cabriole-shaped legs, solid walnut carved frame: £550–700.

Curved back, integral upholstered arms, carved legs and frame. Rosewood more than walnut: £550–1,000.

Left: *open-armed button back, c.1870.*

Bentwood rocker

Historical background

Bentwood chairs have become so much a part of our lives as to be almost invisible. In a simplified form they have been used in so many everyday places – shops, schools, private houses and public places – that it is difficult to imagine that their whole style was once a complete revolution in furniture-making. Today they are turned out in their thousands in factories all over England, but their origins were elite and aesthetic.

Michael Thonet (1796–1871), their inventor, was an Austrian who trained as a craftsman in the South German Biedermeier school of furniture-making. This was established as a reaction against French influence, in part motivated by the aspiration for a united Germany after the Napoleonic Wars, and in part aesthetic, a search for well-designed 'bourgeois' furniture. The parallel desire was felt in England, and was evident in the designs of J. C. Loudon and his school. Biedermeier was particularly successful with seat furniture, which was solid, well-made, elegant and, above all, comfortable. It was Michael Thonet's search for new materials and techniques to make chairs without ornament, carving or traditional construction that led him to experiment with the shipbuilding techniques of steaming and bending wood. His designs were first produced in laminated wood in the 1840s.

Thonet took out patents for his chair-making techniques, but when the patent ran out in the 1860s a London firm of furniture-makers, Hewlett and Company, took it up, and by the end of the century bentwood chairs were being made by many furniture-makers, particularly in High Wycombe, centre of England's chair-making industry.

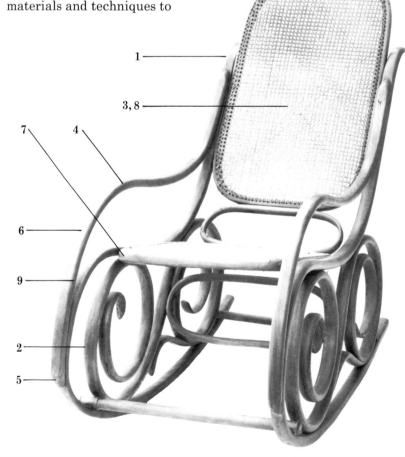

Construction and materials

Michael Thonet's original designs were made in thin strips of wood, steamed and bent into shape and laminated together – a technique which had been known in England for about 100 years, although laminated wood had only been used for parts of furniture and not for a whole piece. Thonet's first commission for these novel, smooth-curving designs was for the Leichtenstein Palace in Vienna, and although they were more detailed and complicated in their sinuous construction, the basic bentwood chair of today differs very little from those prototypes.

In England, the technique of steaming and bending wood had been applied to Windsor chairs for some years, using solid wood as opposed to laminated. The timber was generally birch, traditional wood for chair-legs because it was amenable to bending and was springy enough not to break or split. The cane seat, too, had been in production for country chairs and lightweight seat furniture ever since Sheraton had reintroduced it at the end of the eighteenth century.

Early genuine Thonet bentwood chairs and rockers, for which the technique was particularly suitable, were more curvaceous and elaborate, mainly due to the laminated wood which allowed more freedom than later bentwood chairs in birch, which consisted mainly of a series of hoops and standardized curves.

Variations

Bentwood chairs were particularly suitable for children, and both high chairs and small, miniature versions of the standard shape were made, particularly in the 1920s, for use in schools and nurseries.

Some early, finely designed, bentwood chairs made in England include versions of the sabre-legged S-armed chair, with the back made in a single hoop with the back legs, which are raked well back. Front legs curved forward in imitation of the line of the sabre-leg, but were round-sectioned and taper-turned. The S-curve of the arms was particularly suitable for the new bentwood technique.

Once furniture-making factories had begun to turn out bentwood chairs by the thousand, their finish and style degenerated into the 'tea-room chairs' of the 1920s and 1930s, being reduced to circular hoops and slightly splayed legs, whose timber was no longer carefully chosen for the correct grain, and which have since split and cracked.

Above: *a child's bentwood high chair, c.1870.*
Right: *an original Thonet, c.1860.*

Reproductions

After a considerable spell of unpopularity as 'cheap chairs' there are now many extremely good reproductions of the original bentwood chair on the market, many of them originating in Taiwan and the Far East, where manufacturing is cheap and labour still skilled in traditional crafts such as caning. Their reappearance on the English scene can largely be attributed to the many well-designed small restaurants with imaginative decor, for which they were originally imported.

Price bands

Superb intricate shapes, top condition, with original labels and original, unchipped finish: £850–1,000.

Stripped or plain, simpler shapes with original label: £550–850.

Set of six chairs, original caning and labels: £350–500.

Period singles with labels and authentication: £35–50.

1920s plain but in good condition: £15–20.

Refectory table

Historical background

There was remarkably little furniture of any sort until the sixteenth century in England, apart from chests to hold valuables and clothes, benches and stools to sit on, and a rough 'boorde' or table for eating from. Tables in 'refectories' or halls were dismantled at night and used by knights and squires to sleep on – hence the description 'table dormant'.

At first, tables were of rough-hewn planks mounted on two or more trestles. A stretcher was added for stability, but as the table was destined to be covered with layers of napery its appearance did not matter very much until Elizabethan days when surfaces of polished wood became fashionable. The trestle developed into two solid end-pieces on massive feet, joined by a substantial stretcher, and a top which slotted into the two end-bearers. A tusk-shaped tenon on the outer side of the end-piece, knocked into a hole in the protruding end of the stretcher, held the table rigid. The alternative method of construction for tables was a basic frame made up of legs, low stretchers on all four sides and a top frame on which the table top rested. From these came the 'melon-bulbed' tables of Elizabethan and Jacobean days, so loved and copied by makers of reproduction furniture from the late Victorian days and early years of this century.

Signs of authenticity

1. Some graining, and figuring on all wood where it has been split and not sawn.
2. Timbers shrunk along the grain making them narrower than the cleats or clamps.
3. All timbers, including low bottom stretchers, of same aged wood, patination and colour.
4. Heavy wear on bottom stretchers.
5. Width of two planks only. Some are made from a single plank. From c.1660 these were sometimes framed with cleating on all four sides with mitred corners.
6. In 'frame' construction, dowels sunk or slightly loose, not protruding. Green wood was used so that dowels would not be pushed out by shrinkage of main timbers.
7. 'Bolection moulding' deeply incised, secured to legs with pegs or dowels.
8. Hand-cut dowels and pegs of uneven size and shape.
9. Thick patination on undersurface of table tops where it overhangs and has been handled continuously.
10. Feet blocks are worn, rotted or 'frayed' by damp and constant use on stone floors.

Likely restoration and repair
11. Bottom stretchers on frame construction tables replaced – often entire bottom frame including bases of square-sectioned legs.
12. Planks of table top fitting flush with clamps, no shrinkage, indicates new top or replaced clamps or both.
13. Saw marks on underside of table top or any part of straight timbers means recent replacement.
14. New tops made up from old floorboards with right grain but not much patination. Signs of nail heads where floorboards were nailed to joists.
15. It can safely be said that no table of this age on the market today has survived completely intact without repairs and replacement timbers at some time in its life.

Construction and materials

Most of these solid, heavy and important tables were made in oak. Some were made with elm tops and oak frames, and some of fruitwood for smaller tables if the girth of the tree was big enough for planking. The wood was not sawn, but riven and split into planks and then cleaned off with an adze until a smooth surface was obtained.

Whether made of trestle or frame construction, the table was no more than two planks wide – broad tables were not needed, since the nobility sat on one side of the table only, facing down the hall. The planks were clamped or cleated at either end to finish the raw ends of the wood and reduce warping and bending. The entire frame of a refectory table is held together with mortise-and-tenon joints and thick, handcut pegs or dowels. The uprights on a trestle table were slotted into two cross-bearers fixed to the underside of the table top,

and into two long flat plinths or feet at the bottom. One or two stretchers ran between the uprights and were slotted through and tenoned with a large tusk-shaped wedge to secure them. These wedges could easily be knocked out when the table was dismantled. On tables with frame construction, the base was made up of four thick stretchers, like the bottom of a box, tenoned into the bottoms of the square-sectioned legs very near the ground. The tops of the legs were dowelled into the underframe of the table top.

Detail
Bolection moulding for the swelling melon bulbs was common by Elizabethan times. In order to minimize the girth of timber needed for the legs, the swelling bulbs were added to straight, square-sectioned legs which were then carved and turned above and below the joins.

Variations

If there was little furniture to be seen in grand houses and manors, there was none in peasants' dwellings. Refectory tables were only used in wealthy households, monasteries, and large manor houses.

Some crude side tables were made, usually known as 'harvest tables', for harvest suppers, as well

as some basic X-frame tables of elm, but they were rough and unfinished and very few have survived. Smaller trestle-type tables of applewood and other fruitwoods were also made for farmhouses, but most of the long, scrubbed farmhouse tables date from the end of the eighteenth century, if not considerably later.

Above: *single plank harvest table, or 'boorde', constructed on the trestle principle, with an arcaded, chip-carved frieze.*
Left: *seventeenth- or early eighteenth-century double plank frame table, with rushlight and candle drawer.*

Reproductions

Nineteenth century
Massive melon-bulbed tables were made for the 'Jacobethan' revival of the Victorian age, using traditional methods of construction, but the planks for tops were sawn, not split, pegs and dowels were machine-made and of even size, machine-carving was shallow and not smoothly rounded with use.

Twentieth century
London-made reproductions from c.1900 by furniture-makers employing highly skilled craftsmen are also recognizable for the exaggerated proportions of bulbs and bolection mouldings. Dutch versions of a later period have distinctive pear or acorn-shaped legs, and not straight-sided 'melons'. Later, baluster-turned legs from large tables were combined with frame tops, new stretchers and surfaces.

From c.1925, one finds mass-produced 'refectory' tables with solid end-pieces and square tenons to secure central stretchers, often with knots in planks, usually three planks wide to accommodate people on both sides of the table, now warping and splitting because of unseasoned saw-cut timbers.

Tables of very recent date are often made from old floorboards, usually elm, sometimes oak, correctly split, but without deep patination and with none on the overhang of the table top. Bleached oak versions, mass-produced, greyish in colour, have undersurfaces furry with saw marks where timbers have been sawn as standard planking and then made up.

Price bands

Draw leaf or fixed-top, English c.1600: £10,000 + .

Seventeenth-century frame table, trestle-type: £2,800–3,800.

Eighteenth- or nineteenth-century reproduction: £2,000–3,500.

(All prices for period tables assume some restoration.)

Gate-leg table

Historical background

Coinciding more or less with the Commonwealth period, an increasing number of households began to furnish their houses with relatively sophisticated furniture by comparison with the rather basic pieces of earlier periods. One of the most typical was the gate-leg table, made for the houses of yeomen farmers, manor houses and wealthier households whose whole way of life was changing. The old Great Hall had more or less disappeared by this time and the parlour and dining room had become common in most houses of any size.

The gate-leg table developed from the small side table with a semi-circular flap supported on a single gate-leg, and from the writing box on stand with two gate-legs. Free-standing gate-leg tables first made their appearance at the beginning of the seventeenth century, but were not made in any quantity until after 1648. In the main,

gate-legged tables made in England were round or oval, while those made by the Dutch were often square or rectangular.

Legs and stretchers were simple and square until lathe-turning was mastered by English carpenters and joiners between 1640 and 1660, when

simple column legs, bobbins, twists and then balusters were all used to make more decorative legs. Gate-legged tables were made in all shapes and sizes, from small ones seating four people to very large 12-seaters, usually with four gate-legs to hold the massive flaps.

Signs of authenticity

1. Underframe of same timber as legs, stretchers and gates.
2. Each flap made of a single piece of timber, with the fixed table top also made in a single piece.
3. Signs of wear on framing stretchers where feet have kicked and worn.
4. Legs and legs of gates with grain running right up to underside of table top, with 'gates' tenoned into swinging underframe.
5. Timbers of tops, flaps, and underframe of slightly different thicknesses – hand-cut timber was never of even thickness.
6. Good figuring, grain, speckling, of wood, split not sawn.
7. Flaps overhanging gate legs by several inches when raised.
8. Flaps falling to a line just above stretchers when dropped.

9. Good patination, scratch and groove marks where gates have been swung in and out, flaps and gates have been constantly handled.
10. Feet showing signs of 'fraying' from stone floors, damp and wear.
11. Worn, polished sockets to pivots of gate legs from constant use.
12. Flaps hanging flush with closed gates when dropped.
13. No signs of saw marks, or circular saw cuts on underside of any part of timbers.
14. Gates and legs battered, split and chipped in places. Pristine tables are suspicious.

Likely restoration and repair
15. Replaced flap with commercial thickness of timber – genuine period table tops were at least a full inch thick.
16. Cut down from larger sizes – if well done, only the grander turning and decoration on a small supposedly 'country' table will provide the clue.
17. If poorly done, joins, framing and gates will all be out of scale.
18. Old flaps cut down from larger sizes, added to smaller fixed top and frame. Thumb moulding may only be at either end of original top. If new thumb moulding has been cut, there will be no patination in the groove or join.
19. Wood split from hinge to edge and repaired – new hinges and break in grain will show up weakness.

Construction and materials

Like most furniture up to the end of the seventeenth century, gate-leg tables were principally made in oak, or oak with elm tops. At the end of the seventeenth century some fine quality tables were made in solid walnut.

They were built on a rectangular frame construction, with an underframe, four legs with stretchers and two swinging gate-legs on either side of the frame. Until *c.*1700 the tops were pegged to the underframe with wooden dowels; glue was often used and the pieces were clamped together until they were solid and secure. The gate legs were rudimentary, and swivelled on pivots fixed into the underframe and bottom stretchers.

Until *c.*1670 the flaps and fixed table top had tongue and groove joins with steel hinges fixed with nails. After *c.*1690 finer tables had rule joins with thumb moulding which carried round the edge of the table top as well as on the flaps. Hinges were sometimes brass, sometimes steel, and fixed with hand-cut screws.

Gate-leg tables were made in many different sizes, and the larger ones often had an arched or simple decorative frieze at either end, or a small single drawer, supported on a single bearer, usually without side bottom runners.

Detail

Legs were squared or simple turned columns until *c.*1690, after which decoration was more elaborate with twist-turned, reel and bobbin and baluster-turned legs, but always the joints were made on square-sectioned blocks between decorative turning. Tables with decoratively-turned legs usually had bun or ball feet, unturned square-sectioned legs or simple columns usually terminated in solid block feet.

Variations

The only difference between 'country' and grander versions is the quality and craftsmanship in early versions, until the drop-leaf table with hinges developed in mahogany in the eighteenth century and the gate-legged table became more of a country piece.

Country tables continued the simpler, more rudimentary methods of construction long after grander ones had improved with, for example, rule joints, thumb moulding, turned legs and stretchers. Country versions were more frequently in oak and elm rather than oak only, although this cannot be taken as a rule. Column-turned legs with block feet were more common than ball or bun feet on country versions. Unturned stretchers and less elaborate turning to the legs continued to be the rule for country gate-leg tables. Country versions were often smaller to fit the room sizes in a farmer's house compared with larger provincial houses

Left: *typical style, c.1670, except for small bun feet which were added at a later date.*

Reproductions

Eighteenth century
Two eighteenth-century reproductions are: the plain country drop-leaf or modified gate-leg table of more simple form with hinged bearers to support the flaps, and the early Georgian drop-leaf mahogany gate-leg with curved cabriole-style legs or plain legs, tapering to a neat pad foot. Gate-legged tables continued to be made with modifications in construction right through to the beginning of the twentieth century, when their cumbersome design and awkward leg arrangements made them unpopular.

Nineteenth century
Victorian 'rustic' versions have over-elaborate turning to legs and gates, machine-cut and uniformly regular. They were also made in solid Virginia walnut, a wood that darkens with age and will not take a high polish but remains shallow and dead-looking.

Twentieth century
Straight-legged 'country' gate-legs entirely in elm are almost certainly of recent manufacture. Copies are made in French walnut, more highly figured than English walnut. French walnut was only used as a veneer in England until *c.*1720 and not as a solid wood. Mass-produced coarse-grained oak flap or drop-leaf tables were made from the early nineteenth century until the 1930s.

Price bands

Fine, twist-turned oak, *c.*1670: £3,000–5,000.

Simple turning in oak, or oak and elm, *c.*1670: £1,000–3,000.

Elaborate bobbin-turned and Continental, *c.*1700: £800–1,200.

Nineteenth-century reproduction: £800–2,000.

(Prices are for six-seater tables with rounded flaps.)

Side table

Signs of authenticity

1. Grain running from side to side of table top.
2. On solid woods, considerable figuring where timber was split rather than sawn.
3. Back edge of table top sometimes unfinished, with no overhang.
4. Drawers of oak, carcase wood of oak. Pine drawers or other parts of carcase in period piece indicate Dutch origins.
5. Where there is featherbanding and herringbone inlay, 'arrows' always go clockwise.
6. Simple lip moulding to three sides of table top.
7. Beam moulding to drawer edges made from a single strip with wood grain continuing through each bead.
8. On walnut tables, signs of worm boreholes in solid timbers – walnut is particularly susceptible to worm.
9. Good patination on sides and top edges of drawer where it has been pulled out and handled constantly.
10. No lock or lock rail to drawer frame.

Likely restoration and repair

11. Legs restored, replaced where worm damage has ruined originals.
12. Original veneer planed down to the oak carcase beneath: no depth of patination on surface woods.
13. Solid walnut tops replaced: signs of worm-tracks indicate timber planed down from thicker piece of different origin – wormholes only show on surface of wood.
14. Solid walnut with little patination, wrong construction: may be Victorian copy 'distressed' to look older.
15. Made up from larger table in bad state of repair. No patination on overhang of table top – oddly placed boreholes and marks on underside.
16. Legs repaired or replaced: grain will break on the join – quite often concealed by ring turning.

Historical background

By the beginning of the seventeenth century there was much more 'standing' furniture in most houses. In particular, side tables came into use for many different functions. They stood in spaces between windows, against walls with side chairs, and were used as an early version of the 'dressing table'.

The art of twist turning came to England from Spain and the Spanish Netherlands, together with the fashion for embellishing cabinets and the edges of drawers with 'string of beads' mouldings in ebony or ebony-coloured woods. Sometimes legs of small decorative tables were of a much darker wood than the rest of the piece.

The cup-and-cover shape of table and cabinet stand legs, although principally associated with the arrival of William of Orange in England, had been used for several decades before, from the furniture imported from Holland. At about the same time the art of veneering transformed both the construction and the appearance of English furniture. Side tables span this revolutionary change, being made first in solid woods with twist-turned legs, and later in quartered veneer with serpentine stretchers. Stuart side tables frequently had one full-width drawer in the frieze.

Construction and materials

Side tables, being small pieces of furniture, were made in a much wider variety of woods than large tables. They are found in oak, fruitwood, plane and, occasionally, cyprus. At a later date they were made in solid walnut, and in walnut veneer on an oak carcase and underframe.

Most side tables had a single drawer in the frieze, with one or two handles. Drawers were either plain-fronted or with small fielded or coffered panels, contemporary with chest of drawers of the period. Their construction was still based on the solid frame, with stretchers between all four legs, either decorative or plain.

Around 1680 the cup and cover shape of legs with serpentine stretchers, similar to those on stands for chests, were quite common. There is always a good overhang on three sides of the table top, and the back edge will be narrower, for side tables were made to stand against walls and in recesses, and the back stretcher is plain, undecorated and flush with the edge of the back.

The timber of the legs continues up to form the side frame of the frieze drawer and the corners of the frieze. All joints were simple mortise-and-tenon, secured with pegs or dowels. The drawers had through-dovetails or stop-dovetails, with the bottom boards running from front to back in more than one piece. The bottom boards were nailed to the sides with clout nails and a simple rebate joint.

Detail

Early walnut veneer was usually quarter-cut and framed in a broad band of cross-cut veneer, sometimes edged with feather-banding or herringbone with mitred edges.

Drop handles usually had rosette-shaped backplates fixed to the drawer fronts with two steel shafts driven through and splayed and flattened on the inside.

Reproductions

Nineteenth century
The most common ones on the market today are of Victorian oak, recognizable by decoration such as carving on the frieze, twist turning, polished and darkened to age the wood.

There are also solid walnut copies, stained and bleached where the stain has rubbed off or faded. Many reproductions are in oak, elm, and Virginia walnut, with straight legs or later machine-turned balusters, bobbins or twists and flat stretchers, from almost any date from c.1830. They were made as little side tables for use in passages, halls and dining rooms.

Spanish, Portuguese and Italian tables with ebonized legs, string-of-beads moulding around the drawers, simulating the style of tortoiseshell and ebony chests and cabinets, were imported in large numbers during the mid-Victorian period.

Variations

These traditional 'occasional' tables were made in a variety of shapes, woods and finishes for 100 years or more and the differences in construction, woods and finish rather than stylistic change are the guide to period. Characteristic country-made versions may be of plain oak with square stretchers and no carving or decoration. Others had a semi-circular flap and a plain gateleg on a wooden hinge, opening to an elongated half-circle. Some are found in plain oak with a simple frieze and no drawer. Nice examples can be found in fruitwood, sometimes with a small drawer in the frieze which does not run the full width of the piece.

Dutch side tables, imported during the seventeenth and eighteenth centuries, were veneered or decorated with marquetry and had double-twist legs. Generally they were more elaborate than those in the English style and were usually made on a pine carcase with pine drawers.

Left: *plain oak table of the late seventeenth century.*
Centre: *William and Mary oak table with pierced decorative frieze.*
Right: *an elaborately decorated table of the Stuart period.*

Price bands

Stuart oak, with frieze drawer and good turned detail: £1,200–2,000.

William and Mary oak with good detail: £1,000–1,800.

Country, period oak or fruitwood, c.1700: £2,000–4,000.

Nineteenth-century reproduction oak: £400–800.

Queen Anne drop-leaf table

Historical background

Although popularly known as 'Queen Anne', the drop-leaf table did not really come into widespread use until mahogany became available, after the end of Queen Anne's reign. The earliest drop-leaf tables were also made of Virginia walnut from c.1720 onwards, when supplies of good French walnut ceased. The curving cabriole-like leg, terminating in pad feet or a more elaborate ball-and-claw foot, is distinctive of the period generally known as Queen Anne, but the style continued well into the reign of George I. Not until then were dining habits adapted to the Continental style, with all the diners seated round a large table, with matching chairs, dinner service and glasses. Until then the English custom of serving food from a long buffet-style table was prevalent and smaller dining tables were mainly in use in the morning room and parlour for occasional meals such as breakfast when small numbers of the household sat down at different times. The drop-leaf table was a more sophisticated version of the gate-leg table, with four legs only, two of which hinged out to support the flaps on either side. Drop-leaf tables were circular at first, but from c.1740 square flaps became more popular, because they could accommodate more people in comfort.

Tables for eating off were made in solid wood and were not veneered because of the damage that might be caused by spillages or hot dishes. The advantage of mahogany was that it was immensely dense and strong, did not warp or bend and, unlike walnut, was impervious to worm.

Signs of authenticity

1. Heavy weight of mahogany – San Domingo or Cuban.
2. Grain of flaps and central fixed top all running parallel to joins.
3. Each piece of table top cut from a single piece of timber.
4. Underframe of thick solid timbers of oak or close-grained red pine.
5. Scrape marks on under surface where gate has been opened and closed.
6. No screw holes or bore holes of any description on any part of undersurface.
7. Patination under flaps and on sides of gates where they have been constantly handled.
8. Thickness of timber would be a minimum of 1 in.
9. Flaps correctly proportioned to legs when not raised.
10. Wooden hinges with three 'knuckles'.
11. Rule joints and hinges with thumb-moulding continuing round full circumference of top.
12. Circular tables seating four until c.1740, then squared table tops as well as circular.
13. Correct height – 2 ft 4 in for dining tables.

Likely restoration and repair

14. Legs broken and replaced, particularly on gates. Grain either running right across from underframe or breaking on a line with bottom of underframe where replacement has been pegged in.
15. Gates broken on hinges and repaired with white pine, stained.
16. Flaps split, cracked from weight of wood on hinge. Repaired but weakened. A break in grain, thick streak of fake patination will indicate plugged crack.
17. Replaced flaps with slight difference in thickness, duller patina and signs of old screw holes on undersurface, or new hinges with machine-turned screws.

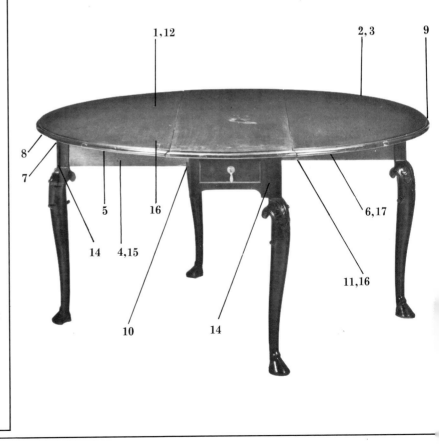

Construction and materials

The technique of making chests and chests of drawers with a carcase of different woods spread to table making, and the drop leaf table is among the earliest to have an underframe of oak or close-grained red pine, with the main parts of solid mahogany or Virginia walnut. A few very fine tables were also made in English walnut, but they are rare to find. As with the gate-leg table, the legs continue up in one piece to the underside of the top, whether on the hinged or fixed leg. The gates of drop-leaf tables formed part of the underframe construction and had wooden or brass hinges with three 'knuckles'.

Most drop-leaf tables were never very large, and at most seat six on later, square shapes, and four on circular tables of the earlier period. There are conflicting dates for the first general use of mahogany, but as a rough guide it can be said that except for isolated and exceptional cases, it was not used for furniture before 1730–35. From that date until the 1750s, when duties and taxes were lifted, mahogany was imported in ballast, and its quality varies considerably, although most furniture-makers preferred to use the best, fine-grained, dense San Domingo or Cuban timber.

Detail
Brass rule hinges set close to the edge of the table, secured with round-ended hand-turned screws, were countersunk into the underside of the fixed top and flap, which had a rule join, with the moulding continuing round the full circumference of the table. Legs were high-curving, virtually cabriole, with plain pad feet or hoofed feet.

Variations

Period country versions were made in oak, or elm, or oak and elm with stretchered frame and gates, as simplified drop leaf tables. The balance of a genuine four-legged drop-leaf table is hard to achieve, and some drop-leaf country versions are found with half-legs folding against each other when the flaps are down, opening to a six-legged table when raised, but few of these have survived.

Simple column turning persisted in oak on legs of Georgian drop-leaf tables, plain chamfered legs being the later period alternative. Good country versions follow the rules of mahogany drop-leaf tables: the grain runs parallel to joins which are thumb-moulded, hinges set well in, approximately over legs when flap is down, but the grain of underframe is vertical for strength; dowelling persisted long after it was replaced with screws in mahogany versions. Traditional methods of construction were used for country pieces long after they had been superseded by improved techniques.

Below left: George II provincial drop leaf in oak, with pad feet, it has slightly wider fixed table top than mahogany versions.
Below right: late seventeenth-, early eighteenth-century country version.

Reproductions

Nineteenth century
Plain rectangular square-legged drop-leaf small dining tables were manufactured from c.1840 onwards in light-weight African mahogany, cheap Honduras mahogany or baywood. They usually have deeper flaps, falling quite close to the floor. The construction of early drop leafs is difficult to reproduce and has a limited market in commercial terms.

Later versions of simplified gate-legged tables have been made continuously through to this century, as general purpose tables for domestic households, hotels and public buildings, and as dining tables for the average home. Poor-quality materials, machine-cut timbers, coarse-grained pine underframes and lack of craftsmanship in detail and proportion indicate mass-manufacture.

Price bands

Fine-quality mahogany: £1,200–2,500.

Country version in oak: £1,000–2,000.

Gate-leg version in oak: £700–1,200.

Fruitwood, yew (flaps in two pieces): £2,000–5,000.

c.1800, reeded leg: £1,200–2,000.

Early nineteenth-century plain mahogany: £800–1,200.

Below: *Late eighteenth-century drop leaf, c.1800.*

Folding card table

Historical background

Separate tables for playing cards became popular during the reign of Queen Anne and were built on the same construction principles as gate-leg and drop-leaf tables, except that the flap folded over the top of the fixed surface. In Queen Anne and early Georgian days their playing surfaces were not always inset with baize or velvet, for these tables were also used for taking tea and were made in solid wood, either walnut or mahogany. By c.1730, however, with a proliferation of small decorative tables for many purposes, the card table was often veneered and lined with baize or velvet, its corners rounded for holding candlesticks, and the playing surface dished with small containers for counters. This type of card table often had cabriole legs, crisply carved with a scallop shell, acanthus or lion's mask, and although not necessarily made *en suite* with chairs of the period, are recognizably contemporary.

The best card tables of the Georgian period have both back legs on hinges which swing out to support the flap, using the same construction as the drop-leaf table, or have both legs on a separate frame which either slides out or opens out with a concertina action. It is sometimes said that the back legs of card tables are of poorer detail because when not in use they stood, like side tables, against a wall. This is debatable, since when in use card tables were free-standing and all four legs were equally important.

Folding card tables were frequently made in pairs, but it is extremely rare to find that the two have remained together undamaged over such a long period of time.

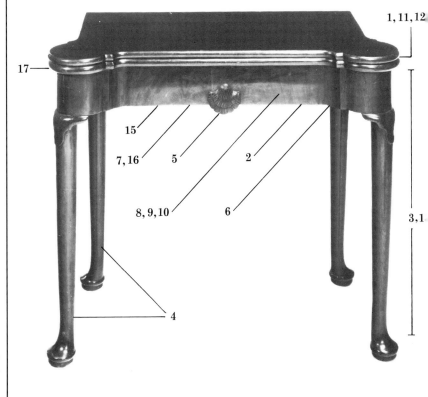

Construction and materials

Card tables were made with several different methods of construction to enable the folding flap to be supported. The earliest method was the same principle as the gate-leg table, with both back legs swinging out on wooden hinges to an angle of 45 degrees so that the back legs squared up with the front legs. From c.1760 many card tables had a separate sliding frame, on to which the back legs were attached, and which pulled out on runners to extend to double the width, and so support the table top. From c.1780 a novel hinged wooden concertina action doubled back on itself to fold neatly into the underframe. Many card tables had a single drawer in the frieze, concealed and without handles from c.1770 onwards.

Detail

Card tables were either rectangular, with elliptical corners to hold candlesticks, or demi-lune opening to a circular table. From the middle of the eighteenth century, in line with fashionable design, many were made with serpentine shapes. The round-cornered rectangular shape and the elongated demi-lune opening to an oval are both of later date.

Early versions had simple cabriole legs and pad feet to c.1740, after which they were more richly decorated with carved scallop shells, acanthus leaves, lion masks, and ball-and-claw feet. Until c.1770, edges closed flush and were undecorated. From c.1770 many were made with carved and fretted decorations to legs and frieze.

Because of their function, card tables had to be smooth with an unbroken surface. The display sides of the flaps were sometimes discreetly veneered, or inlaid with featherbanding or small panels of decorative marquetry, and always edged with cross-cut veneer.

Variations

Almost all country versions continued to be made on the old construction principles long after mahogany and better-quality tables were constructed with improved methods, using screws rather than nails, brass rather than steel hinges, and drawers on runners. Mortise-and-tenon joints and dowelling, drawers sliding on a single bearer, no lock rail above the drawer in the frieze were characteristic.

They are found in a variety of woods: oak, simply made with plain straight legs, undecorated with no moulding or carving to table edges; also in oak and elm, preferably with oak table top and flap, and in elm and fruitwood. If in fruitwood alone, there was minimal decoration and legs were chamfered down the backs.

Pairs: Matching pairs of card tables are worth considerably more than singles. Sadly all too often one of them is a recent copy of the original. The clue is to turn them upside down. There is no way of matching age and patination on a new underframe. Where a skilful hand has been at work, patination and marks may be there, but a carbon copy of the genuine one – an impossibility on a true pair.

Above right: *D-shaped folding card table of late Georgian style, a type much copied in the late Victorian and Edwardian period.* Left: *Sheraton period demi-lune in light mahogany veneer.*

Reproductions

Nineteenth century

Satinwood demi-lune card tables of Adam style have a more fragile construction and are of later date. Card tables were largely supplanted during the Regency period by 'games tables' with fitted compartments, drawers for backgammon, chequers, chess, etc., and the circular 'loo' table named after the fashionable card game of the day.

Many card tables in a poor state of repair have had their flaps removed, their back legs fixed to the frame and have become side tables.

Twentieth century

Edwardian reproductions of later satinwood tables are the most common, and are often known as 'bridge' tables. Few variations or reproductions are in solid woods – most are veneered, and their construction is far more flimsy than the thick-timbered solid-framed.

Price bands

Queen Anne, walnut:
£5,000 + .

Georgian solid walnut, hinged leg, ball-and-claw feet: £1,800–2,500.

Same period and design, with concertina action: £3,000–5,000.

Sheraton period: £2,100–3,500.

Nineteenth-century D-shape: £900–1,500.

Tripod table

Signs of authenticity

1. Made of heavy, dense mahogany.
2. Carving, dishing, piecrust or scalloping integral with table top, standing proud of the surface.
3. Grain of stem running from top to bottom without a break.
4. Proportions correct: when tilt top is vertical the sweep of the curve should not cut into the baluster, carving or decoration, or leave too much showing.
5. Measurements of top should not be precisely circular – timber shrinks along the grain and circle will be slightly flattened.
6. Never veneered – always in the same solid wood, for the top, stem and feet.

Likely restoration and repair
7. Metal brackets pinning underside of tripod or knees where wood has split and been repaired.
8. Wrong proportions – tops too large or small. The eye can judge better when the top is vertical not horizontal.
9. Line of joined timber at collar at base of stem: block added, into which legs have been fitted.
10. Dishing on top surface without corresponding tapering of outer edge of undersurface suggests later copy or dished out from undecorated table.
11. Grain not running in unbroken line up the shaft indicates stem from another piece of furniture with additional piece to give extra height.
12. Tripods of dumb waiters, fire-screens, torchères, teapoys, suitable posts from four-poster beds, inverted legs of dining tables – all these give an idea of suitable beginnings and replacements for stems and tripods. Many period trays are used for tops.
13. Dullish, reddish-coloured walnut, not mahogany – nineteenth-century copy.
14. Lighter-weight mahogany, shallow carving – also nineteenth-century copy.

Historical background

The antecedent of this small table is the candlestand of the sixteenth and seventeenth centuries, standing on three splayed feet. Small tables on central stems and three scrolled feet were made in 'black' Virginia walnut from the late seventeenth century onwards, and in the first two decades of the eighteenth century. But the tripod table did not really come into its own until mahogany had become readily available. Its construction demanded a strong, close-grained timber which would not easily split, and which could be cut in a single piece for the table top.

Of all tripod tables the 'piecrust' is the best known and has been ceaselessly copied in a recognizable, although emasculated form. Genuine 'piecrust' tripod tables are far more massive: the tripod legs are a version of the cabriole leg, with acanthus, scallop or lions mask carving on the knee, which has a pronounced spring. The stem is carved with foliage or cupped leaves around the bulb of the base which rises in a slender, fluted stem. The 'piecrust' itself is carved from the solid timber, and the thickness reduced to a minimum beneath the carving so that in outline the top itself is slightly dished.

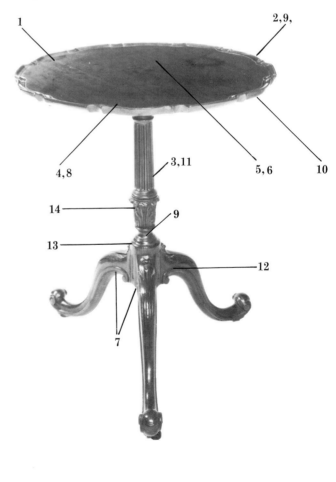

Construction and materials

These are important little tables in terms of construction, so apparently simple that a great deal of detail must be absorbed to be sure that the piece in question really is genuine. The base is made in four pieces: the central stem, cut from a single piece of wood, and three separate legs, secured to the base of the stem with a wedge dovetail, the tops of the joints concealed by the swell of the bulb, or by a circular ring-turned boss below the collar of the baluster.

The top is cut in a single piece with the grain running across it from side to side, and the carving of the rim is integral with the original thickness of the top. On the underside of the rim the wood is tapered so that from the side the shape is slightly dished. The tilt-top construction consists of two parallel cross bearers attached to the underside of the table top, which fit on either side of a small square block mounted on top of the stem, with a pivot running through it into the cross bearers on either side. The top is secured by a brass spring catch to hold it firmly in place when horizontal. On very early, rare tripod tables, the tops were fixed to the stems with a central threaded wooden collar secured to the underside of the top into which the stem was screwed. Revolving tilt tops were mounted on a 'bird cage' gallery, rare to find intact. The top of the stem was enclosed in an open box with wooden columns to all four sides, which revolved, and which fitted neatly into the two parallel cross bearers mounted on the underside of the table, and locked into position.

Detail
Plain-topped or dished tops were mounted on plain baluster stems, sometimes with spiral decoration, with pad feet, or scrolled feet on flat 'shoes' to give stability. The knees of the legs should be high to give the tripod base a good grip. From c.1780 the legs are flattened into soft S-curves, more spread-eagled and sprawling.

Variations

Period country versions were made in fruitwood, yew wood and in mixed woods with oak tops. The construction of the base demanded a close-grained wood which would not split on the dovetail joints of stem and feet, and oak was not suitable. Sometimes walnut was used, but rarely.

If fruitwood and yew wood were used the tops were often of more than one piece owing to the lack of girth of the trees. Simple column turning and baluster turning to stems were characteristic as are plain pad feet on a small rectangular 'shoe'. Rims were undecorated, with no carving on knees of tripod legs. Tops were larger than mahogany versions – tilt tops were used for more practical purposes in the country and small tops were less useful.

Right: *mahogany syllabub or supper table, a Chippendale design which was revived in the nineteenth century.*

Right: *nineteenth-century reproduction with typical sprawling cabriole legs and weak ball-and-claw feet.*

Reproductions

Nineteenth century
Although the tripod is often called 'pillar-and-claw' this is a variation, with flattened curve and flowing unbroken line from tripod base to stem, and denotes a characteristic Regency design of the 'Sheraton' period. The legs were often reeded and, later, curved above the central boss of the stem. Inlaid brass decoration and stringing exaggerated the form of these upward-curving legs, which were joined to a square plinth base from which the stem rose. The tops of these tables were often square or octagonal.

The monopodium pedestal also traces its origins from the tripod base and characterizes a wide variety of Victorian tilt-top tables, usually larger than the eighteenth century tripod table. It is to be hoped that the foregoing points of construction, authenticity, restoration and faking will guide the buyer quickly away from any of the countless reproduction 'piecrust' tables to be found in any department store or general furnishing store. Apart from anything else, the lightest push will tip them over.

Price bands

Eighteenth-century piecrust: £2,500–3,500.

Eighteenth century with bird cage: £2,500–4,000.

Chippendale-style supper table: £1,000–1,800.

Nineteenth-century reproductions: £500–850.

Pembroke table

Historical background

This slender, elegant table was first made, so it is said, at the request of the Countess of Pembroke, around 1750. It was an all-purpose occasional table which was free-standing, unlike side tables of the period, with the added advantage of two flaps to increase the size of the surface. Its original function is unclear, but it was not destined for anything but ladylike use, being fragile in construction and usually richly decorated and veneered.

Pembroke tables did not really become universally popular until the 1770s, when they became some of the finest, most delicate pieces of furniture ever made in England.

The best Pembroke tables are oval in shape with the two side flaps raised. In this case the frieze of the underframe should be bow-fronted, following the curve of the top. They were also made with serpentine flaps and sides, and squared, with rectangular flaps, often richly decorated with inlay and veneer. Whatever their shape, Pembroke tables always have slender square-sectioned tapering legs and their flaps, falling one-third of the height of the table, always have two supporting fly brackets on wooden hinges.

The squat, chunky, two-sided flap tables used in Victorian nurseries, passages and even bathrooms, bear no more resemblance to a real Pembroke table than a packing case does to a coffer. Yet they are far too frequently referred to by their antecedent's illustrious name.

Narrow tables with two flaps supported with a single central pillar-type pedestal, or variations of the pillar-and-claw, or of 'cheval' construction are often also referred to as Pembroke tables. Correctly speaking, they are sofa tables.

Signs of authenticity

1. Legs always tapered from inside only: outside corners of legs form right angles with floor.
2. Tops of legs continuing up to form side-frame of drawer.
3. Single drawer in frieze – sham matching drawer at opposite end.
4. Bow-fronted end friezes on oval tables, matching curve.
5. Two fly brackets to each flap – three 'knuckles' to each hinge.
6. Side frieze inset to take width of closed brackets – flaps falling flush with straight sides of legs.
7. Correct height and proportions – flaps fall one-third the table height and may appear too shallow to the modern eye.
8. On oval Pembrokes, flaps should be generous enough in curve to hide the tops of legs and frieze when not raised.
9. Lock and lock rail to drawer.
10. Undersides of flaps in plain veneer of equal thickness.
11. Narrow overhang of top at either end, not exceeding $\frac{1}{2}$ in.

Likely restoration and repair

12. Most prevalent minor damage is to legs, split and broken on slender extremities. 'Collar' applied to hide and strengthen repair.
13. One or both flaps damaged on hinge near edges, with consequent splitting of flap edge or table top along rule joint – repaired with some impairment to value.
14. Plain-surfaced mahogany veneer cut into with recent decorative panel to increase value. Grain of ground veneer will continue through in same direction.
15. Legs tapering on outsides as well as insides: indicates recent restoration or complete remake.
16. Straight ends to oval topped tables indicates new oval top on original square-shaped frame to increase value. Oval tops are worth more than squared shapes.

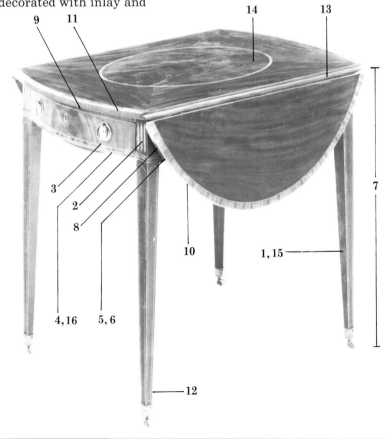

Construction and materials

Pembrokes were made in a wide variety of woods and finishes: satinwood, and mahogany veneer inlaid with rosewood, laburnum, harewood, zebrawood, fruitwoods, delicate floral marquetry in swags and festoons as well as medallions, in many-coloured woods and dyed woods.

The frame was of beech or close-grained red or white pine. Fly brackets were often of plane-wood, which is white and harder than beech. With oval Pembroke tables, the flaps should be sufficiently deep in the curve to hide the frieze when not raised, including the tops of legs. The finest ovals also have a bow-fronted frieze. There was a single deep drawer at one end and a sham or dummy drawer to match at the opposite end.

The square-sectioned legs were always tapered on the inner sides, with the outside corners at right-angles to the floor. Each side flap, however small, was supported with two fly brackets, and each bracket had three 'knuckles', or hinges.

Detail

Undersides of flaps were in plain veneer of equal thickness to that of the surface. With one flap raised, the underside of the other should be clearly visible. The drawer front was inlaid and decorated as profusely as the top and flaps. Height 2 ft 4 in including castors – Pembrokes were often on small cast-brass box castors. The proportions are narrow: the top being just over twice as long as the width, the flaps one-third its total height.

Variations

The ubiquitous two-flap, narrow table with one or two drawers, one either end of the frieze, has been made in a variety of solid woods since the end of the eighteenth century. Square, chamfered legs are sturdy versions of the delicate tapering legs, and in their component parts these little tables may sound similar in description, but they do not in any way add up to the fragile little ladies' tables used in bedrooms, morning rooms for breakfasts, letter-writing and mirror-gazing. The country way of life precluded such luxuries.

Made of oak, elm, fruitwood, occasionally Virginia walnut, they were seldom if ever veneered but sometimes had boxwood stringing. Some country side tables with frieze drawers were made with two flaps extending on either side, but not all small two-flapped tables are Pembrokes. It is the narrowness and slenderness of line which distinguishes one from the other.

Below: *French-influenced serpentine version, c.1800.*

Reproductions

There are two main periods of reproductions: the Victorian Regency revival, during which reproductions were extremely well-made with proportions very nearly right, usually in darker toned West Indian satinwood veneer; and the Edwardian period where the tables were usually emasculated, thinned down to spindly pieces of furniture with no more use than to hold a bowl of flowers and a silver salver for calling cards. Better were the envelope-flapped tables – small square tables with triangular flaps opening out to larger squares.

Above: *Sheraton-style, nineteenth-century reproduction.*

Price bands

Rectangular, satinwood, inlaid and finely veneered: *c.*1790: £5,000 + .

Bow-front, satinwood, high quality, *c.*1790: £6,000.

With fine veneers, *c.*1790: £2,000–3,000.

Plain, with little decoration, *c.*1790: £1,250–1,850.

Serpentine 'French', *c.*1800, £3,500–5,000.

Plain mahogany, nineteenth century: £900–1,500.

Sofa table

Historical background

Sofa tables belong to the last decade of the eighteenth century and the first two of the nineteenth, after which they became 'occasional tables' without a specific function. They were originally designed for writing or playing games while people sat on a sofa, and as such were usually at least 5 ft long, sometimes as much as 6 ft, and no more than 2 ft 6 in high and 22–24 in wide.

Bearing in mind their function, it is obvious that the extra flaps are extensions of length rather than width, since a flap on the sofa side of the table would make it very uncomfortable for anyone to sit at. In order to give as much leg-room as possible, they were of cheval construction, with two end bearers, rather in the manner of the old X-frame trestle table, solidly made and correctly balanced so that they did not sway from side to side. In some, a central stretcher helped stability.

By c.1810, sofa tables were made on the central pillar-and-claw design, usually more ornate, and often with brass stringing inset as decoration on legs and plinth as well as on drawers and surfaces.

Early sofa tables had fairly deep drawers on one full length and matching dummy drawer on each side. Often, drawers were fitted with compartments for games and writing materials. In the later period, c.1820, drawers became shallower as sofa tables began to lose their identity and became merely decorative. Early versions were not very robust, being intended only for genteel use, and it is uncommon to find one without any repair or restoration.

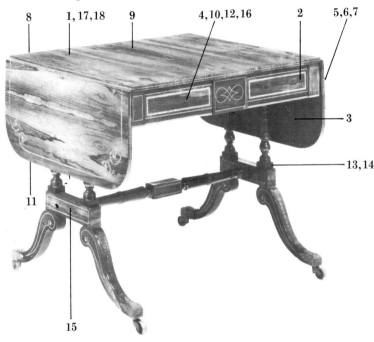

Signs of authenticity

1. Thick, fine veneers on close-grained red pine or Honduras mahogany.
2. Drawers oak-lined, not pine.
3. Undersides of flap plain veneered – visible when not raised.
4. If with locks, steel levers to brass locks and lock casings – brass levers are post-1840.
5. Two fly brackets to each flap.
6. Three 'knuckles' or hinges to each bracket.
7. Underframe frieze inset to take width of closed brackets, allowing flaps to fall flush with cheval supports.
8. Sham drawers on either side to real drawers.
9. Grain running across width, not down length of table.
10. No escutcheons to locks (if fitted) but simple rim escutcheons with rounded bottoms. Squared bottoms to rim escutcheons are post-1840.
11. Cross-cut veneer to edge of tables.
12. Often, cast brass, turned, circular, flat knobs to drawers or lion's masks with rings.

Likely restoration and repair
13. Cheval supports broken, replaced with central pillar support taken from damaged piece of same period.
14. Cheaper cheval supports taken from mass-produced sofa tables of same period, usually not as long, added to a high quality top. Marks of original bearers, screw-holes, chevals set in too close.
15. Made-up cheval supports from Victorian cheval mirrors. Holes where mirror pivoted, usually in square block in cheval, concealed by a rosette or other decoration, where it has been plugged and stained.
16. If both drawers are on the same side, indicates a recent addition.
17. Veneered in pinkish-coloured birch. Cheap Victorian substitute for satinwood, with wavy grain instead of straight or figured.
18. Grain running length of table suggests new top with suitable inlay made up from larger piece of period furniture.

Construction and materials

Sofa tables were made with two different constructions: the cheval and the central pillar support. The cheval type had solid supports dividing into two splayed legs, and was made with or without stretchers. The central pillar-supports often incorporated a half-circle resting on a central plinth with up-curving flattened splayed legs, frequently terminating in lion's paw feet or square box castors with horizontal fittings.

They were made in a wide variety of woods and veneers: rosewood, mahogany and 'black' walnut. There were two drawers, side by side in the width of the table, one sham the other real.

The correct proportions are quite large: 5–6 ft long with the flaps extended, 22–24 in wide and approximately 2 ft 6 in in height. The overall shape is definitely long, lean and sleek, with minimal overhang on either side. When the flaps are down they fall flush with the side supports. The legs splay out in a flattened curve so that they can be pulled close to the sofa, with the legs sliding a little way beneath.

Detail

Early sofa tables resemble writing furniture more than ornamental pieces, and share their smooth, plain surfaces rather than the more elaborate inlays which might lift and catch on soft fabrics of sleeves and cuffs. Simple decoration, such as cross-banded borders, continued on to the flaps, and some fine examples have fly brackets set at the edge of the frieze so that, when opened, the design carries on from the frieze to the ends of the brackets.

From c.1810 they are found in many veneers, including satinwood, light Cuban mahogany, laburnum, zebrawood, amboyna and rosewood. Between 1810 and 1820 brass inlay was very popular, and from c.1815 the fashionable design of the lyre was incorporated, and lyre-ended tables were made with brass rods to simulate harp strings.

Variations

Sofas were not part of the furnishings of smaller agricultural homes until the age of sprung furniture some time after c.1830. Country versions of the card table fulfilled the same function as a sofa table for writing and playing games. Contemporary, cheaper versions were made, in machine-cut woods, mass-produced with thin veneer and poor quality materials, usually shorter in length than high-quality versions.

Legs of chevals in provincial sofa tables tend to be heavy, or machine-cut with decoration on outer surfaces of chevals only, strengthened with stretchers. Legs would often be chamfered to join the upright, then screwed, glued and clamped before being veneered over the joint to look as though they are correctly made.

The basic idea of a narrow all-purpose drawing table has been used in many variations since sofa tables were first designed by Thomas Sheraton and his contemporaries.

Reproductions

The period of the sofa table's popularity comes within the age of mass-manufactured furniture. These tables were more often made in cheaper materials, and of meaner proportions for provincial homes, rather than as country pieces. After c.1850 many unattractive versions of long occasional tables were made all over the country, many of them with side-flaps rather than end flaps. Taller versions were used in libraries behind high-backed Victorian and Edwardian settees and sofas for trays of drinks, etc.

In the 1950s a proliferation of copies of the lyre-ended design flooded the market, but since they went out of fashion they have not been seen around in very large numbers.

Price bands

Top-quality Regency, without stretcher, mahogany: £5,000–7,000.

Finely veneered satinwood, c.1810: £5,000–8,000.

With central support, fine quality, c.1810: £3,500–4,500.

Rosewood or walnut, fine quality, with stretcher, c.1830: £2,000–3,000.

Poorer quality veneered: £800–1,200.

Left: *turned stretcher and cheval legs have probably been added.*
Centre: *superb early Regency Thomas Hope design.*
Below right: *fine, early nineteenth-century, on central support with inlaid brass decoration.*

Library table

Historical background

In its most general meaning, a library table is simply a table used for writing or reading in the library of a grand house. The term covers a wide variety of tables, from the slender eighteenth century writing table derived from the French *bureau plat*, to the solid drum-shaped tables which were smaller versions of the rent tables used in the offices of large estates. All were leather-topped, all had drawers in the frieze to hold writing materials and were 2 ft 6 in to 2 ft 8 in high.

For immediate identification only the derivations of the French *bureau plat* will be considered in detail: a writing table with a leather-covered surface and three drawers in the frieze. *French bureaux plats* are similar to the English lowboy, having two deeper drawers on either side of a shallower drawer, but the 'kneehole' is less pronounced and they are much longer. English library tables have a straight frieze, are free-standing and have drawers on both sides, often three to one side and two to the other. Often there is a pull-out writing slide which can be lifted to make an easel over the centre drawer. Sometimes the whole central leather-covered panel lifts to rest on easel struts as a bookrest or 'architect's table'. Regency libraries were equipped with library tables and, from that period onwards, designs of all sorts were made. The Regency archetype is the design described below.

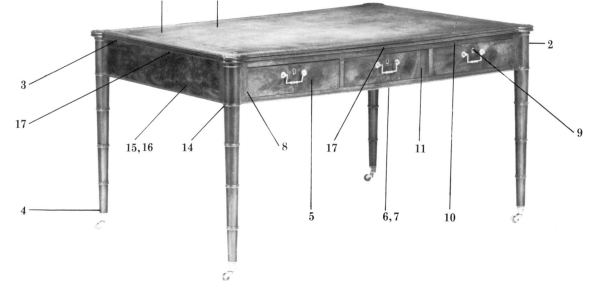

Signs of authenticity

1. Solid, close-grained dense woods with good figuring.
2. Tops of legs continue to form end pieces of drawer frieze, set proud, rounded or square.
3. Minimal lip above frieze, usually less than 1 in.
4. Legs terminating in simple peg foot below a turned collar.
5. Drawers lined with oak.
6. Underside well patinated where knees have rubbed.
7. Underside of drawers enclosed with pine or mahogany with strengtheners and corner pieces.
8. Good patination on inside front of drawer and drawer sides where they have been handled.

9. Lock escutcheons set centrally above handles on single-handled drawers.
10. Lock and lock rail.
11. Drawers are usually same width.

Likely restoration and repair
12. New leather inset panel.
13. New top with panel planed out of damaged solid surface and inset leather panel added. Grain will continue through in one direction.
14. Legs broken at frieze level: break in grain on point of join, often concealed by ring turning.
15. Top section of small pedestal desk mounted on legs. Grain of

all legs will stop short at frieze level, underside of drawers with new wood, or patched and stained where tops of pedestal were originally.
16. Library table tops reset on cheval supports – could have been altered during Victorian period, but more likely to be a recent event.
17. Cut down from more massive Victorian piece: drawers of equal width where centre drawer has been reduced. Tell-tale crack on underside of small overhang beneath veneered top edging where width and length have been reduced.

Construction and materials

Library tables were made in solid mahogany, or mahogany veneer on a mahogany carcase, and in rosewood or Brazil wood (closely resembling mahogany but of a redder, more chestnut colour). Library tables are distinctive and differ from all other tables. The legs were set out from the frieze, giving unusual lobed corners. The same is true of the French *bureau plat* where the legs are usually squared and set slightly proud of the frieze. The English favoured a smoother line, with rounded corners, undecorated except for a thin line of double stringing, framing and emphasizing the curve.

Detail

Drawers were oak lined, outlined in double stringing, often with squared handles on cast brass bolt heads with rosettes, octagonal or circular small backplates on either side of the handle. Legs were always elegantly turned and reeded or fluted, terminating in plain peg feet. The table edges were never carved or decorated, and there is almost no lip or overhang above the frieze drawers. Usually the edge of the table was decorated with two single thick reeds, continuing round the lobed corners. The drawers were usually edged with thin cockbeading or half-round beading, and the leather writing surface is inset and edged with cross-cut veneer.

Variations

Most common are circular rent tables used in the offices of large estates, with small drawers in the circumference of the frieze. Plain oak or oak-and-elm tables of solid construction often had drawers set in the ends as opposed to along the length and square chamfered legs. Country versions should be wider than a side table and may have plain square stretchers for extra stability.

Below: *a late Regency design, probably provincial.*

Above: *drum or rent table.*

Reproductions

Victorian

Variations are legion: octagonal leather-topped tables set on pedestals with drawers; drum tables set on central pedestals with bow-fronted drawers set fairly far apart (usually four on a small drum table, and not tapering in shape towards the centre); leather-topped tables on almost Davenport-type pedestals with two flaps, one on either side. Also popular were 'architect's tables' with tops lifting on easel supports. Victorian versions of the *bureau plat* had ornate, over-curvaceous serpentine lines, often with mass-produced mock-ormolu embellishments. 'Gothic' Victorian library tables with pillared legs on square plinth feet had carved edges to tops and applied or shallow machine-cut decoration on side friezes.

Twentieth century

Edwardian library tables were well-made and often quite well-proportioned but of mahogany veneer which was darker than earlier veneer. They often have a bigger overhang and lip moulding, and the grain of the veneer running vertical and not horizontal on frieze and drawer fronts, which can cause wrinkling, chipping or splitting.

From the turn of the century, there was a plethora of mass-produced reading/writing tables for public libraries, hotel reading rooms and public institutions. Many library tables have been 'made up' from other pieces of furniture, so it is particularly important to examine similar-shaped pieces and styles with great care, and to scrutinize materials, detail and construction of the piece under consideration.

Price bands

Fine quality, *c.*1790: £3,000–5,000.

Later versions with less detail: £2,000–3,500.

Drum or rent table, *c.*1790: £3,000–3,800.

Pillar-and-claw table

Signs of authenticity

1. Matching tops and pillar-and-claw supports – reeded edges to all pieces of table top including leaves, with reeded feet, legs and pillars.
2. Plain edges to table tops and leaves, with plain pillars, sometimes octagonal or polygonal, plain legs and feet.
3. Squared cast-brass shoes, plain swivelling castors with horizontal sockets more common on period tables than lion's paw, which is often a sign of Victorian Regency revival.
4. Four legs and not three to each pillar for the best examples.
5. No cross-bearers visible near edge of table tops – always chamfered so that they could not be seen.
6. Squared tops to pillars in same timber as the rest.
7. Patination, particularly on leaves, the depth of a hand on undersurface of table top where table and leaves have been handled.
8. Grain of tops and leaves running parallel with rule joints, not down the length of the table in any part.
9. Ring turning on pillars above leg joints.
10. Height of table, 2 ft 4 in.

Likely restoration and repair

11. Mismatched tops and pillars: reeded with plain, or vice versa, means a marriage of more than one table. Even if correct period, worth considerably less.
12. Replaced pillars from later bulbous Victorian shapes, cut down and reeded. Reeding will be rough, no patination in grooves.
13. Replaced legs and feet: ring turning may be directly above leg joints where wedge dovetail has been recut.
14. Bearers visible too near edge of table: top cut down from larger size.
15. Bearers not chamfered indicates new top or replacement.
16. Edge moulding rough, no patination indicates Victorian machine-carving cut away.
17. Carved edges to tops and leaves indicates later Victorian table tops. Period tables were undecorated except for reeding or thumb moulding.

Historical background

The method of supporting table tops with one or more central columns on splayed legs was the natural development of the tripod table, combined with the great strength of mahogany. The greatest innovation in the design was that an extra leaf could be supported on the rule-join of the two endpieces, with nothing more than bolt-and-fork fastenings and no supporting pillar beneath it. This had obvious advantages for seating arrangements, as legs and chairs did not have to contend with a forest of uprights below the table.

The best examples of the pillar-and-claw construction are those with pillars terminating in four splayed legs rather than three. The square base of four legs suited the more symmetrical style of the Regency period and the whole appearance of these tables is characteristic of the 'Sheraton period' of simple, undecorated, glossy mahogany, with smooth tapering lines and restrained reeded decoration. Dining tables of this period were designed to set off the quantities of silver, crystal and porcelain reflecting light from chandeliers and table candles – hence the emphasis on richly veneered surfaces.

Brass shoes and castors are an integral part of the design of pillar-and-claw tables – sometimes with lion's paw feet but more often a simple squared shoe was preferred, with the castor horizontally beneath it.

Pillar-and-claw tables are sometimes known as pedestal tables, but strictly speaking the pedestal was a solid affair without separate splayed feet and belongs to a later period. No pillar-and-claw table measures less than 4 ft across and their height is always 2 ft 4 in. The smallest pillar-and-claw table measures about 9 ft long with the extra leaf inserted.

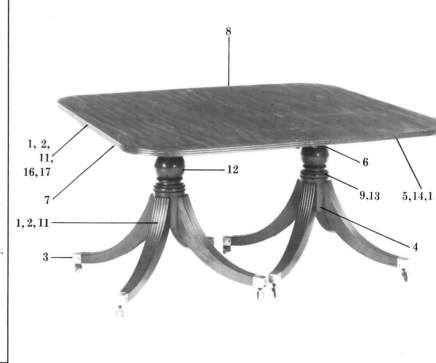

Construction and materials

The function of the table demanded a massive, heavy mahogany. San Domingo or Cuban mahogany was also used and is nearly always darkened from rich chestnut brown to deep gloss with age and polishing. Each piece of table top was cut from a single piece of timber, planed and rubbed with brick dust or sand until perfectly smooth, and then oiled and polished with beeswax until it shone like silk.

Legs fitted into the pillar on the same principle as the tripod table construction – each curving splayed leg dovetailed into the base of the pillar with a wedge dovetail, glued and clamped for extra strength.

Pillars ended in a square platform of the same piece of timber, and were mounted between chamfered bearers under the table top. There was a hairline join between the two halves, a fixed top and extra leaves, with rule joint and bolt-and-fork fastenings below the table top on either side. Large spans had additional bolt-and-fork fastenings further towards the centre. With all extensions, the progression of numbers is: two pillars with one extra leaf, three pillars and two extra leaves, four pillars and three extra leaves or five pillars and four extra leaves.

Detail
The tables were always solid – never veneered – because of the potential damage from spillages and hot dishes, which could lift veneer. The edges to tops were plain, as were the circular pillars with their narrow band of ring-turning above the leg joints; legs were also plainly shaped. One sometimes finds reeded edges to table tops with matching reeded pillars and legs. There was no frieze to any section of the top.

Variations

The method of construction demanded the use of expensive mahogany which allowed the extra leaves to be inserted without supporting pillars, and therefore these were expensive tables used only in large houses for large numbers of diners.

Country tables of any size at this period were usually of the draw-leaf variety, descendants of the seventeenth-century draw table, with leaves at either end which slid out from beneath the table top on bearers. By the end of the eighteenth century the two extending leaves joined in the middle under the table top when they were pushed in, and when pulled out the table top dropped into the well between them.

They were constructed with the traditional square or rectangular frame, with stretchers and plain square legs or minimal decoration.

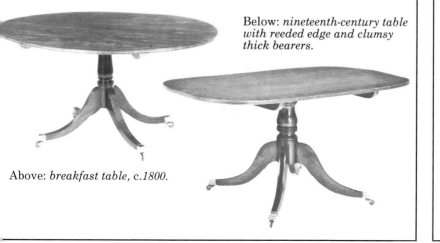

Above: *breakfast table, c.1800.*

Below: *nineteenth-century table with reeded edge and clumsy thick bearers.*

Reproductions

Nineteenth century
Versions came in many forms, often with three-legged pillar-and-claw, lion's paw feet, indicating Victorian Regency revival. Pillars were thicker and more bulbous, with more ring-turning. Legs were curvaceous and cumbersome, with castors set on base of upward-curling feet. Victorian draw-leaf tables sometimes managed a combination of the old solid X-trestle with central stretcher, bulbous in shape and added nothing to construction. Better versions had legs which tapered inward at the top, echoing the old triangular trestle shape.

Whatever the pillar or pedestal, it has to run on castors so that it can be moved about for inserting and removing extra leaves. Thus the triangular, solid-stem of later Victorian 'tripod' based tables were not suitable. The only other period variation during the early nineteenth century was a pillar constructed of three or four pieces, clustered together to form a single support.

Twentieth century
Smaller versions (less than 4 ft wide) are still made today, and are often quite well reproduced, but in poorer-quality woods with machine finishing, sometimes even with rough undersides to the table top.

Price bands

Four-claw, two pillar table on solid mahogany, George III and Regency: £8,000–10,000.

Three-pillar, two leaves: £10,000–12,000.

Four-pillar, three leaves: £9,000–11,000.

Single pedestal, rectangular, c.1840: £2,000–3,000.

Circular, c.1840: £850–1,000.

George III-style reproduction: £800–1,500.

Tilt-top table

Historical background

The predecessor of the Victorian tilt-top is the eighteenth-century tripod table and its contemporary cousin, the breakfast or supper table, also known as a 'snap-top' table. In its original form, like all dining-room furniture, the snap-top was made in solid, well-grained mahogany with little embellishment except for cross-cut veneered bands of contrasting inlay. They were more often rectangular with rounded edges than circular or oval: four to six people could be seated round a rectangular table, but a round one could only seat four in comfort. However, by the turn of the century, the advantages of display had become evident, and from William IV onwards table tops became more and more decorative with intricate designs and inlays, shown to advantage when the table was in an upright position, like a huge firescreen.

By the mid-Victorian period, the table tops were still immensely fine and decorative, but the restrained bases had become bulbous and heavy, or were thick monopodium shapes on squat paw feet. The better designs adapted a plinth base with outreaching feet terminating in scrolls, dolphins, lion's paws, or flattened claws with round, square or triangular plinths. Tops were oval, round or rectangular, with rounded corners. Some larger tilt-tops dating from the early nineteenth century are known as 'loo' tables and were designed to seat eight people to play the card game, 'loo'.

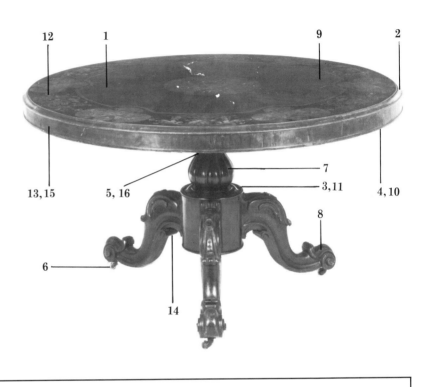

Signs of authenticity

1. Good-quality veneer and inlay on solid mahogany.
2. Cross-cut veneer edging to borders.
3. Well-made, well-designed base, plinth or monopodium support.
4. No signs of tampering with top and base – screw-holes, marks, signs of cross-bearers being moved, on underside.
5. Correct proportions, both when table is horizontal and vertical.
6. On circular 'loo' tables and square supper tables, horizontally fitted castors on cast-brass shoes.
7. Central column in one piece with grain continuing up to the fixing block.

8. Good incised carving base with no chipping or damage.
9. No damage, replaced veneer, chipped or cracked round circumference or any part of table top.
10. Veneered on good quality Honduras mahogany or on oak, not stained white wood.
11. Bases, plinths, monopodium, in solid mahogany, not stained-up cheaper woods, brightly gilded.

Likely restoration and repair
12. Later inlays cut into plain veneers to increase value – grain will run in one direction only.
13. Bases married to better-looking tops, out of proportion, too decorative for base. Signs of

tampering on top undersurface.
14. Bases restored, repaired – metal braces under legs, knees, feet, castors reset where feet have been damaged.
15. Rectangular tops replaced with circular and vice versa. Proportions will be wrong, overall design incorrect. Best seen when table is vertical, not horizontal.
16. Replaced square platform on pillar where it has broken. New catches and snap-top fastening – no immediate disadvantage, but a weakness which will reduce value and may break with use.

Construction and materials

The earliest snap-top tables, rectangular in shape, and circular 'loo' tables, were usually on castors, so that they could be moved to the centre of the room for breakfast or supper or for playing cards. From c.1840 many tilt-tops were made without castors, on flattened, triangular or circular bases with ornamental feet. Generally they were heavy and not designed to be moved about. They usually had highly decorated table tops and were probably seldom used, since they looked better in the vertical position and were probably designed more for display than for use.

Victorian tilt-tops, for breakfast or supper tables, were made in solid mahogany, well-figured with good graining, in solid rosewood, solid walnut and in lighter-weight South American and African mahoganies, more reddish in colour than eighteenth-century mahoganies.

The snap-top fastening was a stouter version of the small tilt-top tripod fastening, with parallel cross-bearers fitting either side of a square platform on the top of the central plinth or pillar, secured with a heavy brass catch.

Detail
Tilt-tops for occasional use or for display were made in many veneers, including rosewood, walnut, burrwood, amboyna, tulipwood, kingwood, bird's eye maple, with zebrawood, harewood, ebony, coromandel, satinwood, laburnum and many other exotic and dyed woods for inlays.

There was a wide variety of pillar supports, ranging from flattened pillar-and-claw to triangular plinth with gilt-brass or bronze decorative feet, lion's paw, dolphin's head, bear's paw and many versions of a scrolled foot, as well as reeded columns and decorated monopodium plinths. Later versions were more bulbous, over-ornate and ostentatious.

Variations

Provincial tables were often richly decorated in veneer and inlay for display, but their central supports lacked the finesse of good furniture-makers and were often badly proportioned. Country versions of the tilt-top are much the same as larger versions of the tripod table. They were most often made of plain oak, or in well-grained yew or fruitwood, the tops in more than one piece, but the grain being highly prized.

Reproductions

Tilt-tops span a period of over 100 years of continuous manufacture, some with quarter veneer framed with decorative, restrained borders, some of simple, plain, good-looking veneer or solid woods, some with machine-stamped ground veneers and showy, poor-quality 'inlay'. They were not made much after the beginning of the twentieth century, but such a large quantity had been manufactured that there was little need for reproduction. Labour was cheap and machines could reproduce many of the more difficult processes. Brass inlay and decoration could be inset by hand, painstakingly by craftsmen, or poured in a molten state into grooves in the solid timber and sanded down and polished by machine.

It is a question here of quality an eye for a good design and good materials, not really of authenticity. These tables have recently enjoyed a surge in popularity, and although it is doubtful if any are being made today, it is certain that table tops and bases are being exchanged and replaced to achieve a better-looking table than the original might have been.

Price bands

Rectangular breakfast table, in fine, plain veneer, c.1780: £2,000–3,500.

'Loo' table, circular, plain, c.1800: £1,800–2,500.

Victorian, with rich, decorative veneer, inlay: £1,400–2,200.

(Mahogany is the most expensive, followed by rosewood, then walnut.)

Variations, left: *A circular George III snap-top breakfast or supper table, in well-figured mahogany veneer and broad cross-banding.*
Right: *Flamboyant Victorian decorative inlay and veneer.*

Sutherland table

Historical background

These slim, practical folding tables were reputedly named after Harriet, Duchess of Sutherland, Mistress of the Robes to Queen Victoria during the early decades of her long reign. The combination of a cheval-type construction and gate-leg is far more successful and elegant than it sounds and they are among the few really successful designs of the Victorian period.

The top of a Sutherland is so narrow that it is able to stand against a wall without taking up much space, yet when the flaps are up and supported on two swinging gate legs, it is large enough for a small supper or breakfast table. The frame is almost like a heavy Victorian clothes horse in construction: one or two slim baluster-turned uprights join a simple frieze below the table top. On the best, the gate legs tuck in beside the bracket foot. Others have half-gates with two legs swinging closed in the centre on either side of the central stretcher.

Sutherland tables were such strong little work horses that many of them have only survived in a dilapidated state and some of the more decorative, with slim bands of contrasting veneer, have been broken up to make the tops of questionable pairs of card tables.

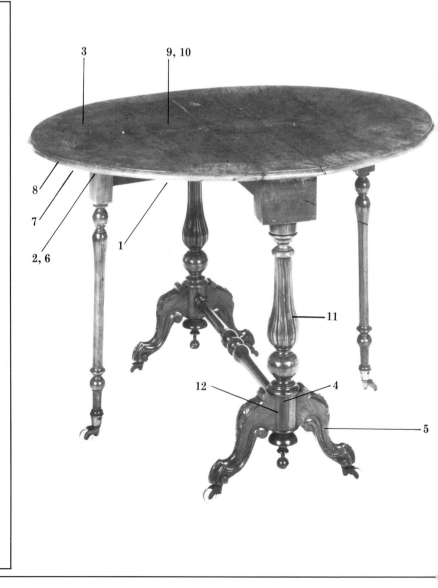

Signs of authenticity

1. Undersides of flaps with scoremarks, pronounced where top of gate leg has been swung out and back.
2. Good patination on undersides of end overhang where it has been frequently lifted and moved.
3. Dark, glossy woods with very little decoration.
4. Cheval construction stoutly made with well-turned, simple decoration.
5. Splay of legs compact, not sprawling.
6. Solidly made underframe of mahogany or oak, to withstand hard use.
7. Flaps falling to correct height, just above curve of bracket, to show an inch or two of leg.
8. Good patination under flaps where they have been continuously handled.

Likely restoration and repair
9. Edge of flap split with weight of flaps and constant use. The repair likely to split again with the weight of the flaps after some use.
10. Repairs to join on edge of rule hinge.
11. New turned uprights, replaced uprights from parts of other table legs, even staircase balusters, stained and polished with mottled results, not caused by age or wear.
12. Made up from solid Victorian mahogany clothes horse, built on similar lines, with new top and underframe.

Construction and materials

Sutherlands are usually about 3 ft 6 in long – a comfortable size to be lifted by one person. They were made in plain mahogany with mahogany cheval supports, feet and gate legs, with flattened bracket feet joined by a turned stretcher. They were extremely narrow, not more than 9 in across when the flaps were down, which were very deep and fall to a line just above the stretcher. The two gates on either side are recessed into the underframe, and swing out on wooden hinges. The flaps have brass hinges on a rule joint, set close to the ends of the joins, with one or two additional hinges under the flap to support the weight when lifting and lowering.

Detail
The upright supports are usually turned or baluster shaped, or twin turned legs socketing in to a single bracket foot at either end. Sometimes, on more ornate versions, there is a small drop finial on the undercurve. Sutherlands are always on castors, sometimes set beneath slightly outward-scrolling feet, or a compressed inward scroll. They are usually about 2 ft 4 in – more the height of dining furniture than writing furniture, and early versions were always in solid woods and not veneered. Later versions for provincial drawing rooms and parlours were veneered in the ubiquitous birds' eye maple and were much more showy and not so elegant.

Reproductions

Small spindly Victorian and Edwardian 'tea tables' are low enough to be used by people sitting in sprung armchairs or sofas. These were sometimes round-leafed, sometimes square or rectangular, but the principles of construction are basically the same: narrow top, often on four turned legs with thin stretchers, and two gate legs to support the flaps. Heavier, chunkier tables of full height, also on four stretchered legs, usually have flaps of less depth. They are almost a cross between the delicate Pembroke and the functional, unobtrusive Sutherland.

Variations

Often the tables are found in oak, and very pleasing when well-polished and aged. However, oak tends to split quite easily, and the weight of the flaps imposes a considerable strain to flap edges and table-top edges at the hinges. Others may be found in yew wood with elm tops, and in fruitwood with oak tops.

Broader versions of this simple design melt into narrow gate-legged tables with deep flaps, made over a century earlier in standard 'country' woods and combinations of woods. Usually the cheval supports are abandoned in favour of four simple straight legs, joined with stretchers. The flaps may be rectangular or rounded.

Price bands

Ornate frames, veneered tops: £500–750.

Nineteenth century, plain, solid wood: £350–500.

'Spider-leg': £600–1,000.

Below: *the black paint and excessive turning is characteristic of a late Victorian Sutherland.*

Below: *in contrast to the table on the left, this elegantly turned and inlaid piece dates from c.1870.*

Blanket chest

Signs of authenticity

1. All wood split or quarter-sawn, with more figure and grain than planking.

2. Timbers were not clamped or cleated – the lid in particular should show signs of bowing, curving and shrinking across the width.

3. Feet of both board chests and frame construction worn and frayed with use and wear on stone floors, and from damp.

4. Uneven shape of pegs and dowels, hand cut from green wood.

5. Good patination on underside of lid where it has been opened and handled over a long period of time.

6. Wood around lock and hasp, worn and polished with use and age.

7. On frame construction, panels with grain running from top to bottom.

8. Panels chamfered to slot into frames – should be slightly loose on end-grain from shrinkage of timber.

9. Interior wood with no splintering along grain – worn smooth and dust-dry from age and use.

10. Front and back timbers overlapping side edges.

Likely restoration and repair

11. New lids where originals have split or cracked. Timber will not be thick enough and lack bowing or curving.

12. Back timber of lids split where hinges have taken the strain and may be patched, replaced, pegged or repaired.

13. Made up in whole or part from bits and pieces of old panelling and timbers. Hard for novice to detect, but clear signs of saw marks on edges; lack of patination on inside and around lock and hasp are usually obvious.

14. On frame construction, original plain panels replaced with cut-down pieces from church panelling or house panelling. Particularly prevalent with 'linenfold' panelling, which, if original, should butt on to frame and not finish decoratively above and below it.

Historical background

Oak coffers and chests owed their origins to the 'sumpter chests' or trunks which were strapped to baggage animals to carry the goods belonging to the household when travelling. However, the term 'blanket chest' is of eighteenth-century origins: blankets as we understand them were not known until the seventeenth century.

The earliest form of coffer was simply a slab-sided box or 'coffin' known as a 'boarded chest'. The sides extended to the ground and were cut in a plain V-shape to form feet. They were held together with wooden dowel pins or clumsy iron clout nails, and each piece of the chest was made from a single piece of wood. The lid had two big iron or steel strap hinges, and there was an iron lock and hasp fixed to the outside of the chest. Framing and panelling replaced this crude construction in the sixteenth century, a technique learned by carpenters for house building and for embellishing churches.

'Wainscot oak' was imported in large quantities from the mid-sixteenth century onwards, and coffers and chests were made with frames of sawn timber and inset panels of riven wood, chamfered to fit into grooves in the frame. Panels were carved in 'linenfold' and arched Gothic decoration, and everyday coffers and chests had four short legs, extensions of the side frames, and became less clumsily made and more decorative.

Until the end of the seventeenth century chests were restricted to the richer classes who had possessions which needed to be stored. With the growth of the middle class they became more prevalent as storage for the more elaborate dress of the day and richer households were often equipped with chests with separate drawers for ruffs, collars, doublets, stockings, hose and gloves. Poor families kept their best clothes in simply made chests constructed in the same way as a century before.

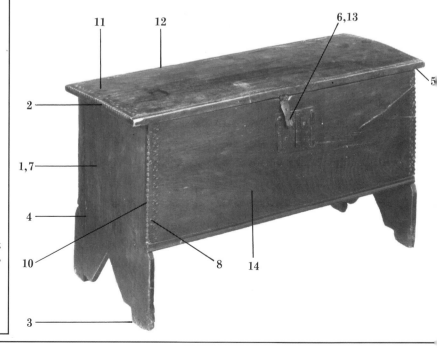

Construction and materials

Chests and coffers were made in oak, the principal wood for most early English furniture until the mid-seventeenth century. Some were made in chestnut, and elm was also used, but it is not an entirely suitable wood since it tends to split and crack with changes of temperature and humidity. Grander Elizabethan chests were also made in cypress, known to repel moths, and from the beginning of the eighteenth century, in cedarwood. Even in later years, blanket chests were often lined with cedarwood.

The slab-sided construction of board chests continued well into the eighteenth century in country districts, but in general it was superseded in the sixteenth century by frame-and-panel construction which remained the basis for all storage furniture until well into the eighteenth century. All joins were made with wooden dowelling pegs or iron nails, with mortise-and-tenon joints from the end of the sixteenth century.

Detail
Panels were decorated with carving and chamfered on the back surface so that they would slot into the frames. Early panel shapes varied, but in length rather than in depth. Elizabethan panels were smaller and squarer, but by the seventeenth century they were much bigger.

Many early board chests were originally painted in bright colours, but some have bands of simple chip-carving in arches and geometric shapes. The legs of frame and panel chests were a continuation of the side frame and were not decorated or shaped in any way. Iron or steel locks were mounted externally, or internally with a square lockplate on the outside and a hinged hasp fastening, all secured with iron nails. Lids had simple edge moulding, but from c.1610 onwards, were finished with lip moulding.

Variations

Continental
While oak was the principal national timber for English furniture in the early years, so walnut and chestnut were extensively used on the Continent, particularly in France, and pine and deal in Scandinavia. Chests of these woods are almost certainly not English, as can be seen from their size, shape and decoration. The most common chests, usually of a later date, tend to be Flemish, often constructed from richly decorated and carved Gothic panelling from churches, or from the bottoms of built-in dressers and cupboards of panelled rooms. A few very rare chests and coffers were made in chestnut before the sixteenth and seventeenth centuries, but one is unlikely to come across these rare originals. Pine was not used in England until the mid-nineteenth century.

Below: *oak 'mule chest', with carved timber frames, characteristic of Continental pieces and Victorian 'improvements'.*
Below left: *this is almost a dresser base, ornately decorated with applied moulding in seventeenth-century Flemish style.*

Reproductions

Nineteenth century
The great age of reproduction oak was the Victorian Tudor revival, when, from c.1830 onwards, simple furniture of an earlier age was faithfully reproduced, as well as being made up from bits and pieces of genuinely antique panels. There was a great vogue for 'old oak' in the 1860s and 1870s, still occasionally referred to as 'Wardour Street oak' from the famous firm of London reproduction furniture-makers who had their workshops there.

The Victorians often 'improved' the appearance of original chests with carving, which was often quite skilful, but the grooves will lack the patina and roundness one would expect on a really old chest.

Price bands

Below: *frame-and-panel linenfold chest in solid, well-worn oak.*

Court cupboard

Signs of authenticity

1. All timbers of same age, colour, patination, distinctly hardened with age and smoke from wood fires.
2. Adze marks on chamfered panels on insides of doors – they should not be smooth-planed.
3. Base showing considerable signs of damage from kicking, knocks from brooms, and damp.
4. No locks on doors originally: these cupboards were accessible to both servant and master.
5. Backs in roughly fitting boards or planks, shrunk across the grain with age.
6. All joints mortise-and-tenon with dowels. Backs nailed to frame with iron clout nails, usually with rectangular heads.
7. Shelves held by dowelling pins to sides.
8. Bottom planks of cupboards marked and smoothed with use, same age as back boards and approximately same colour.
9. Bulbs on column supports attached with glue and wooden pegs, or turned and finished by hand, often of slightly irregular shape.
10. No marks on top timber of any sign of another tier. Look for dowel holes and discolouration of wood. Timber of top should be same age as rest of piece.
11. Plain panelled sides with cross-frames corresponding to rest of frame.
12. Pin hinges of iron or steel on cupboard doors.

Likely restoration and repair
13. Replaced panels from larger pieces of panelling or another piece of furniture of later date.
14. Upright column supports replaced – colour will be different, lack rich dark patina and feel rough to the touch.
15. Base of piece replaced – bottom of base cupboard will be of newer wood. Suspect more restoration if this is the case.
16. Marriage of two pieces of furniture to make one whole. Check side panels and cross frames for difference in colour, frames not matching up.
17. If completely made up from old timbers, this will show up as the patchwork it is.

Historical background

Court cupboards – the forerunners of the 'buffetier' and sideboard – were made for keeping and displaying food and dishes from the mid-sixteenth century onwards. Originally they stood in the hall, where most meals were taken, and later in the parlour. Their name is possibly derived from the French word *court* meaning 'short', since they often stood on tables. Their generally accepted form is that of a deep two-doored cupboard below, with a stepped single or double tier of smaller cupboards above, supported on pillars. Earlier food cupboards, such as the aumbry, show a similar function, as do 'food hutches' and 'livery cupboards'. All these had pierced or slatted doors to allow air to circulate around the food inside.

By the time the court cupboard had evolved, meals were taken in a room apart from the hall, where there was a need to display fine plate, porcelain, 'delft' and pewter on the shelves of an imposing piece of furniture.

Court cupboards had a relatively short lifespan in English houses, but its Welsh equivalent, the *cwpwrdd deuddarn* or *cwpwrdd tridarn* (depending on whether it had two or three tiers) survived for far longer.

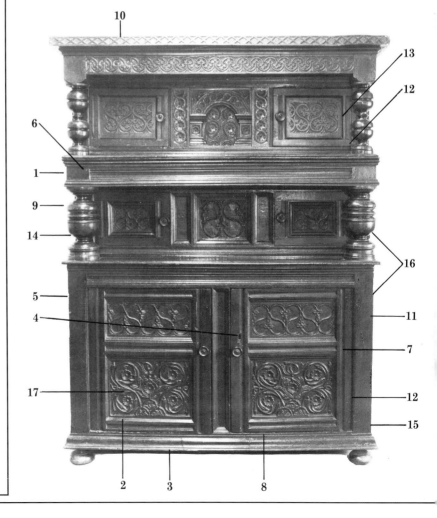

Construction and materials

Without exception these massive, impressive pieces of furniture were made in oak, constructed on the same principle as frame and panel chests. Sides were left plain and simply panelled; the back was boarded with planking, and inside, the shelves themselves were often no more than $\frac{1}{2}$ in thick, edged with deep moulding to give the impression of solidity.

Quite often, in the overhanging top, there was a shallow hidden recess or shelf, which can only be reached from the inside, and which may have served the same function as the hidden cushion drawer of later chest-on-stands: as a secret compartment for documents and small objects of value.

Detail
The technique of bolection moulding was at its height during the second half of the sixteenth century, and cherubs heads, masks, figures, foliage, and the imposing bulbs themselves were applied to the framing timbers with strong glue and wooden pegs. S-scrolls and C-scrolls were used in profusion, either carved shallowly in the timber, or applied in relief. Decoration was still recognizably derived from stone-mason's work, with typical arched shapes, and ogee and strapwork decoration. Door panels were divided into smaller shapes with symmetrical designs on either side.

On many court cupboards, intricate carved detail has been applied as 'strapwork' or strips of decoration, often copied from the earliest pattern books of designs from the Netherlands.

Variations

Food hutches, like old-fashioned, wire-gauze meat-safes, served to keep food away from rats, cats, dogs and mice. 'Bread hutches' and 'dole hutches' were used in religious establishments to preserve the sacramental bread, and can be distinguished by their barred or railed doors and their relatively small size. Large establishments, both religious and secular, possessed food hutches or aumbries, usually with pierced patterns in the doors to allow air to circulate and help prevent stored food from going mouldy. If they were fitted with rudimentary drawers, these were more likely to contain candles or rush dips than cutlery.

Below: *court cupboard, with typical arcaded decoration and late seventeenth-century turned supports. Framing timbers were usually undecorated except for simple moulding.*

Below: *the carved decoration on this aumbry is reminiscent of early Gothic roundels, but the drawers and moulding on the framing timbers indicate a later date.*

Reproductions

Eighteenth century
By the eighteenth century country versions of court cupboards were being made, as well as hall cupboards and parlour cupboards, in plain oak, with the heavy pillars replaced with pendant knobs, and frequently with a row of drawers in the top frieze. Panels of doors were often 'coffered', with the chamfering on the outside and not inside, and used as simple decoration. Although brass screws and advanced furniture-making techniques were being used for sophisticated furniture, the country carpenter continued to use nothing more than mortise-and-tenon joints, dowelling and crude iron nails.

Nineteenth century
As with all furniture of this period, the greatest period of reproductions was from c.1830 onwards, with particular emphasis on 1860–70 'Wardour Street oak'. Even later, more grotesquely exaggerated 'Tudor' furniture was made in considerable quantities in the 1920s and 1930s, but today it should deceive few people, since the timber lacks seasoning, it is stained, saw-cut wood lacking patination, and the machine-drilled dowelling and machine-cut applied strapwork are still raw and rough to the touch, usually because the wood has been cut with no regard to grain.

Price bands

Elizabethan oak: £3,000–5,000.

Elizabethan oak with restoration: £900–1,500.

Seventeenth-century, plain panels: £2,000–3,000.

Genuine aumbry: £1,200–3,000.

Victorian 'Gothic': £500–1,000.

Made-up, nineteenth- or twentieth-century: £250–500.

Chest-on-stand

Historical background

The revolution in the art of veneering was quite spectacular, both in terms of craftsmanship and in design. Veneering, marquetry and parquetry originally came to England from the Netherlands, and gained in popularity when Charles II returned from The Hague in 1660 with a retinue of foreign craftsmen, artists, silversmiths and designers. With the succession of William of Orange to the English throne in 1689, the two countries were even more closely connected.

The technique of veneering, of which marquetry is a part, required a complete change in the construction of chest furniture, from the traditional frame construction to the carcase method. In England, carcase wood was almost exclusively close-grained Baltic pine with drawers lined in oak until the beginning of the eighteenth century. The Dutch, by contrast, used red or white European softwoods for their veneered furniture which, from the seventeenth century onwards, they made in far greater quantities and of varying qualities.

Marquetry seems to have arrived fully fledged in England, for there are no surviving examples of clumsy, early work while English craftsmen learned the new technique. From this it is perhaps fair to assume that skilled craftsmen from the Netherlands crossed the Channel and established the craft of 'cabinet-making' in England, teaching English carpenters and joiners a new skill. Previously their only method of decorating woods had been by inlaying.

Signs of authenticity

1. Interior surfaces more brightly coloured than exterior, which has been faded by light.
2. Oak drawer linings.
3. Locks inset into thickness of cabinet doors, drawer in base. Keyholes, escutcheons, should not break into decorative pattern – knobs, drawer-pulls should be set within drawer panels, rather than cutting into featherbanded or herringbone edging.
4. Steel or brass pin hinges to cabinet doors.
5. Steel locks and lock casings to c.1700, thereafter brass lock casings with steel levers.
6. Wide variety of woods for inlays: cherry, laburnum, olive wood, harewood, (dyed sycamore) and, from c.1685 boxwood, holly, burrwood, ebony and yew wood.

7. On quartered veneer panels, such as the insides of doors with a central marquetry panel, the ground veneer is in four separate pieces: grain should not run through decorative panels in continuous line.
8. Featherbanding or herringbone cross-cut veneer around drawers and doors running to central point at top and bottom, not continuing round without change of direction.
9. Veneer thickness almost $\frac{1}{8}$ in – and same thickness on both sides of doors.

Likely restoration and repair
10. Exterior veneers scraped down to remove discolouration or fading, sometimes concealing parts which have been reveneered in new wood.

11. Drawer linings, of red or white pine indicates Dutch or Continental origins.
12. Plain veneer on inner surfaces of doors where original has lifted, bubbled and cracked, beyond repair.
13. Cornice directly above doors where cushion drawer has been damaged and removed.
14. Stands replaced with frieze-drawers, newly veneered to match up with cabinet: veneers are thinner, colours and cutting of marquetry will vary slightly from original.
15. Damage to carcase wood from weight of doors on hinges. Hard to detect, but important because weakness can recur. Veneer steamed off, wood repaired and veneer replaced, leaving no dirt around hinges.

Construction and materials

With the advent of carcase construction, not only did the old frame-and-panel method of making furniture change, but so did the construction of drawers. The old through dovetail was abandoned in favour of the stopped dovetail or lapped dovetail, and drawers ran on bottom runners instead of grooves on drawer sides, so that the thickness of drawers could be reduced and to give a smooth surface to which veneer could adhere.

As with chairs of the same period, many sound construction principles and the fine finish were sacrificed for the sake of appearance. The twist-turned legs of the stands were often no more than dowelled into the base of the carcase wood, and not surprisingly few have survived intact. Most of the stands were made in walnut, another reason for their disappearance, since walnut is very susceptible to woodworm.

Detail
All decoration was on the surface, in the fine figuring of the veneer and the intricately cut marquetry designs. Chests were almost completely flush-surfaced, with the exception of the cushion drawer beneath the cornice. It comes as quite a surprise to find that the interior finish of these grand cabinets is often comparatively rough and ready, with crude iron nails still securing the sides and bottoms of drawers, unfinished wood, and coarse saw-cut oak planking nailed to the back.

Variations

Continental
Dowry chests without stands were imported in considerable quantities from the Netherlands from the end of the seventeenth century onwards, usually made in pine or poplar and inlaid with pale-coloured woods with motifs of hearts, doves, and tulips. Small chests of drawers with two doors were more commonly made in England, in oak with fielded or coffered panels and drawers, for keeping small articles and precious possessions. They are very similar to spice cabinets of later date.

Right, above: *a full view of the open chest-on-stand opposite – a superb Charles II piece with cushion drawer. Inlaid panels of tulips, flowers and scrolls of leaves, all mounted on a twist-and bobbin-turned stand.*
Right, below: *a fine quality, late seventeenth century chest-on-stand in oyster veneer.*

Reproductions

Nineteenth century
Chests-on-stands had a much longer life on the Continent than they did in England, although the nineteenth century saw a revival in popularity. Few were actually made in England but, either elaborately fitted with small drawers, or with two doors and an ordinary shelved cupboard, were imported in considerable numbers. The taste of the time was very much inclined towards the Gothic, and more chests-on-stands from southern Germany came into England at this period than their more traditional counterparts from Holland.

Twentieth century
Spanish and Portuguese *varguenos* have come into England more recently, as well as cheaply made but impressive-looking Italian versions using tortoiseshell instead of veneer. The veneer is frequently surrounded with ebonized string-of-beads moulding, similar to the fashion in England during the William and Mary period.

Most showy chests-on-stands of recent manufacture have not been made or reproduced in England because they are extremely time-consuming to make and the costs outweigh any ultimate profit.

Price bands

Charles II marquetry with fine interior fittings and original walnut stand with drawer: £9,000–12,000.

Charles II with restored or later stand: £4,500–6,500.

Chest on low stand with oyster veneer and fine inlay: £4,000–6,000.

As above but on restored or later stand: £1,800–2,500.

Carolean chest of drawers

Signs of authenticity

1. Mellow, rich colour of timber, hardened with age.
2. Graining, rippling and figuring of wood where it has been split or quarter-sawn, rather than cut as planks.
3. Base should show signs of heavy wear, knocking and 'fraying' of timber.
4. Applied moulding and decoration, cut from single piece of wood with continuous graining, not in individual sections with change in grain.
5. Marked signs of wear on drawers and runners.
6. Dents on front below drop handle where it has fallen and swung over years of use.
7. Patination on sides of drawers through handling.
8. Side panels slightly loose from timber shrinkage.
9. Top of chest not completely flat, showing signs of curving and bending with damp, changes in temperature, shrinkage along the grain.
10. Drop handles corresponding to holes in drawer-fronts – no other signs of screw holes or bore holes, where handles have been moved or replaced.

Likely restoration and repair

11. Three small drawers in top flight indicates that the piece is the top half of a chest-on-chest. This applies to walnut-veneered chests of drawers only.
12. New top too flat and even, denotes the same: tops of chest-on-chests were of unfinished planking.
13. Moulding and reeding, secured with brass pins – usually a Victorian 'improvement' to a plain-fronted chest or a Victorian 'original'.
14. Side-panelling frames do not match up with drawer-frames – newly replaced, or new frame from old timbers.
15. New timbers in base seen when bottom drawer is removed – should be same age as the back plank. Suspect other replacements if this is the case.

Historical background

Chests with one long drawer beneath them are found from the mid-seventeenth century onwards, variously described as 'mule chests', 'dowry chests' or 'counter chests', each with various explanations for their names. A 'mule chest' is recent terminology, a 'dowry chest' is self-explanatory, and 'counter chests' were believed to have been used by merchants, with drawers for money and documents. Some credence may be attached to the last, since early inventories refer to drawers as 'tilles', the word still used for money-drawers today.

By the Restoration, the whole frame of the chest was taken up with drawers, although some early chests have two drawers in the base, made as one piece, and a hinged top to a more shallow chest which fitted above the drawers. Others have a single deep drawer in the top half, and two drawers in the base. Even when they were proper 'chests of drawers' they continued to be made in two pieces, in a manner similar to early bureaux.

In principle, chests of drawers were either made of oak, with fielded or coffered panels and drawers running on a side-runner, with the traditional frame and panel construction, or in veneer or marquetry with carcase construction and drawers on bottom runners. Chests of drawers of this period had four flights of drawers, often with a pair of shallow drawers in the top flight. They were taller than those of later periods, and were usually mounted on plain block feet or bun feet from c.1690. Few chests of drawers were made without locks, for they were intended as places of safe-keeping as well as storage.

Construction and materials

Of the two types, the solid wood chest of drawers is more interesting in its construction, since carcase construction became the standard method of making veneered chests of drawers from the eighteenth century onwards.

With oak chests of drawers, the frame construction can clearly be seen, with panelled sides, cross-frames, and the drawers decorated with applied mouldings to conceal through dovetails with reeding, string-of-beads or half-round beading. The top was made in a single piece. Drawer bottoms were usually joined with a simple rebate to the sides, reinforced with iron nails and with the grain of bottom boards running from front to back. Drawers for clothes and storage did not run the full depth of the piece, but there was a space of two to three inches to allow air to circulate inside the chest.

Detail
At this period, simple drop-handles were most common, with small circular or rosette-shaped backplates. The cast brass drop-handles were secured to the drawer fronts by a rudimentary split pin, called a tang, which was pushed through a hole in the drawer front and then hammered flat on the inside. The top edges of drawers were smoothly rounded, the runners nailed or pinned to the interior sides of the carcase. In heavier pieces, drawer sides had a groove into which side-runners fitted. These drawers are sometimes known as 'hung' drawers. Tops showed vestiges of the cornice shape, with moulding below the overlap, although by the end of the century they were also made with simple lip-moulding or edge moulding. Backs were of plain oak planking, nailed to the frame.

Variations

The oak chest of drawers with frame construction was the prototype for much country-made furniture for several centuries. Plain-fronted oak chests of drawers with simple reeded or half-rounded mouldings and small turned wooden knobs were made well into Georgian days. Some smaller chests of drawers in yew wood, fruit woods and beech, as well as the familiar country mixture of oak and elm were made at a slightly later period. It is as well to remember that chests of drawers implied considerable possessions and clothing, and that until the mid-eighteenth century relatively few people needed more than a single chest in which to store their 'Sunday best'.

Below left: *late seventeenth-century oak chest of drawers made in two halves.*
Below: *William and Mary chest of drawers on bun feet.*

Reproductions

Eighteenth century
Oak chests of drawers with more elaborately decorated panels are usually of a later date and are Flemish or Continental. Many marquetry chests of drawers are on pine carcases, indicating that they stem from Dutch or German origins where they were made long after they had gone out of fashion in England.

Nineteenth century
During the Victorian Tudor revival, countless copies of early oak furniture were made, among them chests of drawers from old panelling and timbers with stained frames of coarse-grained, poorly seasoned oak, which has cracked and split and may mislead the novice into believing it to be of a far earlier period. The drawer timber in particular will show up its relative lack of age from the almost black lines in the grain of commercially seasoned oak.

Twentieth century
Marquetry and decorative veneer enjoyed (if that is the right word) a boom during the 'twenties, when many fine, flat-fronted chests of drawers of the Hepplewhite period were stripped of their plain mahogany veneers which were replaced by vulgar, machine-cut 'marquetry' and inlay. The essential clue to this disastrous period is that the carcase wood is pine and not oak. The veneer was thin and cut in sheets with the grain running through decorative panels and inlay.

Price bands

Oak with coffered or fielded panels, c.1680: £1,500–2,500.

Oyster veneer, laburnum, olive or walnut with stringing, c.1700: £2,500–3,500.

Veneered front, plain sides, c.1700: £1,200–1,800.

Oak with sectional construction, c.1700: £1,200–2,200.

Flat-fronted chest of drawers

Signs of authenticity

1. Perfectly matching veneer across the whole front.
2. Well-matched veneer on both sides, of corresponding thickness and colour as the front.
3. Half-round moulding down side edges and across drawer rails.
4. Mitred joins to cross-cut veneer around drawers indicating high quality. Poorer quality workmanship had butt joins.
5. Cross-cut veneer set at a sharp 45° angle indicates early pieces from c.1680–1705.
6. Cross grain combined with herringbone indicates c.1695–1710. Cross-grain veneer banding alone after c.1710.
7. Plain plinth base with thick double or single half-round moulding with mitred edges.
8. Top flaring with shallow cornice-type moulding until c.1740.
9. On veneered pieces, drawers of oak with bottom grooves for runners.
10. From c.1720–35 some lesser-quality chests with drawers of close-grained imported pine, but drawer construction must be right for period.

Likely restoration and repair
11. If three drawers in top flight rather than two: almost certainly the top half of same period tallboy.
12. New top with later moulded edges – confirms above point. Tops of tallboys were of unfinished carcase wood.
13. With three flights of drawers only. If top drawer is full width, it most probably comes from the bottom half of same period tallboy. With two drawers in top flight, examine closely for alterations, plugged screwholes of original single drawer.
14. Oak carcase: likely to be late eighteenth–early nineteenth century chest with newly added walnut veneer in early Georgian style. A popular 'restoration' in the 1920s and 1930s.
15. Pine carcase sides with pine drawers indicates Continental, probably Dutch.
16. Thinner timber sides: suspect Victorian replacement.

Historical background
There were two distinct periods during which flat-fronted chests of drawers were fashionable. Both periods can quite correctly be called 'Georgian', although nearly a century may separate them. The earliest of these was during and immediately after Queen Anne's reign, and the second was during the Regency, when Hepplewhite reintroduced plain rectangular lines as a relief from the curved and serpentine shapes which had dominated the middle of the century. Of the two, the former are rarer to find and more interesting, since many minor, but important, structural changes occurred between early methods of construction and the Georgian period. By the time Hepplewhite reintroduced the flat-fronted chest of drawers, construction was firmly established and furniture was being made in commercial quantities.

Early Georgian chests of drawers were still being made in walnut veneer, although its popularity was waning. By c.1735 some furniture was already being made in mahogany, which was clearly set to oust walnut, since supplies had virtually ceased to be imported. There were still stocks of seasoned walnut and walnut veneer available, but from 1720 France, England's main supplier, imposed a total ban on exports. Thus, virtually without any change in construction, the same design was made in mahogany from c.1740 onwards.

Construction and materials

It is believed that not a few of these fine early Georgian walnut-veneered pieces were made with sides of solid walnut as well as in veneer. Perhaps this accounts for their relative rarity, since walnut is very susceptible to woodworm, and large quantities of fine walnut furniture has been quite literally reduced to dust. Veneers were carefully chosen to match over the entire front of the chest; tops were veneered in a single piece and not quarter-veneered, with bands of cross-cut veneer with mitred corners.

Drawer linings were of oak until the mid-eighteenth century. Dovetails were smaller stopped or lapped dovetails, and the sides of the drawers now enclosed the bottom boards, which were grooved on the outer edge to form bottom runners. Drawer pulls had improved from the rather insecure tang fixtures, and were now fixed to drawer fronts with flat-ended, thick, hand-cut screws terminating on the outside in a cast knob bored

to take the drawer-pull, and on the inside with a nut, notched to take a special tightening tool. These fixings are known as 'pummel pins'.

Detail

Early Georgian chests of drawers still display many design features of an earlier age, notably the popular bun feet and simple plinth moulding found on much Queen Anne furniture. Tops were made with echoes of cornice moulding, as in the previous century, splaying outward from the sides and front. Side edges finished flush with the front and drawers were edged with heavy cockbeading. But there was still half-round moulding on the drawer rails, and drawers were also bordered with cross-cut veneer or herringbone banding. Many chests of drawers of this period have long since had their original bun feet replaced with bracket feet as fashion changed, and probably also as the veneered plinth moulding became chipped and damaged.

Variations

Chests of drawers were still fairly rare pieces of furniture in all but wealthy households. Some were made in oak, with plain-fronted drawers except for added cock-beading, otherwise much the same in construction as earlier oak chests of drawers. Smaller in size because of the smaller rooms they were intended for, they were often made originally with plain turned wooden knobs, and sometimes with herringbone inlaid banding around drawers, but no other decoration. Plain plinth bases were mounted on bun or bracket feet.

Country chests of drawers of this period were often still made in the traditional fashion, in two halves, with panelled sides. They are easy to distinguish from later country-made chests of drawers by their fine workmanship, the lines of half-round moulding along the drawer rails, and the quality of the timber which is much finer, more close-grained and smooth-surfaced.

Reproductions

Most common is the later Hepplewhite-period flat-fronted chest of drawers in mahogany veneer, usually on a red or white pine carcase, or on cheap Honduras or baywood mahogany for the better-quality versions. Inevitably, these well-designed late eighteenth-century chests of drawers merge into later, cheaply made and mass-produced nineteenth-century pieces, easy to detect from their thin, almost figureless veneer, machine-cut shaped aprons, stamped-brass handles, often with bone or ivory escutcheons. Edwardian copies which are distinguished by badly fitting drawers and plywood backs.

It might be added here that many of these, originally veneered in thin machine-cut veneer but with good, solidly made Victorian pine carcases, have been stripped and sold as original pine. Pine chests of drawers were not made until the end of the eighteenth century, and can easily be distinguished by their early methods of construction and detail.

Price bands

Sectional construction in oak: £400–850.

With walnut veneer: £2,500–3,500.

Mahogany, late eighteenth century: £1,000–1,800.

Variations, top left: *Plain, early Georgian oak chest of drawers, made in two halves, with locks on the bottom drawer of each half, small, turned, wooden handles and simple, panelled drawers.* Bottom left: *An eighteenth-century chest of drawers mounted on a low stand with a single drawer. The drop handles are from an earlier period, but the graduated drawers are early Georgian.*

Lowboy

Historical background

The lowboy and the tallboy both derive their names from the French *bois* meaning 'wood', and came into use at the beginning of the eighteenth century. Just as the tallboy was a development of the chest-on-stand, so the lowboy could be said to be a smaller version of the tallboy stand by itself: a half-table, half-chest on simple cabriole legs. The shape of the lowboy is quintessentially of the Queen Anne period, with its simple elegant lines, practical design and smooth surfaces. Two deep drawers were set on either side of a simply shaped frieze with a central drawer, but not so delicately made that it could not stand up to considerable knocking from the person who sat at it, and from the stool which was pushed underneath when not in use.

All surfaces and decoration were kept as smooth and simple as possible so that richly embroidered clothes, with lace, fringes, tassels and brocades, did not snag against them. Lowboys, which were equally suitable for men or women to use, always stood with their backs to the wall on which the mirror hung. Kneehole dressing tables were more sophisticated and on them stood little dressing mirrors mounted on swivels to two uprights above a delightful miniature chest of drawers. Kneehole dressing tables often had pull-out hinged dressing flaps to provide extra space for toiletries.

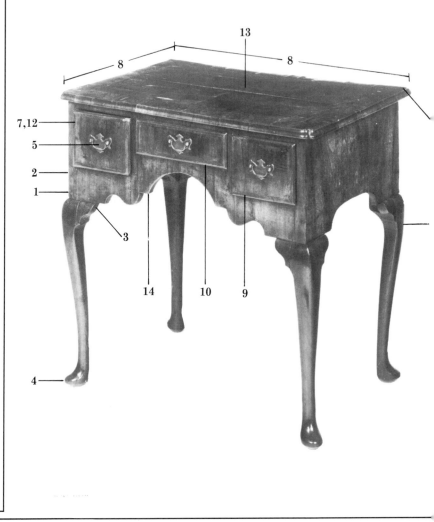

Construction and materials

Lowboys were made in solid walnut, in oak, and in walnut veneer. They were never decorated with inlay or marquetry, although the top was often quarter-veneered with a broad band of cross-cut veneer framing it.

The lowboy has one exceptional detail in construction: the side timbers have the grain running horizontally and not, as with most other chest furniture, vertically. This is because the side frames are a continuation of the legs, and it was not possible to join side-grain to side-grain without the timbers splitting. The mortise-and-tenon joint frequently carries through to the front of the side frame above the leg, where it is neatly finished and almost invisible.

No screws were used in the construction, only dowelling pegs and iron nails to secure the drawer runners to the inside, and the drawer bottoms to drawer sides to reinforce the simple rebate join.

Drawers were usually without locks, and the underframe was of sturdy construction, including the back which was of solid timber and not planking, though roughly finished.

Detail
Simple curved cabriole legs terminated in neat pad feet which were not ornately carved. Edges were finished with simple thumb or lip moulding, and drawers had ovolo lip moulding projecting round the drawer to conceal any signs of damage when it was closed. This 'overlapping' technique was first used on veneered drawers, where damage frequently occurred, but it was also used on solid woods for a smoother finish.

Variations

Contemporary variations of the lowboy are limited to the kneehole dressing table, with a central door to the kneehole and two flights of three small drawers on either side. These pieces were also made as writing tables, with a top drawer that pulled out in the style of a secretaire.

Period country versions
Very pretty plain oak versions of the lowboy were made throughout the first half of the eighteenth century – the only difference from walnut pieces being the lack of spring in the cabriole leg (which is much stiffer and straighter in shape, since oak is not entirely suitable for fully sprung cabriole legs). Small all-purpose side tables with one or two drawers, sometimes in fruitwood or yew wood, with turned rather than cabriole legs, were also made in considerable numbers.

Reproductions

Curiously, the admirably simple lowboy has not been much reproduced, possibly for the same reasons as the early Queen Anne cabriole-legged chair – the thick, well-seasoned wood is no longer available and standards of craftsmanship required are high. Functionally, they are perhaps no longer suitable as dressing tables, nor quite big enough for writing tables for there to be much demand for reproductions.

Price bands

Queen Anne, fine quality, solid walnut: £3,500–6,000.

Queen Anne with veneered top and drawers: £2,000–3,000.

Country-made fruitwood: £1,500–2,500.

Kneehole dressing table in plain walnut veneer: £2,000–3,000. (Seaweed, oyster, other fine veneers, more.)

Kneehole secretaire, c.1730–50: £2,800–4,000.

Top left: *Eighteenth-century kneehole dressing table is identical in appearance to a kneehole secretaire, except that the writing drawer is fitted for toiletries and performs the same function as a brushing slide.*
Left: *Country-made lowboy with stiff cabriole legs, pad feet and a simple shaped frieze.*

Above: *Chippendale mahogany, c.1760.*

Tallboy

Historical background

The tallboy, or chest-on-chest, replaced the Queen Anne chest-on-stand from c.1710. The cabriole-legged stand-with-drawers was replaced by a solid chest containing three single drawers, running the full width of the piece. Tallboys were first made in walnut veneer, but their finest period was during the early part of the 'mahogany period', that is from c.1735. The wood itself was far more suitable for such double-height pieces of furniture, being immensely strong, close-grained and heavy. Tallboys often had canted corners, and were richly carved on cornice, frieze, apron and feet.

By the middle of the eighteenth century, mahogany veneer had largely replaced solid wood, and ebullient decoration gave way to restrained architectural motifs, characterized by reeding, fluting, and dentil cornices. With typical ingenuity, furniture-makers of the period often incorporated a small pull-out writing drawer in the top of the base, and it is not hard to imagine professional cabinet-making workshops designing interchangeable pieces for double-height furniture.

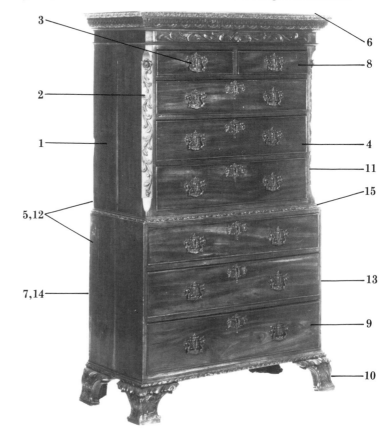

Signs of authenticity

1. On walnut or mahogany-veneered tallboys, well-matched grain on front and sides.
2. On solid mahogany, incised decoration crisp and showing signs of wear and knocking on base apron and feet.
3. Handles, backplates, escutcheons correct period for piece. No unexplained holes on insides of drawer fronts where handle may have been moved or replaced.
4. Drawers of right construction and timber for period. Bottoms of drawers and runners showing considerable wear from use.
5. Base slightly larger than top, but fitting closely together.
6. Surface above top drawers, within cornice, rough and unfinished. As it was above eye-level, it was unpolished wood.

7. Oak, pine or cheap mahogany planking on back, same age on both halves. Nailed to framing, sides of main timbers.
8. Top drawers either a pair or three small drawers – never a single full-width drawer.
9. Bottom drawer always deeper than all others.
10. Bracket feet, often curved, echoing cabriole leg.

Likely restoration and repair
11. Plain mahogany tallboys with later shallower carving on chamfered corners, frieze and base apron to increase value. Carving will not stand proud of profile.
12. Flush sides without stepped join indicates tallboy of much later date with moulding added to 'improve' piece and make it look Georgian.
13. Carved, serpentine or shaped corners to base without corresponding decorated chamfered corners to top half suggests it has been cut down and made up from later, cumbersome wardrobe. Search for evidence in newly made-up drawers, signs of handles, escutcheons, being moved, hence plugged screw holes.
14. 'Marriage' of two pieces of more or less same period: check match of decoration on base and top, also check age of back planking.
15. Top half of Queen Anne chest-on-stand married to chest base, often with 'brushing slide', which tallboys seldom had.

Construction and materials

Tallboys or chest-on-chests were made in both solid woods and in veneers. At the beginning of the eighteenth century, while walnut was still in fashion, finely matched walnut veneer on Baltic pine was typical, with restrained herringbone or featherbanded decoration, sometimes with a cavetto moulding in the base drawer similar to some secretaires of the same period.

By c.1735 tallboys were being made in finely figured solid San Domingo or Cuban flame-grained mahogany, with oak-lined drawers and incised carved decoration. Like most double-height furniture, tallboys were made in two halves, and even when the construction changed later in the century and they were made in one piece, the dividing line lingered on to break the rather severe shape. Often there were three small drawers at the top rather than two. The cornice was always incised, never applied.

Detail

By the middle of the eighteenth century, mahogany veneer had largely replaced solid wood, and the lively decoration changed to restrained architectural motifs. Drawers were smoothly cock-beaded, and ornate, pierced and decorated brass handles, backplates and escutcheons were replaced with simple bail handles.

Variations

The demand for imposing double-heighted furniture increased from c.1710 when the chest-on-chest began to replace the chest-on-stand. Hitherto, most clothes presses had been built onto the panelling as general-purpose storage cupboards, but when mahogany became the all-purpose timber for double-heighted furniture, often a linen press was incorporated above the chest base.

Below: *Queen Anne walnut veneered chest-on-stand, c.1710, with square-kneed cabriole legs and pad feet. The oak-lined drawers have ovolo lip moulding.*

By c.1760 the basic tallboy design was also combined with a pull-out secretaire drawer, believed to be for the use of the housekeeper – by this period a very important person in households of any size. The versatility of the basic tallboy design can be seen in the many functional combinations of the top and base.

Reproductions

Ninteenth century
The tallboy was a standard piece of furniture in the nineteenth century, in a full range of qualities, from well-made to cheaply veneered on pine or cheap mahogany carcases. They were more frequently made for gentlemen's bedrooms and dressing rooms, but the top flight of drawers was not too easily accessible, and the alternative gentleman's wardrobe, or clothes press, was equally common. Many massive pieces of bedroom furniture were made for Victorian and Edwardian bedrooms, as well as for suites of hotel rooms.

In recent years a considerable number of Continental provincial 'armoires' have been seen in salerooms and antique shops. Most of them date from the early nineteenth century, although by their carved panelled doors they may appear to be at least a century older.

Price bands

With original stand, walnut veneer, good quality: £3,000–5,000.

Marriage of different pieces, or heavily restored: £1,300–1,800.

With restored stand or legs: £1,500–2,000.

Late Georgian tallboy with fluted, canted corners: £3,000–5,000.

Fine quality with decorative carving, ogee bracket feet, Chippendale period: £4,000–6,000.

Left: *Georgian tallboy in solid mahogany with dentil cornice, canted corners with fluted decoration, swan-neck handles and ogee bracket feet.*

Clothes press

Signs of authenticity

1. Fine, dark-figured mahogany veneer, well-matched on doors, drawers and sides.
2. Applied half-round or reed moulding simulating panels with small decorative rosettes on cutaway corners of rectangles.
3. Matching moulding around drawers.
4. Slim, stepped profile with half-round or reeded moulding on base of cupboard where it joins the drawer section.
5. Brass locks with brass bolts and levers, all inset into door timbers.
6. Mitred joins to door frames, perhaps showing some signs of timber shrinkage.
7. Well-fitted interiors of smooth-planed oak with rounded top edges to drawers and trays.
8. Good patination on inner surfaces of tray-fronts where they have been handled.
9. Locks and lock-rail to drawers in base.
10. Well-made solid bracket feet with no decorative apron.
11. Friezes, cornices, in simple architectural motifs.
12. Back planking of same aged wood and colour on top and base.

Likely restoration and repair

13. Oval satinwood cross-banded inlay to 'improve' plain pieces. Ground grain will continue as single piece.
14. Inlaid satinwood oval panels in later, thinner veneer, sometimes of 'satin birch' and sometimes even inlaid marquetry panels added to 'enhance' appearance. A typically Edwardian addition.
15. One or both bottom drawers removed, fronts left as 'shams' and interior fittings removed to make full-length hanging space.
16. Bracket feet and plinth moulding replaced where damaged.
17. Large breakfront wardrobe cut down to central piece only – new sides and added bracket feet. Original wardrobes were on plinth bases without feet.

Historical background

A 'press' is no more than a cupboard with shelves – an earlier version of the clothes press was the linen press and a later one the wardrobe. 'Wardrobe' is an ancient term, originally applied to clothes and not the cupboard in which they were stored. It also included linen, wall-hangings and table linen – the Keeper of the Wardrobe was an important person in a large household.

Until the last quarter of the eighteenth century, built-in hanging cupboards and chests-on-chests were the standard equipment for the gentleman's dressing room. Only from c.1770 were these augmented by a clothes press – a low chest of drawers surmounted by a cupboard with double doors, inside which were open shelves or trays, on runners.

Freestanding hanging cupboards for clothes in bedrooms and dressing rooms are a late development. Sadly, many handsome Regency clothes presses were knocked out to full-length hanging cupboards by the early Victorians, the drawers turned into 'shams' and the insides completely gutted of fittings.

More monumental breakfront wardrobes were built during the Regency period, with two slim, tall, cupboards flanking a chest with three flights of drawers and a cupboard with double doors above. The flanking cupboards were fitted with shelves on one side and clothes pegs on the other, probably for full-length 'dressing gowns' worn by gentlemen while they dressed, put on the wigs and powdered their hair. Until the nineteenth century full-length outdoor clothes were usually kept downstairs or in passages in built-in hanging cupboards.

Construction and materials

Plain dark mahogany is most usually associated with clothes presses of the late Georgian period, although some were made with plain dark figured walnut veneer. The carcase wood was usually cheaper Honduras mahogany or close-grained red pine, always solid and well-made. From *c.*1770 the traditional stepped shape of double-height pieces was incorporated into the design of clothes presses, although they were in fact made as a single piece.

Interior shelves and drawers were of oak, finely finished and smooth, on oak runners, often in the manner of the old 'hung drawer' construction, fitting into grooves in the sides of clothes trays.

Drawers in the base were also of oak, usually a flight of two, sometimes with a pair of drawers below the cupboard. Plain half-rounded or reeded astragal moulding on the right-hand door concealed the join: the left-hand door closed with brass slides at top and bottom.

Detail

Half-round mouldings and small corner ornament echoed the earlier panelled doors of linen presses, while both bases and cupboards were often made, like tallboys, with canted corners. It was Hepplewhite who first used inlaid satinwood decoration from *c.*1780, in oval as well as rectangular shapes on the doors instead of half-round moulding, and Sheraton who introduced the oval inlaid panel which was to be so endlessly copied.

Variations

The communal clothes press in smaller country houses and farmhouses was still built in, often taking up half a small dressing room or closet, housing all the clothes of the family. Downstairs in large and small houses there were built in hanging cupboards for overcoats and capes with turned pegs for hanging. Freestanding oak cupboards of any age are likely to be made up from the doors of built-in period hanging cupboards, or are of Continental origins. Some provincial presses were made in walnut, but they are French and not English.

Below, left: *early Georgian walnut veneer clothes press with well-figured, quarter-veneer panelled doors.*
Below: *George III secretaire linen press in mahogany veneer.*

Reproductions

The true clothes press with drawers and fitted cupboard continued to be made, along with other massive bedroom furniture, well into the beginning of the twentieth century. Hanging cupboards or 'wardrobes' are predominantly Victorian. Later versions of the clothes press are taller than Georgian and Regency cupboards, with fitted shelves and trays on one side of the cupboard and full-length hanging space on the other. These usually had two half-doors in the base as well as the top half, as opposed to drawers.

The all-too-familiar shiny, thinly veneered 'hotel bedroom' type of fitted hanging cupboard was mass-produced in a variety of combinations and permutations of shelving, trays, drawers and hanging space as a typically Edwardian piece of furniture, often mimicking Sheraton's oval inlaid satinwood panels with panels of cheap maple or dyed sycamore, also known in the trade at that time as 'maple'. Dutch, bulbous-shaped, serpentine-fronted, top-heavy clothes presses, often inlaid with marquetry, date from the early nineteenth century and are not of the English 'marquetry period' at all.

Price bands

Early Georgian, fine walnut veneer with good detail, made in two halves: £4,000–6,000.

George III plain linen press with drawers in base: £1,500–2,000.

George III press with fitted secretaire drawer: £1,700–2,500.

Plain linen press in the 'Sheraton' style: £1,000–1,500.

Victorian wardrobe: £500–1,000.

Serpentine chest of drawers

Historical background

Curving shapes began to come into furniture design from the reign of Queen Anne onwards, as can be seen from the pediments of secretaire bookcases and, in particular, the spoon-back chair with cabriole legs. Techniques of cutting wood into curved shapes took time to master, and it was not until the Chippendale period, when many features of French design were incorporated into English taste, that serpentine-fronted desks and chests of drawers came into fashion, around c.1750 onwards.

Those at the top of the social scale in England who were privileged enough to own and enjoy beautiful, immaculately furnished houses were not allowed to keep them all to themselves however. All the country seats of wealthy landowners and aristocratic families had 'open days' when groups of people came to look over every room in the house,

bedrooms included. Provincial ladies and gentlemen arrived to demand entry whether the owners were in residence or not, and all furniture became as much a part of the show as the house itself. Chests of drawers, up to now no more than functional domestic pieces of furniture, evolved into the English equivalent of the French 'drawing-room

commode', and even the plainest pieces, derived from Chippendale's grand designs, had curved aprons and feet, and were made in beautifully figured woods and veneers.

The serpentine-fronted chest of drawers was made throughout the mid-eighteenth century and was only replaced by the bow-fronted design during the Sheraton period.

Signs of authenticity

1. Fine-grained, well-figured San Domingo or Cuban mahogany on cheaper mahogany carcase, or imported red Scandinavian pine.
2. Flush-sunk escutcheons to locks with no ornamental surround.
3. Drawer handles with plain swan-neck handles, cast-brass bolt-heads with pummel pins, small circular backplates.
4. From c.1770 drawer bottoms with grain running side to side with central bearer for extra support.
5. Drawers and dustboards not running, full depth of, piece.
6. Dustboards in two joined pieces with front shaped piece added separately.
7. Where chest of drawers has canted corners, matching canted corners to bracket feet.
8. Where there are carved pillar motifs on sides with rounded

bases, there is a corresponding rounded profile to bracket feet.
9. Graduated drawer depths, sometimes with baize-lined fitted top drawer.
10. Brushing slides with polished surface, cleated edges, small loop handles.
11. Lip, thumb or reeded moulding to tops with good overhang, sometimes serpentine-shape on sides.

Likely restoration and repair
12. Plain canted corners with later carving or reeding to increase value. Wood will seem rough to the touch compared to rest of piece.
13. Dustboards in single piece of timber indicates a replacement for originals. Suspect more restoration if this is the case.
14. Plain square-cornered bracket feet replacing originals

with rounded or canted corners where originals have been damaged.
15. New tops where originals have been damaged with alcohol-based lotions, etc. or reveneered for same reason. Back edges of new top will not have same patination as sides, the veneer will be thinner.
16. Brushing slides damaged and removed: lock rail to top drawer should be examined for disturbance, top edges of sides with reeding or carving may finish abruptly.
17. Cockbeading too thick and secured with pins indicates replacement of originals, or new drawer fronts.
18. Drawer-front carcase with grain of wood running in continuous line – made from steam-moulded timbers of considerably later date.

Construction and materials

Serpentine-fronted chests of drawers were made in a similar way to spoon-back chairs. The timber was cut in curving shapes which were then veneered because of the partially exposed end-grain. The construction of carcases began to change from the mid-eighteenth century onwards, with new joints for sides, such as the mitred dovetail which joined woods at right-angles on the end-grain and allowed the sides of chest furniture to be built with vertical timbers, as opposed to the earlier method of horizontal frame and panel construction.

Many of these new techniques became possible because of the use of cheaper mahogany as carcase wood which did not split as easily as more coarsely grained oak. The tops of chests of drawers were no longer made to conceal the joins with small cornice moulding, but could be laid over the carcase and secured, then edged like table tops with thumb or lip moulding. Canted corners were often part of the design of serpentine-fronted chests of drawers as an aid to construction as much as a decorative feature.

Detail
Drawers were edged with elegant cock beading, handles were simple swan-necked brass with cast-brass bolts and pummel pins, bracket feet were joined with shaped aprons following the graceful lines of the serpentine front. Bracket feet were often curved and referred to as 'French feet' because of their resemblance to the scrolled feet of French commodes.

Variations

Curved shapes of any sort were difficult to make without sophisticated tools and techniques, and serpentine-fronted furniture of any sort is extremely rare among genuine country pieces. Some late eighteenth century plain-fronted, well-made oak chests of drawers might have tops cut in serpentine shapes as a concession to fashionable styles, but in general chests of drawers of the period continued to be made in traditional fashion, often still using the frame and panel technique which had long been superseded by mitred dovetailing on more sophisticated furniture.

If serpentine-fronted pine chests are found, they are sadly most likely to be later nineteenth-century pieces, originally veneered and recently stripped. By that period it was possible to shape softwoods by steaming and clamping them into shape and the timbers seen in the top edges of drawers will have the grain running in a continuous line.

Below left: *an early George III chest in fine, well-figured walnut veneer.*
Below: *an example in the Chippendale manner, c.1770.*

Reproductions

Nineteenth century
The serpentine front is the least copied and reproduced of all chests of drawers. The bow-front is much easier to manufacture, and serpentine-fronted designs are more heavily constructed and the shape is less commercial or convenient to manufacture. Nineteenth-century, so-called, serpentine-fronted chests of drawers on pine carcases with thin mahogany veneer were made in some quantities, but the positive sinuous curve is reduced to a mere wavy line lacking any authority. The bases presented problems, and were sometimes exaggerated with thick mouldings which protruded several inches out from the bottom drawer.

Many reproductions are Continental: French versions were much larger, originally well-veneered, but often on poor-quality oak carcases. Dutch 'commodes' in over-decorated marquetry, usually with a bulbous curved shape known as 'kettle-shaped', were made continuously and well into the nineteenth century. Ornate French serpentine commodes with heavy ormolu decoration on the canted corners, heavy drawer-handles and ornamental escutcheons were very popular at one time with the Victorians and there are still large numbers of them around.

Price bands

Finest quality mahogany with veneered drawer fronts and shaped bracket feet, *c.*1770: £3,000–4,000.

Georgian mahogany with fluted and canted corners, shaped bracket feet and brushing slide: £3,800–4,500.

Georgian with fine detailing and veneering: £4,500–6,000.

Nineteenth-century versions: £800–1,500.

Dresser

Historical background

In the late sixteenth century, while wealthy households separated their dining rooms from the large hall and displayed their fine plate and porcelain on impressive court cupboards in their parlours, yeomen farmers moved to brick-built farmhouses with fewer rooms and servants. In their parlours were 'side boordes' – long shallow tables with a single row of drawers and a boarded base.

By the turn of the eighteenth century these elongated side-tables had found a place in country manor houses. They were elegant pieces of furniture, usually in gleaming polished oak, with shining brass handles and escutcheons. In the North of England, they had storage cupboards in the base, either with a central flight of three or four drawers, or with a central cupboard flanked by two flights of drawers, made in elm, oak and elm, and sometimes in ash.

In the southern counties, often a separate set of hanging shelves was fixed above the dresser base. In the North, solid shelves with backs seem to have been more common. Late eighteenth century oak dressers with fixed shelving and no backs were often handsome pieces. However, by the end of the century, most dressers had been relegated to the kitchen, and by the nineteenth century were made in cheap soft pine as part of built-in cupboards and shelving.

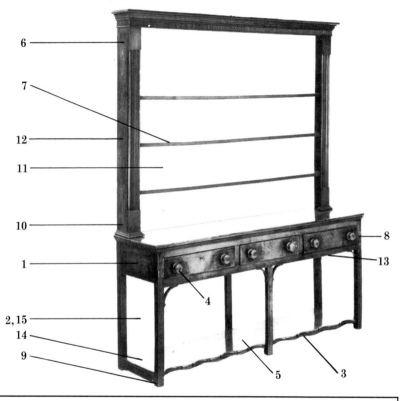

Signs of authenticity

1. Timber of sides with grain running horizontally on dressers with frieze drawers only.
2. If dresser has cupboards or drawers, the sides are often in more than one panel for extra strength and stability.
3. Simple curving shapes to frieze and apron, in wood of matching colour and patination.
4. All parts showing signs of heavy use and wear: build-up of grease and dirt on plate-stays, grooves, top corners of cupboards, around drawer handles.
5. Signs of 'distressing' on base boards: dents, scratches, where heavy pots and pans have been dragged over surface.
6. Mortise-and-tenon joints of shelves running through uprights to show as thin rectangular shapes on the outer surface of the upright.
7. Accumulation of dirt colouring inner surface and underside of top frieze, and on top of dresser shelving.
8. Deep patination on sides of drawers, marks of knife-points, sharp instruments, on insides of drawers.
9. Bases well-used, with signs of 'fraying' on block feet from damp, knocking with mops and brooms.
10. Dresser shelves and backboards of same-aged timber as base, on to which it fitted.

Likely restoration and repair
11. If backboards have been added, they are usually of even width, commercially cut timber, wire-brushed down the grain and polished to look old.
12. Whole tops added to dresser bases – may be a period addition or a more recent one, to add value.
13. Added friezes and aprons to increase value – saw-marks can be felt on unfinished underside, timber will not be as hard and seasoned as original timbers.
14. New base boards and legs – inspect closely for other repairs, such as new underframe.
15. If there are board-backs to bases with frieze drawers, suspect new legs and aprons where original doors and drawers have been too badly damaged to restore and have been removed.

Construction and materials

In all but a very few pieces, dresser construction lagged considerably behind more sophisticated pieces of furniture, and drawers were made with thick through-dovetails, projecting lip moulding and simple rebate joints reinforced with coarse iron nails from the local smithy. Mortise-and-tenon joints continued to be used with wooden pegs or dowels long after brass screws were common on most furniture. There was probably also a practical reason for this traditional form of construction. In the constantly changing temperature and condensation of the kitchen, with consequent continuous movement of timber, it would have served far better than later methods of construction.

Dressers were made in oak, finely finished and without fixed shelving from c.1690 onwards, sometimes much in the style of contemporary chests of drawers, with fielded and coffered doors, drawers, reeded and mitred mouldings and twist-turned legs or baluster-turned legs. By the early eighteenth century some had well-fitted shelving units with small spice cupboards and grooves or plate-stays.

Between c.1690 and 1710 some grander dressers heralded the shape of sideboards, with a raised backboard, sometimes with shelves or small drawers. From the mid-eighteenth century, shelving above the dresser base became an integral part of the design, though these seldom had backboards.

Variations

Regional styles
Most dressers were country-made, in varying degrees of skill and craftsmanship. Most interesting are the regional variations, such as the 'Welsh dresser' proper (as opposed to the *tridarn* and the *deuddarn*) from South Wales with elaborately pierced and fretted aprons and friezes. Southern dressers without backboards could stand flush against a brick-built wall. North country dressers with backboards stood against rough-cast or stone walls. North Wales dressers often had a pair of cupboards below three frieze drawers in the base, as opposed to the North country dressers with cupboards and one or two flights of drawers.

Countless kitchen dressers were built by the resident carpenters on large estates for all the tenant farms, frequently of a very high standard of design and craftsmanship, often using odd pieces of fruitwood or fine timber left over in their workshops from panelling and boarding from the 'Big House'. These may date from the last two decades of the eighteenth century up to the beginning of the twentieth.

Below: *North Country pine dresser, with two fielded panelled doors in the base, and panelled sides. The shelves are tenoned through the shaped side-pieces which support the simply moulded canopy.*

Reproductions

Nineteenth century
Oak dressers were reproduced during the Victorian period in commercial plank oak, usually stained. Some of the more interesting pieces date from the end of the nineteenth century and were made by the Arts and Crafts Movement as all-purpose pieces of furniture. They are closer to sideboards than dressers in concept.

By the end of the nineteenth century all kinds of kitchen cupboards were built into the large service quarters of Victorian houses, some with glass-fronted doors with cupboards or drawers beneath; some with open shelves and cupboards. Many of these have been neatly converted into 'antique pine dressers', stripped of their many layers of paint.

Pine
The ubiquitous pine dresser was first made as a built-in piece of furniture destined to be painted from the mid-eighteenth century onwards. By the end of the century it was being made in smaller, more finished versions for use in farm houses and town-house kitchens.

Price bands

Dresser, with decorative frieze, potboard, turned legs, excellent quality, late eighteenth century: £2,500–3,500.

Good oak with decorative canopy, c.1820, oak: £1,800–2,500.

North Welsh, oak, enclosed, c.1850: £4,500–6,000.

Cottage oak, with potboard and simple legs c.1820: £2,000–3,000.

Simple pine, c.1840: £500–1,000.

Corner cupboard

Historical background

Corner cupboards would appear to be of Dutch origin, made by cabinet-makers who, until the eighteenth century, were far more skilled than their English counterparts. The earliest corner cupboards made in England would seem to be early eighteenth century, when the difficulty of making bow-fronts was made simpler with the use of pine for 'lacquering' or 'japanning'. Pine is far more amenable to shaping than a hard wood.

Queen Anne walnut hanging corner cupboards were triangular, and usually blockfronted, with prettily shaped shelves inside, although some were made with Vauxhall mirrored glass. It is unlikely that many of this period were made with glass doors and glazing bars. Small, bow-fronted, walnut veneer hanging corner cupboards with very simple moulding were made almost throughout the eighteenth century – a neat, space-saving cabinet to hold treasured pieces, opened proudly to show the elegantly shaped shelves.

During the Georgian period, corner cupboards were designed as part of panelled rooms, of double height with the break on a line with the dado panelling and decorated with simple Greek key or dentil moulding to accord with the architecture.

By the end of the eighteenth century, corner cupboards had been relegated to libraries, or were made as storage cupboards for many corners in the house, usually of double-height with glass doors in the top half and block-fronted panelled doors in the base. The most likely reason for their swift departure from important reception rooms was the use of wallpaper and the end of panelling from the mid-eighteenth century onwards.

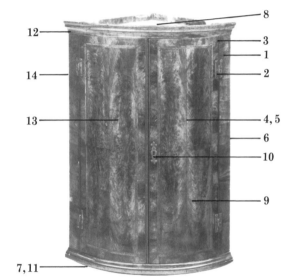

Signs of authenticity

1. On bow-fronted corner cupboards, the curve continues to the side frame in matching wood or veneer.
2. H-hinges, cockshead hinges or butterfly hinges on outsides of doors until c.1760 and much later in many country pieces.
3. Mitred corners to finest flat-fronted doors with chamfered panels.
4. Bow-fronted doors made up of narrow (4 in) planks, joined with tongue and groove, as with match-boarding.
5. Shelves with serpentine or curving shapes.
6. Signs of original paint – eighteenth-century red, green, yellow or blue – in the graining of the back planking and on the edges of back planks where they have shrunk with age.

7. Underside of base in genuine hanging corner cupboards polished, well-finished, visible from below.
8. Tops of both double height and hanging corner cupboards unfinished behind raised moulding.
9. Double-doored bow-fronted veneered cupboards from c.1720 – no English single bow-fronted doors except occasional rare japanned ones on pine.
10. Escutcheons placed exactly halfway from top and bottom on hanging corner cupboards with double doors – half-round or reeded astragal moulding on the join.

Likely restoration and repair
11. Underside of bases unfinished or recently planed and stained, indicates it was originally the top of a double-height piece.
12. Heavy rim moulding without outward flare to top of hanging corner cupboard, often on double-doored bow-fronts: indicates it was originally the base of a double-height piece.
13. Glazing bars or plain glass doors on walnut veneered piece means the original blockfront or Vauxhall mirrored glass has probably been replaced.
14. Back planking of even width, rough and identical in thickness: backs added to originally built in piece, or made at much later date.

Construction and materials

To all intents and purposes, corner cupboards consisted of a façade and a frame. There are exceptions, and some double-height corner cupboards were built with barrel backs from *c.*1740. But in the main, corner cupboards were built as an integral part of a room, at least until panelling at first sunk to a dado and was then completely ousted by wallpaper around 1750 – the beginning of the Chippendale period. From that date the height of tall corner cupboards was no longer dictated by the height of the panelling or the dado and, for a short period, elegant mahogany corner cupboards were raised on bracket feet. Bow-fronted designs curved to the wall, the frames continuing the curve. Flat-fronted corner cupboards had chamfered sides, often decorated in the same manner as tallboys, bureau-bookcases and secretaires of the same period, with fluted columns often running up to an arched or broken pediment, with airy glazed doors displaying 'cabinet pieces' of fine porcelain.

Even by splitting the door into two, the curved surfaces could not be cut, as with serpentine-fronted chests of drawers, from a single piece of timber. They were built up from narrow planks joined with tongue and groove, and then veneered in finely matched mahogany. Smaller hanging corner cupboards made earlier in the century on the same principle were quarter-veneered to prevent lifting and surrounded with featherbanding or cross-cut veneer inlay. Oak hanging corner cupboards remained traditional in design, harking back a century to fielded panels.

There is one common denominator in this multiplicity of design: corner cupboards were always backed with unfinished wood, even when made as free-standing pieces. It is rare to find a corner cupboard of any age without shaped shelves, and almost without exception the interiors, and often the exteriors too, were originally painted. Many early hanging corner cupboards were difficult to secure firmly to walls because of their weight. This is because they were originally made to be partially supported by the jutting top edge of panelled dadoes.

Variations

H-hinges, butterfly hinges and cockshead hinges were used in country pieces long after they had been replaced by less visible ones in grander pieces. Corner cupboards were made in a variety of country woods: walnut, fruitwood, and occasionally yew wood, but mainly in oak. Few double-height pieces were made, and bow-fronted country hanging corner cupboards are rare because of the difficult construction. The most traditional shape is flat-fronted with a plain, arched or cupid's bow fielded, chamfered panel, showing some good figuring or grain where the wood was split or quarter-sawn. Few country pieces have bolts or slides to hold the left-hand door closed – these date from the nineteenth century, before which there was often no catch at all, or only a clumsy wooden one.

Above: *Georgian pine corner cupboard which, originally, was probably painted.*

Reproductions

Nineteenth century
The most common reproductions of hanging country oak corner cupboards were made during the Victorian period, from artificially seasoned or partly seasoned timber, more coarsely grained and showing dark lines on the grain where the half-seasoned wood has discoloured. Both double-height and hanging corner cupboards were made, flat fronted, often with straight rather than mitred joins to door frames, and machine-cut chamfering of even width and depth to central fielded panels. Bow-fronted hanging cupboards were also made in reddish-coloured nineteenth-century walnut which darkens with age to a mahogany colour, with well-reproduced copies of original hinges and escutcheons.

Reproductions of 'lacquered' bow-fronted cupboards were also made in the second half of the nineteenth century, rather brightly painted in imitation of Angelica Kaufmann's style, on carcases of soft American pine, often the victims of stripping in recent years. Most common in the last 50 years are 'Georgian', arched, double-height corner cupboards in pine, with glazed doors and applied glazing bars, good copies of the original except for the proportions which usually have higher base cupboards.

Price bands

Queen Anne walnut veneer, highest quality: £1,500–2,500.

Georgian pine, double height, of excellent quality: £700–1,200.

Georgian pine, lesser quality: £450–650.

Georgian oak, double height: £800–1,600.

Early Georgian, mahogany: £1,200–1,800.

Hanging corner cupboard, eighteenth century: £350–650.

Sideboard

Historical background

In England, dining-room furniture only began to develop as functional purpose-made pieces from *c*.1730 onwards, with side tables made specifically for serving rather than merely displaying dishes. The first recognizable sideboards were contemporary with the work of the Adam brothers (the middle decades of the eighteenth century) and consisted of a heavy side table flanked by two pedestal cupboards topped with urns in the classical manner. These were ingenious all-purpose dining-room fittings, with knife urns, lead-lined containers for keeping hot and cold water for washing glasses and cutlery, racks for hot plates, cellarettes for bottles and, frequently, pot-cupboards for the gentlemen's after-dinner use.

From *c*.1770 the size of the sideboard became more manageable and the most common shape began to emerge:

two deep drawers or cupboards (sometimes with drawers above), raised on legs, with a central frieze drawer above an arched or shaped apron. Many of them had a 'splash board' at the back, or brass rails with pleated-silk panels, and brass candle-holders. It is Sheraton who is most often connected with the design of sideboards,

although Hepplewhite, Shearer and George Smith all designed very similar pieces.

By about 1790 the most instantly recognizable and most copied shape for sideboards had become generally accepted. The interiors were fitted with many clever devices, including in some cases a heater beneath tin-plate racks.

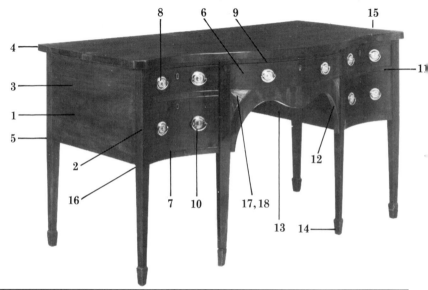

Signs of authenticity

1. Glossy, well-matched mahogany veneers on Honduras mahogany or imported Scandinavian red-pine carcases.
2. Grain of all legs continuing up to form sides of frame.
3. Grain of side carcase wood running horizontally.
4. Flush-edged top with good overhang, thicker than table top.
5. Back timbers unfinished and of same age and colour, showing gaps on joins where wood has shrunk.
6. Frieze drawer lined with baize and with original compartments.
7. No signs on inside bottom of carcase, which forms the flanking cupboards and drawers, of circular wear and scratchings where swing-out, fitted cellarettes have been removed.
8. Accumulation of dirt and patination around drawer

handles – good patination to insides of drawers.
9. Drawer bottom with timber running from side to side with central strengthening bearer.
10. Flush drawer fittings and handles with stamped brass decorated backplates.
11. Cockbeading edge to plainly veneered doors and drawers.
12. Undersurface edge of shaped apron veneered to match the edges of top serving surface.
13. Inner underframe of side sections either side of central arch visible and therefore plain veneered.
14. Signs of damage, scuffing to feet, particularly central ones.

Likely restoration and repair
15. Common in many variations is the massive sideboard cut down to more suitable sizes: many were over 6 ft long. Undersurface of overhang may

provide evidence. If fingers detect a 'crack' or break, check interiors of drawer fronts, central frieze drawer for newly made holes for handles without accumulation of dirt around them; examine underframe for evidence of cutting down.
16. On genuine smaller sizes, legs repaired where they have broken, or cut down where breaks have occurred on line with spade feet, and repair concealed by collar.
17. Added inlay and other decoration to original mahogany veneer. Harder to find material evidence, since ground veneer of this period often runs across whole surface, but style and proportions of later inlays are often quite wrong.
18. Aprons replaced with more elaborate design, or with later inlaid corner-pieces.

Construction and materials

The construction follows the traditional pattern for standing furniture, with the legs continuing up to form the sides of the carcase, with two additional legs in the front only, forming the central frame to support the elongated shape.

Sideboards were often serpentine-shaped, curving inwards at the centre, or with two concave side pieces and a central bow to the frieze drawer. Legs were usually tapered, fluted, reeded, or square-sectioned and tapering to small spade feet. On some genuine Sheraton furniture the veneer is laid with the grain running in the opposite direction to the carcase-wood, particularly in the case of satinwood.

Both the central drawer and side drawers or cupboards contained a variety of fittings. Cupboards often swing open with circular racks to hold bottles, or tin plate racks. Deep side drawers are often lead or zinc lined: the central drawer is baize-lined and fitted with compartments for cutlery. Sideboards should not be less than 30 in high, and are more often 33 in.

Detail
From c.1770 the sideboard had become a regular item of dining-room furniture, made in fine dark figured mahogany veneer with little decoration except for drawer handles, which were often quite elaborate, and shaped central aprons below the frieze drawer. By c.1780, with the trend towards more decorated furniture, the mahogany was often inlaid with satinwood, tulipwood, plumbago and boxwood. Hepplewhite favoured lighter colours, and satinwood veneer inlaid with decorative panels was used for sideboards at the end of the eighteenth century and the beginning of the nineteenth.

Variations

Dining-room or parlour furniture was still sparse even at the end of the eighteenth century, and the most common alternative to sideboards were side tables with frieze drawers, similar to dresser bases, or heavier side-cupboards with plain tops, sometimes with a flight of drawers in the centre.

Regency sideboards were even more massive than late eighteenth-century designs, often made on the same principle as pedestal desks, with heavy plinth-based pedestal cupboards supporting a great sweep of lustrous mahogany, no longer curved but with straight lines, and a central arch beneath which stood a heavy sarcophagus cellarette.

Above: *George III, with concave central bow and frieze drawer flanked by two deep cross-banded drawers.*

Below: *George III serpentine sideboard with oval inlaid top, tapering legs and spade feet.*

Reproductions

Victorian
By the Victorian period, the sideboard and chiffonier had become inextricably mixed. Sideboards were built with towering superstructures in a cross between a court cupboard and a dresser, to suit the Gothic and Elizabethan revivals.

Parallel with these huge pieces of furniture were the mass-produced dining-room suites, on pine carcases, veneered in shiny thin mahogany, or in stained oak with elaborate machine-carved decoration. They often have square-sectioned legs, which were not in solid wood, but veneered. Labour was so cheap it was less expensive to veneer cheap wood than use solid timber.

Twentieth century
By the Edwardian period there was a plethora of sideboards, often with inset panels of light-coloured cheap veneer such as birch or maple masquerading as satinwood. Some were well-made and respectably solid, but many had clumsy proportions, spindly legs, badly fitting doors and drawers. Today the reproductions of the so-called 'Sheraton sideboard' continue unabated, made of heavy veneered chipboard and veneered in woods unknown to the furniture trade until the last 50 years, many of them coming from Africa.

Price bands

Sheraton-period mahogany: £3,000–5,000.

Serpentine-fronted, George III period: £2,800–3,500.

Small Regency bow front with demilune ends in the 'Sheraton' style: £2,000–3,000.

Bow-fronted chest of drawers

Signs of authenticity

1. Fine, well-figured solid mahogany with well-matched mahogany veneer on drawer fronts.

2. Oak-lined drawers to *c*.1800 with slim cockbeaded outline and plain swan-necked drawer handles. Oval backplates from *c*.1810.

3. Delicate, double or triple reeding or thumb moulding to sides of the top on the overhang. Plain back edge is flush with backing planks.

4. Backs in unfinished timber of same age and patination, with gaps where shrinkage has occurred with time.

5. Curved fronts of dustboards in separate piece.

6. Graduated drawer depths.

7. Four full-width drawers to *c*.1800 when a pair of top drawers replaced the single one.

8. Bracket feet made separately to *c*.1800 with a thin line of moulding around the base. From *c*.1800–*c*.1840 feet are integral with side timbers.

9. After *c*.1830, chests of drawers taller, often with five flights of drawers, on round, turned feet.

Likely restoration and repair

10. From *c*.1850 made in much larger sizes, which may be cut down to better-looking 'Sheraton' shape. Top pair of drawers removed, piece raised with splayed bracket feet to add height; new top with 'Sheraton' reeding often added as a separate fillet which can be seen from the back.

11. Later, five-flight chests of drawers cut down in similar fashion, with turned feet replaced with splayed bracket feet and shaped apron added – the join will show on the sides.

12. Drawer handles set too close to edge on small chest, which indicates it has probably been cut down, the turned wooden handles removed and new brass backplates added to conceal the original holes. No patination around the new backplates.

Historical background

It is probable that the bow-fronted chest of drawers was an evolution of the flamboyant French commode and the bombé shape so favoured by the Dutch. The bombé shape, with its double curves and sinuously swelling sides, was never as popular in England as plainer, serpentine shapes, although Chippendale incorporated the curved sides into many of his French-influenced designs. There is evidence of Hepplewhite's use of bow-fronted shapes, particularly in his designs for bedroom and boudoir furniture, but it would seem that it was Sheraton who first produced this enduring shape which has become, like his sideboard, a standard piece of English furniture.

Few bow-fronted chests of drawers can be directly attributed to a particular designer, and most of the fine early examples are more often described as 'George III', a generous label since it covers 60 years, from 1760 to 1820. The finest early mahogany examples fall into the early part of this period, when they were made with curving bracket feet, fine cockbeading on the graduated drawers and brushing slides. Later versions are of the more familiar early nineteenth-century design, with shaped aprons and slightly splayed feet, made in mahogany veneer on a red pine or, sometimes, a cheap mahogany carcase.

Bow-fronted chests of drawers are seldom found in any other wood or veneer except dark mahogany, and it is fair to assume that they were intended for gentlemen's dressing rooms and bedrooms, at least until the end of the nineteenth century.

Construction and materials

Early bow-fronted chests of drawers followed the same construction principles as serpentine-fronted chests of drawers, in that they were made in solid wood with veneered drawer-fronts and deep thumb moulding around three sides of the top. There was no overhang at the back. A line of moulding ran round the base, which was mounted on curving or slightly splayed bracket feet. From c.1780 reeded moulding was introduced around the tops, and was believed to have been originated by Thomas Sheraton. Drawers were still oak-lined and veneered, and were outlined with a thin, typically late eighteenth century, line of cockbeading.

There were four graduated single drawers until c.1800 when frequently a pair of drawers replaced the single one in the top flight. Up to this date the slim top drawer was sometimes fitted as a writing drawer, with the brushing slide serving a double purpose.

Drawers had runners on small blocks on either side of the dustboards. They were made in two pieces, with the curved front edge cut separately. As with all other storage pieces, the drawers and dustboards did not run the full depth of the piece, but stopped a little short to allow air to circulate inside. Backs were of unfinished planking, oak or cheaper-grade mahogany. From c.1820 the bow-front became more accentuated as techniques of bending and steaming timber began to be used, and from this date carcases were often made of red pine.

Detail
Plain brass-rimmed locks were replaced with Victorian Bramah locks from c.1846, and all drawers, at least until the end of the nineteenth century, were fitted with locks. From c.1850 the front edge of the top was often given an exaggerated curve to add visually to the line of the bow-front. Top edges of veneered chests of drawers were mainly flush from c.1810–30, while solid tops had rounded moulding. Few bow-fronts after c.1820 incorporated brushing slides, and by c.1850 turned wooden knobs often replaced brass drawer handles, and rounded turned feet replaced the splayed bracket feet and curving apron.

Variations

There are many Continental variations of the bombé-shaped chest of drawers with its double curve and swelling front. They were often made in walnut, and were sometimes late variations of earlier walnut marquetry pieces. They tend to have very decorative handles and escutcheons and oak-lined drawers, but although at first glance they seem to resemble a bow-front, they are more serpentine in shape.

It is extremely unlikely that bow-fronted chests of drawers were ever originally made in pine. The main point about pine furniture in the nineteenth century was that it was cheap to make in quantity, which would not have been true of a bow-fronted piece. If these are encountered, it is more likely that they were originally well-made carcases of chests of drawers which have been stripped of their thin veneer to add value during the fashion for stripped-pine furniture.

George III bow fronted mahogany commode.

Reproductions

The most common reproduction is the Sheraton copy, with the familiar late Victorian or early Edwardian version of the conch shell or spray of flowers inlaid in paler-coloured panels, as seen on other bedroom furniture of the same period. The mahogany veneer is thin and without good figuring, the escutcheons frequently of bone or ivory, and the piece may well have been French polished to increase the glossiness of its appearance. American pine carcases were common for these reproductions, and the quality of the finish in many cases is poor, with rough edges under the machine-cut curved apron, and drawers which do not fit properly.

However, much good-quality 'Sheraton revival' furniture was made during the first decades of the twentieth century, and among the favourite pieces for gentlemen's dressing rooms and bedrooms was the bow-fronted chest of drawers, in many cases far better made than those of the late nineteenth century. They were made by furniture-makers who supplied the main furnishing department stores of the day. Once seen and handled, they are not easily confused with the cheap run-of-the mill reproductions with shoddy workmanship of the same period.

Price bands

Hepplewhite period, fine figured veneer and brushing slide: £1,200–1,800.

Satinwood veneer, top quality, some inlay and decoration: £2,500–4,000.

George III splayed feet, good veneer: £900–1,700.

Early Victorian good quality, c.1850: £800–1,200.

Late nineteenth-century, variable quality: £300–600.

Display cabinet

Historical background

Glass-fronted display cabinets ranged from soaring architectural pieces to delicate little inlaid versions of chests-on-stands, but one of their most desirable forms was as part of a desk or bureau. The influence of William Kent's architectural designs for furniture (starting c.1720) meant that many kinds of tall, elegant pieces began to be made in England. Some of the earliest display cabinets resemble stonemason's work, with glazed 'windows' beneath severe architectural pediments, and though suitable for houses built in the very grand manner, were soon replaced by the cabinet-maker's lighter, more decorative work. Among these are many variations on the secretaire or bureau-bookcase, with glass-fronted doors embellished with decorative glazing bars.

These 'china cabinets' formed the top halves of both writing furniture, cupboards and chests with drawers in different combinations. At first, glazing bars were in simple geometrical shapes, of fairly thick half-round moulding, but when newer, thinner 'crown' glass became available and mahogany was better understood and worked, (from c.1750 onwards), some very fine effects were achieved, of which the most adventurous were probably during Chippendale's 'Gothic' period. However, with a return to more severe architectural pediments after c.1760, glazing bars were more often in geometrical shapes.

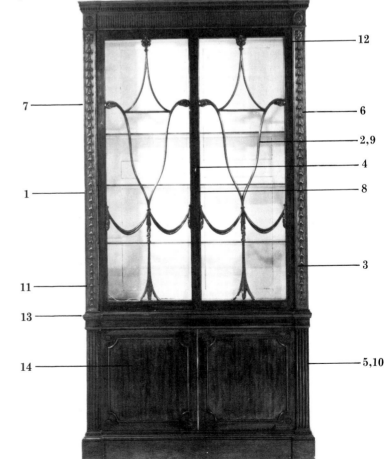

Construction and materials

Beautifully made in matching, finely figured walnut veneer for a brief period, display cabinets soon joined the range of pieces in mahogany veneer, on carcases of Honduras mahogany.

Inside, the shelves were of oak, with grooves or plate-stays on adjustable pegs, with shelf edges finished with thin mahogany astragal moulding. Inside surfaces of the sides of the cabinet were veneered in plain, dark mahogany, and the base of the cabinet was usually in a single piece of solid mahogany for strength and stability. The cabinet was stepped and considerably narrower than bases with drawers and cupboards or bases with secretaire drawers.

Detail

From c.1750 the thick glass and heavy glazing bars were replaced with thinner 'crown' glass and delicate mahogany glazing bars, reduced to minimal width and built up in two layers on the outside and a single thickness on the inside of the door, each shape enclosing individually cut panes of glass. At first the designs were geometrical, but from c.1750 glazing bars were arched, curved, and sometimes interspersed with thicker, carved swags and garlands.

From c.1770 display cases were often mounted on low, plain, cupboarded bases, ending on a line with panelled dadoes, and with the glass-fronted doors taller in proportion. Cupboards were usually severe, virtually undecorated except for rectangles of moulding to resemble panels or sometimes with cutaway corners and small rosette decorations.

Variations

Dressers served the same purpose as display cabinets in country dwellings, and glass-fronted cupboards of any kind were not usually made or used except by more sophisticated households. Some single-doored bureau-bookcases, originally with blockfronted cupboards were converted into glass-fronted cabinets, often by the Victorians, when there was a great need to display mass-produced 'cabinet-ware', such as small figurines and profusely decorated plates, hitherto only made for the wealthy. These will be of simple, good-looking oak with fairly wide frames to doors and heavy glazing bars, without any form of decorative pediment except a plain cornice.

Left: *A typical George III design with astragal glazed doors.*

Right: *Display cabinet-bookcase, reminiscent of the 1880s Arts and Crafts Movement.*

Reproductions

Mass-produced versions of display cabinets of every size and shape were made from c.1835 onwards, on carcases of imported American pine or deal with thin, shiny veneer, often French-polished, with double doors beneath, sometimes en suite with bureau-bookcases. Inlaid oval panels of lighter-coloured woods may be found on the doors of the base. The conch shell or spray of flowers seen on bureaux and bureau-bookcases was often repeated within these panels.

Smaller dressers with glass-fronted doors were made from c.1860, often in a jumble of left-over woods by estate carpenters for tenant farmers. Experience has often shown that these painted pieces will not strip down to be sold as 'stripped pine', since some of the wood was red pine, some white, some even cheap mahogany or 'black' Virginia walnut.

Many display cabinets dating from c.1830 onwards are no more than part of wall-length library fittings originally built into Victorian mansions, cut down, with new sides and often glass doors added where there were originally open shelves.

Some very fine-looking display cabinets, library furniture and desk furniture was produced by the Arts and Crafts Movement, as well as some nicely designed 'country furniture' by J. C. Loudon from c.1830, usually in plain unstained oak in Gothic revival styles.

Price bands

Georgian mahogany with architectural columns, cornice, ogee bracket feet and fine veneer: £7,000–9,000.

Georgian-style, well-made and veneered, nineteenth century: £2,500–3,500.

Provincial, nineteenth-century oak: £900–1,500.

Chiffonier

Signs of authenticity

1. Carcases of Honduras mahogany or Scandinavian red pine.
2. In solid rosewood from *c.*1830, inlaid or decorated with brass inlay, often to a specific pattern like a stencilled design.
3. Inner surfaces still planed and finished by hand until *c.*1835.
4. Veneers still hand-cut until *c.*1830, after which they were machine-cut, with consequent loss in quality and thickness in cheaper versions.
5. Pillar supports lathe-turned and finished by hand, not absolutely identical nor mechanically symmetrical.
6. On plinth-based chiffoniers, decoration does not continue on the plinth itself, which is always plain.
7. Narrow frames to silk-panelled doors with or without grilles.
8. Reeded, fluted or half-round astragal moulding to right hand door on double-doored versions.
9. Doors of single-doored cabinets opening left to right with hinges on right.
10. Rule hinges to doors, brass locks with brass levers.

Likely restoration and repair
11. Added brass grilles to pleated-silk door panels may have been done any time from mid-nineteenth century onwards.
12. Converted from late nineteenth-century Italian credenza – flanking shelves may be curved or serpentine, originally with glass doors. Central door, originally veneered, painted or inlaid replaced with pleated-silk panel and brass grille. Often they were originally mounted on small feet with a shaped plinth base and inlaid brass decoration continuing down on to base.
13. Made up from sections of library bookshelving with new doors, or with glass removed, silk and brass grilles added.

The above points refer to the low chiffonier, sometimes referred to as 'side cabinets' which are easier to sell and more popular than the taller version.

Historical background

English chiffoniers are of two kinds: the enclosed, stepped cabinet with shelves above and doors below, used as occasional furniture in morning rooms and dining rooms, and the low, slim, marble-topped version, frequently incorporating bookshelves, which stood in halls, passages and libraries, usually with an important mirror or picture hanging above it. Generally assumed to be part of English Regency furniture, the chiffonier is a purely French design, and the name has nothing to do with the fact that English chiffoniers often have open-pleated silk door-panels. Originally, the French chiffonier was a commode with doors to conceal its drawers. If there were seven drawers it was known as a 'semanier'. It emerged during the Directoire period immediately after the French Revolution, and blossomed during the First Empire. The reason for its development was the almost complete absence of craftsmen to carve, inlay and work in wood, together with the post-Revolutionary desire to create a new style of severe, classical taste. And so, the swinging curving shapes of bombé commodes were replaced with flat-fronted lines, embellished with ormolu and gilt-bronze mounts (metal-workers were still plentiful after the Revolution) depicting classical symbols of victory, or Egyptian-inspired palmettes.

English designers toned down the ormolu and gilt, substituting inlaid brass stringing and decorative inlay, and replacing the solid doors with pleated silk panels to accord with the backs of sideboards. The ubiquitous brass grilles are almost without exception later additions, dating from the early Victorian period onwards.

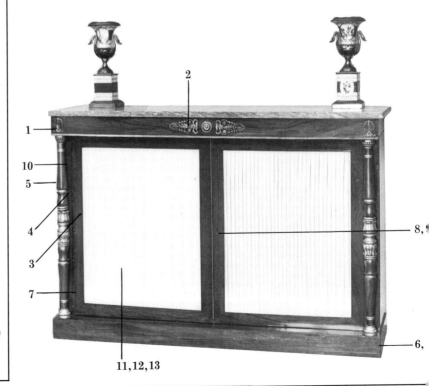

Construction and materials

It is most common to find chiffoniers of the taller variety in rosewood from c.1815, although both versions were made in rich plain fine-grained San Domingo mahogany on Honduras mahogany carcases. The low chiffonier was a sleek elegant piece of decorative furniture, originally made with mahogany or rosewood tops which were almost without exception replaced with marble in the first half of the nineteenth century. Designs differ widely, although the form remains the same: some are on plinth bases, some have ornately gilded pillar supports and decoratively carved feet, some are stepped with bookshelves on either side, others may be intricately inlaid with brass. The silk-pleated doors usually conceal shelves rather than drawers: the tall chiffonier surmounted with shelves have storage cupboards beneath, and it is these which merge with the ebullient sideboards of the second half of the nineteenth century.

It is interesting to note that French furniture of the same period was made with poor-quality oak carcases, since the English blockade of France made the importation of foreign timber virtually impossible.

Detail

From c.1818 brass inlay and decoration became profuse and intricate after Robert Clayton patented his method of pouring molten, non-tarnishing alloys directly into grooves and channels in the wood.

Brass grilles became almost mandatory from c.1840 – the brass was laid in a lattice pattern and soldered together with studs to conceal the joins. Eighteenth century brass grilles were notched on each intersection and no solder or studs were used.

Variations

The chiffonier has no place in a country furniture-maker's workshop, since it demanded veneering and good solid fine-grained imported woods. As with the sofa table from Hepplewhite's designs in the 1780s, neat side-cupboards were made for the small town house without the ornament or pleated silk door panels. They were often used as bookcases by the growing literate population, and sometimes used as substitute sideboards with cupboards below.

Should any 'genuine oak chiffoniers' be encountered, it is fairly safe to say that these were originally veneered, with heavy ormolu mounts, and made in France where oak was used as a carcase wood in the first quarter of the nineteenth century.

Left: *Regency, rosewood chiffonier with rising top and small, brass gallery.*
Below: *early Regency rosewood breakfront side cabinet or chiffonier with pleated silk door panels, brass rosette inlay and table top.*

Reproductions

Nineteenth century
The French Empire style so popular during the Napoleonic period also took root in Italy where it endured far longer than in France itself, or in England. Credenzas, heavy, over-ornate side cabinets based on the sleek original low chiffonier, were still being made almost until the end of the nineteenth century in Italy. Many of them were imported into England and have become popular again, and smaller, more restrained credenzas have begun to fetch relatively good prices.

Victorian chiffoniers of both the low and high variety continued to be made throughout the nineteenth century, particularly in what was at one time disparagingly called 'Louis the Hotel' style for the corridors, halls, morning rooms and reception rooms of hotels and public assembly rooms. They gradually became more degraded in form and more elaborate in design. In particular, the vast Gothic chiffonier/sideboard pieces flanking a large and ornate mirror are still found in provincial hotels to this day. The slim, low, marble-topped chiffonier, flanked by bookshelves with a stepped front is an elegant piece of furniture, recently increasing in popularity and commercial value. There are quite a large number of them on the market of a considerably later date than the originals, but none the worse for that.

Pine 'sideboards' with curved pillar supports and blockfronted doors may well turn out to be the carcase bases of tall Victorian chiffoniers.

Price bands

Regency, rosewood, with brass inlay: £2,500–3,800.

Regency, mahogany veneer: £1,200–2,000.

William IV or early Victorian walnut: £1,100–1,600.

Military chest

Signs of authenticity

1. Made of solid mahogany, cedarwood, camphorwood or padouk wood.
2. Cast-brass backplates recessed into drawer fronts with square, flush-fitting, hinged drawer handles. Brass corners and reinforcements set flush into the wood, secured with countersunk screws.
3. Flush escutcheons, locks with brass cases and brass levers.
4. All sides of chest in solid wood built like a trunk, with no backboard planking.
5. Oak-lined drawers with reinforced pine runners, half-round moulding on insides, drawer bottoms with grain running from side to side with central strengthening batten.
6. Fitted helmet drawer, or small secretaire fall-front, either the width of the top drawer or fitted centrally between two small flanking drawers.
7. Iron carrying handles fixed with steel screws on backplates.
8. Both surfaces of top and bottom and corresponding brass corner-pieces scratched and scuffed with wear.
9. Where there is a secretaire drawer or writing compartment, brass catches to secure fall-front, cleated sides to writing surface, usually inset with tooled leather, brass double-hinges to flap. Both halves of equal depth.

Likely restoration and repair
10. Original fitted drawers damaged, new drawer-linings or top drawer-front repaired, joined or replaced where fall-front or helmet drawer has been removed or converted.
11. Iron carrying handles replaced with brass ones.
12. Turned or bun feet added at later date, usually late nineteenth century.
13. Top and base of different depths: usually some of the central section has been damaged and the second or third drawer and frame cut down and repaired.
14. Brass corner-pieces replaced with thinner, more yellow brass than originals, lacking any sign of patination, build-up of dirt or corrosion around edges.

Historical background

In sharp contrast to the ebullience and indiscriminate mixing of almost every period and style by the nineteenth-century furniture designers, the travelling furniture made for the officers in the Napoleonic wars has endured as a reminder that Victorian design could be plain, simple and eminently practical. Whole suites of campaign furniture or military furniture was made between about 1800 and 1870. Some were quite elaborate and all were hinged, folded or divided into more or less regulation-sized chests with brass-reinforced corners to prevent damage in transit. Voyages across the Atlantic still took many months: important passengers furnished empty sea-cabins with similar travelling furniture. A few examples of these grander pieces remain, such as glass-doored display cabinets or bookcases folding to the size of cabin trunks, but most of it has not survived. Best known are military chests, made in two halves, with a variety of different fittings, such as small secretaire drawers or deep helmet drawers.

Similar in concept were the tall specimen cabinets known as Wellington chests, with hinged side flaps which lock over the drawer edges to prevent them from opening in transit. There is, however, no evidence that the Duke of Wellington ever owned or used such a chest on any of his many campaigns.

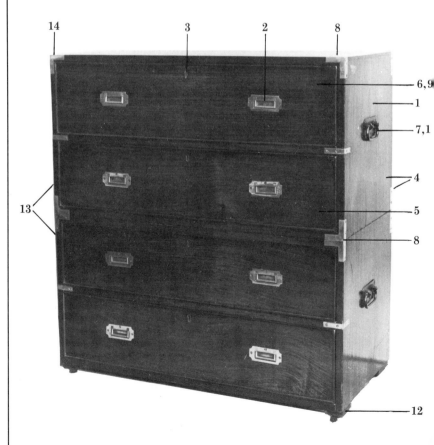

Construction and materials

Military chest
Military chests were always made in solid wood, usually mahogany, although padouk, cedar and camphorwood were also used, for they were proof against damp and moths on long campaigns and distant journeys. The construction is solid, with mitred dovetailing. Drawers have oak linings with pine-reinforced runners and half-round corner mouldings on the inside, firmly glued to the sides and bottom. No nails are used in the main construction – after joints had been cut they were coated with strong glue and clamped together. The two carrying handles on each half were originally of iron, but most of them have been replaced with brass handles to match the flush, sunk drawer fittings. For obvious reasons, military chests were not mounted on any kind of feet or base. Occasionally they might be fitted with small castors mounted on additional blocks.

Wellington chest
Wellington chests were also originally made in solid wood, either mahogany, rosewood or imported walnut, but from c.1850 onwards, having been adopted as a piece of library furniture or as specimen chests, they were frequently also veneered. They were as solidly made as military chests, with no decoration except for small 'capitals' at the top of the hinged side-flap and its corresponding upright on the other side. Drawers always had small, turned, wooden knobs, and many of them were originally lined with velvet, divided into compartments and sometimes fitted with grooved glass lids. In the second half of the nineteenth century, veneers were on good-quality carcases of 'baywood' or red pine, in walnut, rosewood, mahogany and maple. There was no cockbeading round the drawers, which fitted flush without escutcheons. The only lock was in the hinged side-flap.

Reproductions

Although not campaign or military furniture, contemporary pieces for use in libraries, draughtsmen's offices and for keeping documents and maps are of the same family as military chests in their totally functional design, lack of ornament, beautiful finish and excellent craftsmanship. It is as well to remember, however, that multitudes of small shops were equipped with beautifully made, built-in flights of drawers which, with little effort, can be transformed into very similar-looking pieces.

The attractive, clean lines and elegant brass finish has been copied by many small furniture-makers in small chests of drawers.

In relatively recent years American reproduction furniture manufacturers have produced some good pieces of similar appearance, but they are almost always made in heavy chipboard, veneered in 'cherrywood' or 'yew wood' and made with modern techniques and with bonded joins, which are not intended to deceive or masquerade as genuine.

Variations

Military chests were unique to a particular echelon of society, whether in military service, travelling or going abroad on consular or diplomatic business. The rank and file in the army had no such luxuries, neither did poor emigrants who undertook long voyages in extreme discomfort. Its parallel is the brassbound chest, made and used by all types of traveller, sometimes in brass-studded, leather-covered wood, or plain, iron-bound, wooden chests. Military chests probably evolved from the plain chests of drawers made in two halves of the late seventeenth and early eighteenth centuries. The most singular difference was the lack of lock and lock rail to the top drawers of both halves of the traditional chest of drawers.

Far right: *library document chest in solid walnut, c.1870.*
Right: *plain mahogany Wellington chest with graduated drawers and hinged locking flap.*

Price bands

Wellington chest, plain, solid mahogany: £800–1,200.

Veneered in walnut or bird's eye maple, c.1800: £1,000–1,600.

Library chests in walnut, mahogany or rosewood: £750–1,000.

Military chest in padouk, cedar or camphorwood: £850–1,500.

Escritoire

Historical background

After the Restoration (1660) desk furniture developed with the writing box on stand and the escritoire – or scrutoire – built on the same principle as the chest-on-stand so typical of the William and Mary period (1689–1701). The large exterior surface of the fall-front provided a magnificent opportunity for the new art of veneering which had been introduced to England from the Netherlands.

The decorative stands proved too unstable to support these grand writing chests and by the end of the seventeenth century escritoires were mounted on chests of drawers. They were still made as two separate pieces, with the join concealed with plinth moulding which matched that on the base.

The cornice mouldings surmounting the escritoire show the beginnings of an architectural influence on furniture design, and the interiors demonstrate the skill of early cabinet-makers.

Escritoires were made all over Europe and although they were superseded in England by the bureau and the secretaire, they continued to be made in Holland, Germany, Italy, Spain and Portugal until the beginning of the last century.

Construction and materials

As with chests on stands and chests of drawers of the same period, escritoires were made with a carcase construction, with finely figured walnut veneer on soft imported oak. The backs of both component parts were of saw-cut oak planking fixed to the carcase with iron nails. The sides of the top and base were in well-matched veneer. The fall-front had cleated sides to prevent warping and bending. A cushion drawer was concealed in the moulding above the fall-front and below the cornice, occasionally with an escutcheon and lock.

Until c.1700, escritoires stood on plain bun feet, but after that date bracket feet formed an integral part of the base moulding. The base had a flight of three drawers, made of oak with cross-cut veneered surrounds and mitred corners.

Detail
Interiors were made with a wide variety of fittings – usually numbers of tiered small drawers and friezes which often concealed secret compartments. A central door with a lock provided secure storage for documents. Wide bands of cross-cut veneer framed the central panels of the fall-front and, on the interior, was a writing surface of velvet or baize cloth.

From c.1660 to 1685 parquetry veneer in richly figured walnut was typical, where geometrical patterns fitted together like a jigsaw. From c.1685 to 1715 oyster veneer and seaweed or scrolled marquetry replaced earlier patterns and from c.1700 inset panels of lighter woods with leaves, flowers and birds in the central panels were also characteristic.

Brass chains or elbow hinges took the weight of the open fall-front. Up to c.1700 steel lock casings and brass escutcheons were used, but after that date lock casings were made of brass.

Variations

Dowry chests without stands were imported in considerable quantities from the Netherlands, crudely made and inlaid with pale woods in primitive designs such as doves, hearts and flowers. The stands for them were made in England. Chests of small drawers with two doors instead of a fall-front were more common in the average household where writing was not a daily or regular habit. Otherwise the writing box on stand or portable writing box with sloped front – hardly comparable with the grand escritoire – served the same purpose.

Reproductions

Nineteenth century
Cheaply made, imported Dutch, German, Spanish, Italian and Portuguese escritoires on made-up bases had coarse-grained pine carcases with pine drawers, sometimes stained to look like red pine. Italian versions often favoured tortoiseshell in place of veneer, surrounded with ebonized string-of-beads mouldings

A close relation to the escritoire is seen in the 'secretaire de dame' or 'secretaire à abattant', made mainly on the Continent but also in England during the late eighteenth and early nineteenth centuries.

Escritoires on stands had a certain vogue during the early Victorian period when considerable numbers were imported from southern Germany and mounted on bun-footed, twist-turned stands made in England and conforming to the old William and Mary pattern.

Price bands

William and Mary. Fine figured walnut veneer: £3,500–6,000.

Early eighteenth-century walnut with marquetry panels: £3,000–5,000.

Nineteenth-century secretaire à abattant: £1,500–2,200.

Spanish, Italian, German, Dutch, nineteenth-century cabinet on stands: £1,200–1,800.

Far left: *walnut, c.1700.*
Left: *walnut fall-front escritoire on bracket feet, c.1710.*

Queen Anne secretaire

Historical background

The increasing skill of the cabinet-maker and the change in style to loftier and more spacious houses brought new variations to writing furniture, increasing their height with elaborately fitted cabinets surmounted with elegant curves or broken pediments. These pieces were designed to stand between the high windows of architect-designed houses and were always tall and slim.

The base consisted of a much smaller fall-fronted or slope-fronted desk with three or four drawers below it. Above, there were block-fronted or mirrored-glass doors behind which were shelves for books or elaborate arrangements of small drawers and pigeonholes for ledgers and documents. Miniature architectural features such as columns and architraves concealed secret drawers and compartments. Particularly in vogue were lacquered Queen Anne secretaires which have a strong appeal to the copyist.

Signs of authenticity

1. Plinth moulding with matching moulding on joins of component parts.
2. Side veneers matching on component parts.
3. If with serpentine apron incorporating bracket feet, piece made after *c*.1715.
4. Flush edges to writing flap and doors.
5. Wide-bevelled 'Vauxhall' mirrored glass.
6. Oak bearers to support writing flap.
7. Early oak bearers square in section with small brass knobs.
8. Later oak bearers equal in depth to top drawer with small fan-shaped handles.
9. If single door, it always opens left to right.
10. Brass slide fastenings with steel bolts on left-hand door, lock on right.
11. Dust boards between drawers in base.
12. Interior fittings of veneered cabinets and desks usually in oak or walnut, with bone or ivory knobs.
13. Locks and escutcheons to all drawers in base.
14. Only two pin hinges on each cabinet door, top and bottom.

Likely restoration and repair

15. 'Marriages' between component parts of several damaged pieces – sides of secretaire are often in a single piece, cut on the joins.
16. 'Marriage' when top is proportionately too small for base – a deep 'bandage' and bracket feet are often added to increase height.
17. Elaborate cabinet fittings too badly damaged to restore – often replaced with later bookshelf fittings, or with glass-fronted display cabinet.
18. Part or whole of original lacquer flaked and damaged. It is often replaced, repainted with modern materials.

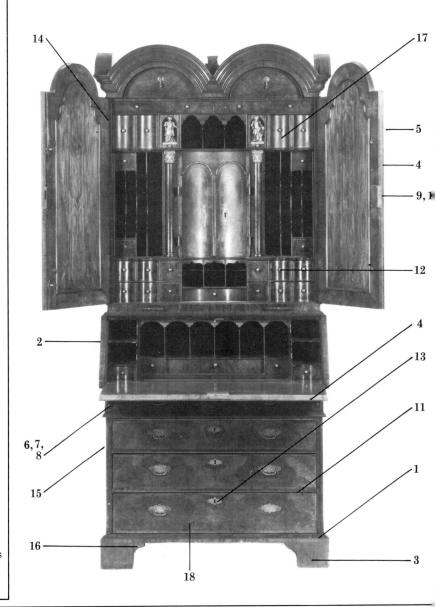

Construction and materials

A secretaire was made in two or three separate pieces: the base, the fall-front or slope-fronted desk and the cabinet. Sometimes the desk and base are made in a single piece, sometimes in two, as with early bureaus. The cabinets are always separate, slotting into moulding round the top of the base. They were made in finely figured walnut veneer on close-grained pine carcases, with pine or beech for lacquered versions. The back of each component part was of relatively thin oak, pine or beech planking, nailed to the carcase. Drawers were of oak or oak and pine. The doors of the cabinet were hung on two pin hinges, and the writing flap had flush edges with cleated sides and an inset velvet or cloth panel. Bun feet were typical until *c.*1710, when they were superseded by bracket feet.

Detail
On veneered secretaires, the interior fittings of desk and cabinet were usually made in oak or walnut, frequently with boxwood stringing or bone or ivory inlay. Narrow bands of cross-cut veneer edged the drawers and a broader band framed the writing flap. Lacquered secretaires were equally elaborate and on both veneered and lacquered cabinets the insides of the cabinet doors were as lavishly decorated as the rest of the piece. Lacquer was often applied to a gesso base, built up in relief for decorative features such as dragons, pagodas, buildings, trees and birds. Red grounds were popular, black less so for secretaires, blue was seldom used and green and yellow only occasionally – the varnish discoloured and dulled them to a dirty khaki.

Variations

The proportions of provincial pieces are not the same as those of their grander counterparts. The writing compartments are usually slope-fronted and deeper. The overall effect makes the secretaire look remarkably narrow. A block-fronted cabinet was more common than glazed doors, and mirrored doors were the rarest.

Provincial pieces were not as tall as grander versions and frequently lacked a decorative pediment. The finest country examples may have simple architectural moulding and lunettes to bottom drawers of bases, inlaid with decorative stringing. Similar-shaped desk-and-cabinets were also made with block-fronted doors, with simple walnut veneer on an oak and pine carcase.

Right: *secretaire-bookcase, c.1720.*
Far right: *elaborate walnut veneered secretaire, c.1710.*

Reproductions

Some excellently proportioned reproductions are being made today, both lacquered and veneered, particularly for the American market. The methods of construction will be entirely modern, incorporating steamed and bonded woods, sometimes even veneered on chipboard.

'Made up' versions or copies of country-made secretaires are likely to give themselves away by the most fundamental errors. In striving for what the maker sees as the 'right' proportions, the overall height of a made-up piece will often be too tall to stand in the relatively low-ceilinged manor houses for which the originals were made.

Price bands

Original and complete Queen Anne, unrestored: £20,000–30,000.

Original Queen Anne but restored: £15,000–20,000.

Nineteenth-century secretaire-bookcase reproduction: £4,000–6,000.

Edwardian copies, in fine condition: £1,200–2,000.

Bureau-bookcase

Historical background

From the mid-eighteenth century, cabinets and bureau-bookcases conformed to the architectural styles and fashions of that period. Although frequently referred to as 'the Chippendale period' it was William Kent (died in 1748) who had the greater influence on these pieces with their adaptation of the classicism of Ancient Greece and Rome. The curved and rounded broken pediments of an earlier age changed to a more severe triangular shape, often with a central plinth on which was mounted a bust, an eagle or some similar classical feature. To accord with Georgian design, cabinets and bureau-bookcases were larger than those of the previous period and there was a preference for fall-fronted writing drawers, as opposed to slope-fronted desks, due to a growing desire for plain and simple shapes.

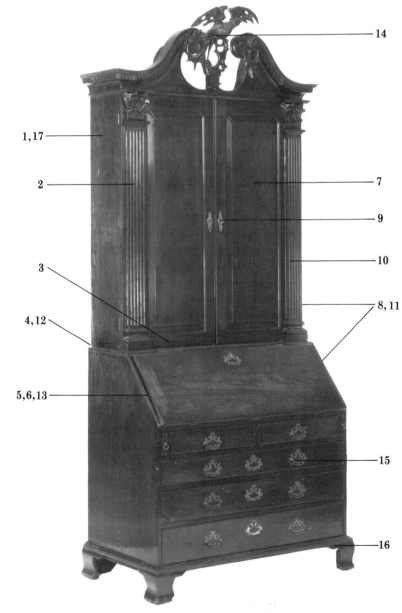

Construction and materials

The strength of mahogany allowed for much simpler construction which reflected the taste for classical simplicity. A bureau-bookcase was made in three pieces: the bureau base, the bookcase, and the decorative pediment. All the lines were sleeker, and there was a less pronounced step between the bureau base and the bookcase above.

The carcase was of cheap Honduras mahogany or baywood, veneered in fine-figured San Domingo or Cuban mahogany. After c.1760 this rich, lighter-coloured wood was used both as a solid wood and for veneer. The backs of the separate components were of saw-cut pine or mahogany planking. When made in solid mahogany, the edges of writing flaps had thumb or lip-moulding. Veneered writing flaps still had flush edges. Drawers in the base were of oak and pine, with dustboards between them. Mahogany cabinet doors were heavier than those of the earlier secretaire, and were hung on three pin hinges instead of two. The decorative pediment was three-sided only, on a frame which slotted into the top of the cornice and was not secured.

Detail
The fine, close grain of mahogany allowed decoration to be carved into the wood: Greek key motifs, reeding, fluting, fretting and dentil cornices were integral and not applied. Pediments were more ornate and so were bases, often with serpentine aprons with a central cartouche, carved paw feet or short, scrolled, outward-curving bracket feet. Canted corners to tops and bases, often fluted or carved, were also typical features. Glazing bars were functional and stood proud on either side of glass-fronted cabinets, holding individually-cut panes of glass in decorative geometrical patterns. If the bookcase had block-fronted doors then the panels would be chamfered. Backplates, handles and escutcheons were of plain, fretted or pierced brass. From c.1750 escutcheons were plain flush plates with little or no decoration. Interior desk fittings had bone, ivory or brass knobs to drawers.

Variations

Some desks and bookcases of the second half of the eighteenth century had double or single cupboards in place of the drawers below the writing flap. In manor houses the plain bureau served the same purpose as the bureau-bookcases of larger households, and a separate hanging shelf accommodated the few books kept by all but educated and wealthy families. As with the previous period, the top half of any double-heighted writing desk was usually glazed to display china and other decorative objects.

Simple square-topped bureau-bookcases with double doors below the writing flap were made in mahogany veneer on pine carcases for modest provincial houses, using the same construction as grander pieces but lacking the ornate carved decoration. Some applied decoration in simple forms was customary, usually a lattice-like design or Greek key pattern.

Reproductions

Nineteenth century
Square-topped library furniture of less height than eighteenth-century originals was made in solid Virginia walnut which discolours and darkens with age. To the untrained eye it may look like mahogany but it lacks the depth of colour and lustre and was often French-polished to a spurious gloss. This classic piece of library furniture continued to be made right through the nineteenth century into the twentieth, with some variations in the combination of display cabinet and desk, bureau-bookcase and base with drawers or double doors containing sliding shelves on runners.

Twentieth century
Modern mahogany veneer is thinly cut by machine. Unlike original bureau-bookcases, the drawers do not have cross-cut veneer edging but are usually veneered with a single piece and then inlaid with a paler wood.

Left: *a provincial version with display-cabinet top, c.1790.*
Above: *Edwardian reproduction in mahogany with satinwood crossbanding.*

Price bands

Georgian, broken pediment, fine and unrestored: £10,000–15,000.

Late Georgian provincial: £3,000–5,000.

Early nineteenth-century reproduction: £2,500–4,000.

Edwardian, in good condition: £800–1,800.

Bureau

Historical background

After the English Civil War, the increase in literacy, coupled with the extension of the Government postal service to include the whole population, meant an increasing demand for writing furniture which was not as grand as the secretaire and the bureau-bookcase. Manor houses and small town houses needed desk furniture, and thus developed the familiar bureau, with desk-shaped sloping front with drawers in the base.

Early bureaux still bore signs of the same construction as early chests of drawers – they were often made in two parts with the join concealed by moulding matching that on the base. There were sometimes carrying handles of cast brass to both parts. Almost without exception bun feet were replaced with bracket feet by the early eighteenth century, although the fashion for bun and bracket feet has alternated down the centuries. Today, those bracket feet are again being replaced with recently made bun feet.

Bureaux were functional pieces of furniture, seldom elaborately veneered, and until the mid-eighteenth century, were seldom decorated with anything other than crossbanding or thin lines of herringbone or featherbanding veneer. Some extremely fine Chippendale period bureaux may have shaped drawers and canted corners, but in general they were flat-fronted and not shaped or serpentine.

As the literacy of the population increased throughout the eighteenth century, bureaux were made in increasing numbers with few modifications and have continued to be made right through the nineteenth century to the present day. The main clues to date are in the finish, construction, materials and patination of different periods, rather than any stylistic changes.

Signs of authenticity

1. Writing height not less than 2 ft 6 in or more than 2 ft 8 in.
2. Interior fittings often arched with drawers beneath the pigeonholes.
3. No veneer on the back. Bureaux were made to stand against a wall.
4. No overhang to top surface which should be flush with the back.
5. Oak, pine or mahogany back planking shrunk a little across the grain with age.
6. Drawers running full depth of piece.
7. Dustboards between drawers.
8. Lock rail, drawer rail with vertical veneer.
9. Writing flaps with cleated sides to prevent warping, bending.
10. Wear and patination on inner surface and on edge of writing flap, round lock, hinges, where it has been handled over the years.
11. Brass lock casings, steel levers and bolts, square or oblong in section.
12. Dirt and rust marks round heads of nails securing backs to carcases. Screws not used until the late eighteenth century.

Likely restoration and repair
13. New top – timber of different thickness to rest of piece when seen from back. May be the base of bureau bookcase or desk-and-bookcase.
14. Bases, aprons, feet with later carving to add value.
15. Mahogany veneer on oak carcase, indicates it was originally a country oak piece or late Victorian bureau that has been veneered and altered to resemble an eighteenth century piece.
16. Writing flaps cracked and split on hinges.

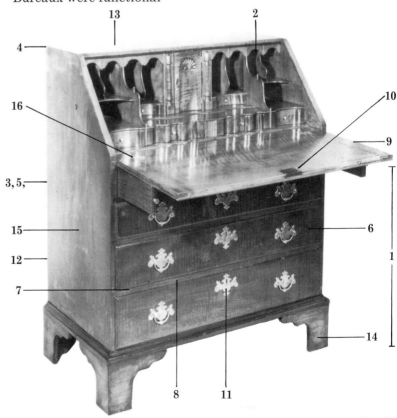

Construction and materials

Bureaux were made in a wide variety of woods: solid walnut in the early decades of the eighteenth century; slightly later, walnut veneer on close-grained yellow Baltic pine with oak drawers and drawer linings and, from the 1760s, solid mahogany and mahogany veneer.

Early bureaux had two top drawers set in pairs, with the writing flap supported with square-sectioned oak bearers set on either side of the top drawers. By c.1725 the pair of drawers was often replaced with a single, rather shallow drawer, or by a well reached from the inside. The bearers were rectangular from this period onwards, usually of oak with brass knobs which replaced the fan-shaped pulls on earlier bearers. On both solid wood and veneered bureaux the writing flap fitted flush until as late as c.1780 when mahogany bureaux had lip moulding round the writing flap.

From c.1750 cheaper Honduras mahogany as well as red pine was used for carcases. Veneers were in fine Cuban curl or well-figured San Domingo mahogany. There was a short period between 1730–40 when there was a return to two-piece construction with carrying handles to top and bases, which sometimes had carved paw feet. In general, after c.1760 the sides of bureaux were made in a single piece.

Detail

From c.1710 the earlier bun feet were often replaced with bracket feet without an apron until c.1720, after which a shallow apron joined the feet. The drawers and pigeonholes of the interior fittings were stepped and sometimes curved until the Georgian period, when the slope of the desk became steeper and the interior fittings were set straight across. However there are always exceptions, particularly with country-made pieces which continued to be made with stepped interiors for some time. After c.1720, bureaux were often veneered in yew and burrwood as well as walnut, sometimes with thin lines of boxwood stringing.

All bureaux, whatever their date or period, had locks to the writing flap and to all the main drawers. On veneered bureaux, the drawer rails and lock rails had veneer set vertically, rather than horizontally.

Variations

Plain oak versions of this classic piece were made of fine quality from the early eighteenth century onwards, embellished by the mid-eighteenth century with a plain, banded inlay and decorative escutcheon to the writing flap. Oak and elm was also used, with oak for the front and elm for the sides.

Interior detail, although of competent workmanship, was less fine and tended to fit less well because of the characteristic movement of oak. Elm was less durable and unsuitable for interiors since it tends to hold the damp. Country made desks of oak had no dustboards between the drawers.

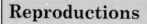

Reproductions

This classic piece of furniture has been made continuously from the seventeenth century down to the present day. Some fine reproductions of earlier styles were made in both the Victorian and Edwardian periods, as well as many cheap versions for offices and institutions, in thin veneer on splintery American pine carcases. During the Victorian period, bureaux were made in artificially seasoned oak which now shows almost black graining when it is stripped of its varnish.

Recently, copies of bureaux in Regency styles are frequently met with in 'yew wood' and 'cherry wood' veneer with flush fitting writing flaps, many of them made in the United States with no intent to deceive.

Price bands

Queen Anne or early Georgian walnut veneer: £4,000–7,000.

Georgian mahogany: £1,800–2,500.

Country-made oak, fruitwood: £1,000–2,500.

Nineteenth-century mahogany: £1,200–1,600.

Far left: *Mid-eighteenth-century oak.*
Left: *George I walnut and featherbanded bureau.*
Below: *Fine Queen Anne or George I walnut.*

Georgian pedestal desk

Historical background

The pedestal desk was not made until *c*.1765 when it can be seen in its grandest form – very large and ornate, and designed by Thomas Chippendale. It developed from bedroom or dressing-room furniture. The kneehole dressing table, a small, extremely decorative piece of furniture, is contemporary with the lowboy of the Queen Anne period.

There was a cupboard in the kneehole for shoes, often a pull-out writing or 'brushing' slide, and two sets of three small drawers either side of the kneehole. A single drawer ran the length of the piece above the kneehole. Rare to find are those with drawers which pull out, their fronts hinged, to disclose a fitted writing compartment.

In simple and ornate versions, pedestal desks have remained part of library furniture in England down to the present day. Although the name 'pedestal' implies that these desks were always without shaping to the bases, from *c*.1765 to *c*.1785 many were made with curving arch-shaped brackets beneath the two pedestals, running in a solid line down the inside of the kneehole to be repeated decoratively at the back.

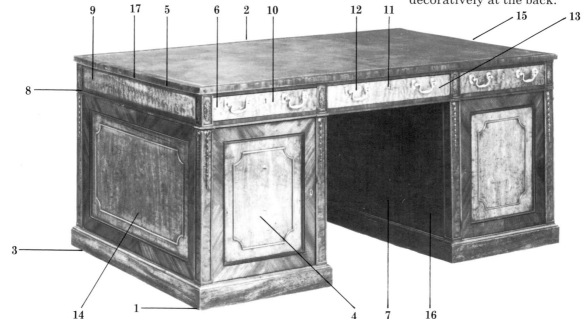

Signs of authenticity

1. Three-piece construction should sit solidly.
2. Backs finished and veneered.
3. Carcase of Honduras mahogany, baywood or red pine.
4. Rich, dark veneer.
5. Lip-moulding overhang to writing surface.
6. Drawers oak sided. Bottom timbers running front to back until *c*.1780. No corner mouldings inside.
7. Inside of pedestal of same wood as rest of piece.
8. Small line of moulding at join of pedestal and top.
9. Veneer and timber grain on sides of top run vertically.

10. No cross-cut veneer round drawers.
11. Locks with rimmed brass keyholes rather than escutcheons. Steel levers to locks, brass casing.
12. Three top drawers, outside pair equal width to drawers in pedestal. Undersurface of central drawer in unveneered carcase wood.

Likely restoration and repair
13. Cut down from larger size. Central top drawer will have had veneer lifted and replaced. New handles may have been added and the holes of the old ones may still be visible inside the drawer.

14. New thin veneer on coarse-grained oak carcase.
15. New tops of solid wood with no frame of cross-cut veneer around stuck-down (rather than stud-fixed) leather panel.
16. Made-up from damaged kneehole desk with one long top drawer. New timber and veneer on inside and either side of pedestals.
17. Cut-down depth. A 'split' can be felt under the lip-moulding where original top has been cut and veneer replaced after lifting.

Construction and materials

Original pedestal desks had three elements: two pedestals and a top section of writing surface with three integral drawers. The carcase of early desks was of cheap Honduras mahogany or baywood covered with a rich, dark veneer. Later desks had a carcase of Scandinavian, close-grained red pine. Early examples had, in each pedestal, a door concealing a flight of drawers, but by c.1790 the doors were often omitted and the drawers, with locks, became the more familiar pattern. As pedestal desks were free-standing, the desk back was well-finished and veneered.

Detail

There was no projecting decoration, such as carved feet or applied fretwork. Canted corners and pilaster mouldings were only incised where there were no doors to the pedestals. Except on very grand versions, there was little ornament unless it was flush with the surface – perhaps a small inset medallion or, from c.1790, brass stringing.

Although some desks had a solid top rather than an inset leather panel, larger versions may be found with three leather panels: one large central piece and two smaller flanking pieces. An overlap of lip-moulding ran round all four sides of the top.

Variations

Pedestal desks were essentially 'town' pieces but they were made in less grand designs, usually of oak on plain pedestals, by most of the leading provincial manufacturers: Gillows of Lancaster, Morgan and Sanders, Thomas Butler, John Mayhew, George Seddon. These same manufacturers would have also made grander versions for more fashionable households.

In country estate offices, pedestal desks and partners' desks, as well as rent tables, were part of the estate manager's general equipment. Kneehole desks, either with plain backs or with the back of the kneehole filled in, were more common in country houses. They were not necessarily free-standing and were often made with lip-moulding on three sides only, unlike their smarter town counterparts.

Above: *George III provincial kneehole pedestal desk with solid back and moulded edge to top. Note the brass carrying handles.*

Below: *Twin-pedestal in mahogany veneer, c.1850.*

Reproductions

As with the classic bureau, pedestal desks have been made continuously down to the present day. Care should be taken when 'period' pieces are offered at high prices because there are far more poorly designed, mass-produced versions around than there are high-quality craftsman-made pieces. Originals were solidly made and, with care, were durable, but many have lost one of their original three elements and have had to be made-up of pieces cannibalized from other desks. Often, this marriage produces something less than the rock-solidness of the original.

The Victorians often made them in plain, coarse-grained 'bleached oak' and the Edwardians favoured inlaid bands of light veneer outlining the drawers. Recently, standard mass-produced desks have been veneered to resemble eighteenth- or nineteenth-century pieces and sold extensively on the Continent. The veneer is likely to lift because it has been applied to the wrong carcase wood. Their tooled leather writing panels are an obvious giveaway.

Price bands

George III mahogany with doors concealing pedestal drawers: £12,000–14,000.

George III with less detail than above, mahogany veneer: £9,000–12,000.

Plain, twin pedestal, early nineteenth century: £1,700–2,220.

Victorian oak with mahogany veneer: £1,200–2,000.

Carlton House desk

Historical background

This extremely elegant piece of writing furniture owes its name to the Prince of Wales' grand London town house which used to stand on the present site of Carlton House Terrace, overlooking St James's Park. A Carlton House desk is a typical Regency design: sleek, elegant, depending entirely on its shape with no added carving – all the embellishment is in the surface treatment.

A drawing for a very similar design appears in Hepplewhite's second edition of *The Cabinet-Maker's London Book of Prices*, published in 1794, six years after his death, and some writing tables or desks of this distinctive shape had already been made before that. In any event, all but three of the 20 illustrative plates in Hepplewhite's book were signed by Thomas Shearer. Thomas Sheraton's *Cabinet Maker and Upholsterer's Drawing Book* (published in a series from 1791–94) also included drawings of a similar desk. Sheraton described it as a lady's drawing or writing table which should be made in two parts, in

satinwood or mahogany with a brass rim around the top part. The name 'Carlton House table' first appeared in Gillow of Lancaster's cost books for 1796. But although it can apparently

be attributed to several furniture designers its form varies only in detail – it would seem that it became almost instantly a 'classic' piece.

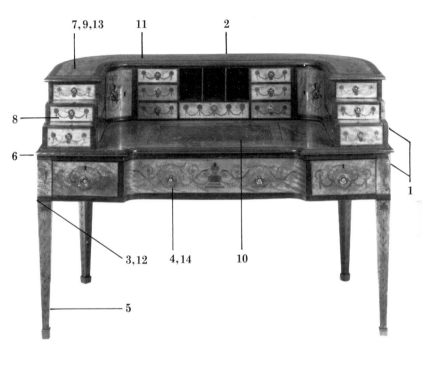

Signs of authenticity

1. Made in two parts, with well-matching veneer on top and base.
2. Free-standing design – the veneer should follow the outside curve in a continuous unbroken sweep around the back.
3. Some early Carlton House desks were made with 'bamboo-ringed' legs and tasselled tops set under the writing top: from *c*.1795 the construction is similar to library tables with legs continuing up to form the sides of the frame, set slightly proud on the corners.
4. Oak-lined drawers with cast brass bolt heads with rosettes, octagonal or circular small backplates, matching in design

on small and large drawers.
5. Legs tapering on insides only – outside corners form right-angles with floor.
6. Small moulded lip running on line of division of top and base.
7. Light-coloured golden satinwood veneer from West Indies with good figuring – light-coloured Cuban 'curl' mahogany veneer, or speckled amboyna.
8. Inlaid or painted decoration.
9. Veneer of top surface slightly faded from sunlight.
10. Inset soft leather writing surface framed with cross-cut veneer banding.

Likely restoration and repair
11. New veneered top and slight

lack of proportion to central pigeon-hole section. Victorian version with higher back removed, new curving top added to give 'classical Regency' horizontal lines.
12. Corners slightly proud with legs set under writing top, indicates original legs broken or replaced with earlier design to add to rarity value.
13. Speckled veneer with inlaid decoration – could be amboyna but may be later Victorian cheaper 'bird's eye maple' with machine-cut inlay.
14. Light-coloured carcase wood, usually pine, with pine drawers, indicates later reproduction.

Construction and materials

A Carlton House desk or writing table is a D-shaped library table with an additional curved tier of drawers, pigeon holes and spaces for books. It is made in two parts: the table base and the D-shaped curving upper part, the back of which should be flat and only curved on the wings. The overall design, so typical of early Regency furniture, is composed of flat planes on the horizontal and stepped or curved lines on the vertical. They are large pieces of furniture, often measuring well over five feet in width, but because of their long low lines, are not overpowering.

Detail

In that they were described as 'ladies' writing tables they are almost the only exception to the rule that writing and library furniture of the period was usually plain and dark. Carlton House desks could almost be termed frivolous were it not for their solidity and excellent craftsmanship. The grandest follow the French bureau-plat tendency to gilt mounts and ormolu, but the finest rely on delicate swags and foliate inlay and the dexterous use of contrasting veneers.

The late eighteenth century delight in hidden features occasionally shows itself in some of these desks where the central block of pigeon holes and drawers slides forward towards the writer. William IV period desks have a tendency to be over-ornate, and many Victorian furniture manufacturers could not leave a good design alone, but gave added height to the central back section, so that the stepped or concave curving sides appear weak and the horizontal line is broken.

Variations

These grand 'salon' pieces had no country-made counterparts. The nearest being large rent tables, usually constructed without any superstructure, used in estate managers' offices. There also exist many cross breeds between the high chiffonier and the Carlton House desk, plainly made in solid mahogany, but in no way country pieces of furniture.

This period overlaps that of the many well-made designs for solid suburban homes, often simplified or adapted from grander pieces of furniture.

Left: *a simpler version, c.1820, made in rosewood, with spindle-turned legs, lion's mask handles to main drawers, inset leather writing surface and decorated with brass beading and gallery.*

Reproductions

Nineteenth century

Once the Carlton House desk had joined the repertoire of English furniture, it was made continuously through to the end of the nineteenth century, particularly in the period c.1860–85 when there was a revival in popularity of both Regency styles and pale-coloured veneers. The Victorian tendency to alter the design has already been mentioned, and taller Carlton House desks were made for a considerable period, alongside the classic design.

The line between 'late original' and 'early reproduction' is almost impossible to define, except from the poorer quality of both materials and craftsmanship of the reproduction: some Edwardian copies were also made with painted decoration and cheaper 'simulated satinwood' veneer, usually birch. Until relatively recently these writing desks have been out of favour, but now that their popularity is again increasing it has become a commercial proposition to restore and refurbish many poorer-quality pieces so that they can take their place spuriously among the originals.

Price bands

Early nineteenth century with simple decoration: £12,000–18,000. (Highly decorated pieces of this age are more expensive.)

Ornate, high quality satinwood copies, late nineteenth century: £7,000–10,000.

Rosewood c.1820: £3,000–5,000.

Edwardian reproduction: £1,800–2,200.

Davenport

Historical background

During the last 30 years of the eighteenth-century, there was a proliferation of writing furniture which was sufficiently elegant in design and compact in construction to be used in rooms other than the library. The most popular pieces were small writing cabinets on slender legs, though these were intended only as receptacles for writing materials rather than to be written at. Typical of these was the 'bonheur du jour'.

All these elegant little pieces were fragile and those that have survived are, almost without exception, restored. A more solid and enduring piece of furniture was the Davenport, an unusually low, solidly made desk, generally assumed to have been made specifically for ladies. In fact the design was initiated by Gillows of Lancaster who made it at the request of a certain Captain Davenport at the end of the eighteenth century. The basic design proved so popular that Davenports were made in many variations throughout the nineteenth century.

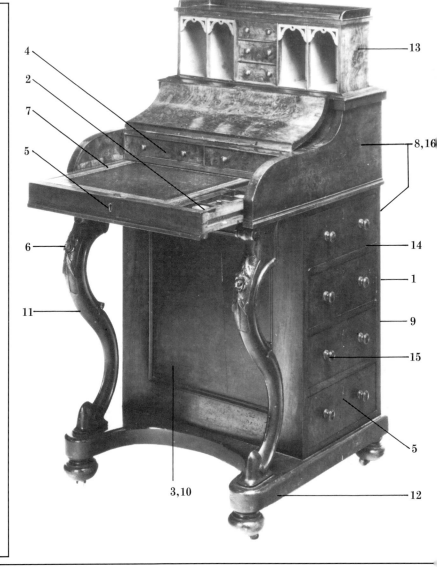

Construction and materials

Davenports were made in solid mahogany, rosewood and imported walnut as well as a wide variety of veneers on a carcase of soft imported oak, close-grained red or white Baltic pine or American softwood. The most characteristic feature of all these sturdy desks is symmetry: sham drawers on one side match drawers on the opposite side, or doors conceal recessed drawers to match the flush side.

Some versions had sliding tops that pulled forward over the knees, while others had a writing desk supported on plain or ornate pillars on either side of the kneehole. Ingenious drawers and slides concealed on either side of the writing slope pulled out to reveal fitted compartments for inkwells and writing materials. Davenports were freestanding and were veneered and finished on all sides.

Later versions had plinth bases or bun feet whereas the earlier Gillow-type designs stood on four small feet. From c.1800 many of them were fitted with castors.

Detail

More ostentatious, florid designs were introduced during the Victorian period, including the piano top, and the galleried rising top with pigeonholes and small drawers. The best Davenports have fine veneering in figured walnut, amboyna, bird's eye amboyna, rosewood, tulip wood, kingwood or speckled veneer. The carving of the base mouldings and other ornamentation is crisp and deep. Inset panels of leather on the writing surfaces have a cross-cut veneered brass and brass stringing, restrained in the earlier versions and more ornate in later ones.

Variations

Variations of the basic Davenport design were made all over the country during the nineteenth century and, with increasing mass-production, the distinction between town and country became blurred. Quality was the main distinguishing factor, then price. Provincial Davenports tended to have lumpier, more ungainly lines and fussy over-ornamentation.

Cheaper versions were made in bleached oak, elm or cheap imported walnut or mahogany, often for use in nurseries and schoolrooms – Davenports are an ideal size for a child. When made in lighter wood and veneers, Davenports were also a favourite item of furniture in ladies' bedrooms.

Reproductions

Until recently these small writing desks were out of fashion and could be bought cheaply. In the last few years, however, their value has risen considerably with a consequent increase in enthusiasm by restorers to make the poor good and the good better. The problem is complicated by the fact that the Davenport's popularity during the whole of the nineteenth century blurs the distinction between 'original' and 'reproduction', since few if any were made without the assistance of machines.

Davenports were made in such quantities that it is possible to make endless combinations and marriages, changing a plain writing slope for a piano top or stripping the ornate ornament from a base to match up with a plainly designed writing desk.

Today the finest examples command high prices for their finish, craftsmanship and a variety of ingenious fittings. A plain, mass-produced poor-quality Davenport can be made to resemble, with relative ease, an early simple design with some well-matched thin veneer. The detail, finish and workmanship can never be achieved and it is these which should be closely scrutinized.

Price bands

Regency, slope fronted, in solid mahogany or rosewood: £1,800–3,000.

Early Victorian rosewood in decorative styles: £1,200–1,600.

Mid-Victorian carved oak with sliding front: £800–1,200.

Late nineteenth century in rosewood or walnut: £650–850.

Variations, far left: *An early Davenport with plain Regency lines, c.1810.*
Left: *Plain provincial version with a sliding writing top. The Bramah locks indicate a date after c.1850.*

Work boxes

1. Nineteenth-century oak 'Bible box', with early iron lock and carved Gothic roundels. £150–190.

2. Lyre-ended lady's writing slope on stand, in rosewood veneer with inset leather writing surface and small brass gallery – a practical Victorian adaptation of the 'bonheur du jour'. £300–700.

3. A beautifully made dressing box, exceptionally retaining all its original period hallmarked silver toilet fittings. The Bramah lock indicates a date after *c.*1850, £1,400 with complete contemporary silver fittings, down to £450 for less well-preserved models.

4. Lady's work and games table, with inlaid brass decoration and brass galleries of the finest quality. The scrolling knee and reeded brass feet date it in the Regency period. £1,200–1,600.

5. Fitted games table of late Regency period design, with well-proportioned pillar and claw support and cast-brass lion's paw feet. £650–1,000.

6. Georgian night table of early design, c.1760, with a shaped tray top, a single hand hole and two brass side handles for carrying. Later night tables incorporated a 'commode'-type, pull-out sham drawer and had doors to hide the chamberpot. £300–500.

7. Victorian walnut, brass bound writing slope, £100–150.

8. Victorian oak stationery cabinet, £90–110.

9. Mid-nineteenth century fitted work table, £300–500.

Mirrors

1

2

3

1. Beautiful example of a William Kent giltwood pier glass, with broken pediment containing a heraldic crest, garlands of formalized fruit and a scrolling shell flanked by two brass sockets for candle arms, *c*.1720–30. £3,200–5,000.

2. Typical Chippendale design for a gilt gesso chinoiserie mirror, with scrolls and leaves entwining columns and the first hints of a later 'waterfall', pagoda and perching ho-ho birds motifs, *c*.1750–60. £1,900–4,000, depending on size, quality and date.

3. Assymetric gilt gesso rococo mirror on a carved limewood base in the French style, with waterfall, scrolling leaves and swags of formalized fruit, *c*.1755–70. £1,800–2,000.

4. The height of rococo chinoiserie, with openwork C-scrolls, rocaille, Gothic pillars and perching open-winged ho-ho birds, *c*.1760–80. £1,750–2,200.

5. Extravagant overmantel mirror, with scrolls, pillars, acanthus leaves and flower heads and incorporating the stylized 'flame', another recurring motif in mid-eighteenth-century mirrors, many of which were made in Ireland from *c*.1745. £2,500–2,700.

6. Relatively restrained carved giltwood and gesso mirror of the Adam period, with swags of bell-flowers, elongated C-scrolls and flaring acanthus leaves with two 'flame' finials, *c*.1780. £1,200–1,600.

Prices given are for genuine period mirrors which have not been heavily restored. Copies of gilt gesso mirrors were made with excellent craftsmanship, particularly at the turn of the century, the prices of which are considerably less than those for originals.

4

6

5

Glossary

Acanthus

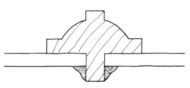

Anthemion

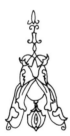

Arabesque

Astragal

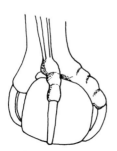

Ball-and-claw

Acanthus The leaf of the acanthus tree featured in both classical and Renaissance architectural design, and was later taken up and used as a decorative motif by furniture-makers. Chippendale used it extensively as decoration on the knees of cabriole-legged chairs. See illustration.

Adze A claw-shaped or axe-head shaped iron or steel blade set on a long handle which was used to smooth the surface of timber in medieval and Tudor times before planes came into common use.

Anthemion A highly stylized presentation of the honeysuckle which was a common feature on furniture, particularly during the eighteenth and early nineteenth centuries. See illustration.

Applied decoration Decorative motifs applied to a surface (rather than carved from it) in ready-cut or carved sections of fret-cut wood.

Apron This is the front (often decorated) of a chair seat. On chest furniture it refers to the decorated or shaped section of the front that runs between the legs or feet.

Arabesque An ornamental design of interlaced lines, often based on a leaf shape. See illustration.

Architect's table In the eighteenth century, this referred to a reading or writing table of which the front legs and frieze pulled forward to enable the top to be raised as an easel.

Architrave The columns and bridging lintel that frame a door or window.

Armoire The Continental equivalent of a wardrobe or large cupboard. It was originally used – as its name suggests – for storing armour.

Arts and Crafts Movement Originally headed by John Ruskin, the movement had a significant influence on furniture design,

particularly during the last decade or so of the Victorian period. The main aim of the movement was to promote a move away from what members of the movement felt to be the badly designed, poor quality, mass-produced furniture of the day, and to encourage a return to more natural forms and craftsmen-designer integrity. Key figures in the movement included designers such as Philip Webb, William Morris, Ford Madox Brown and George Jack.

Astragal moulding Half-round or reeded moulding applied to the edge of the door frame of cabinets and cupboards in order to conceal the join. See illustration.

Aumbry A storage cupboard usually used for food, often with pierced or open-work panels to allow for air circulation. See Food hutch.

Bachelor's chest A small chest, usually with three flights of drawers and a folding top that opened out to form a writing surface.

Back plate A metal plate, usually made of cast or stamped brass, bronze or ormolu, which held the handles or drawer pulls to the drawer front.

Bail handle A drawer pull, similar in shape to a small, flattened bucket handle.

Ball-and-claw A foot shape that probably derived from a Chinese motif of a dragon's claw grasping a pearl. It became particularly popular on cabriole-legged furniture during the Queen Anne and Chippendale periods. In America, an eagle's claw was favoured. See illustration.

Baluster See illustration.

Bandage A description of the moulding that is applied to legs in order to conceal any repair or restoration that has been carried out. It is similar to a collar.

An English **aumbry**

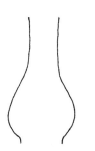

Baluster

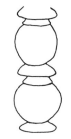

Bobbin-and-reel

Bolection moulding

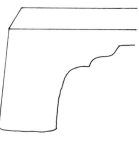

Bracket foot

Banding See Crossbanding, Featherbanding, Herringbone.

Baroque An ornate, if slightly decadent style which was European in origin and became fashionable during the Restoration (1660) up to about 1730.

Bat's wing A drawer pull in the shape of a bat's wing.

Bellflower An ornamental motif of hare-bells in strings or swags. See also Husk.

Bergère A low-backed chair with the arms parallel to the seat. The term usually refers to French chairs, but in England it was also used to describe chairs with caned panels between the arms and the seat, in addition to a caned back.

Berlin work Popular Victorian needlework in wool, usually depicting flowers, landscapes or other pastoral scenes.

Bible box Originally applied to medieval boxes – complete with lid and iron lock – used for carrying and storing the family's bible. The design was later enthusiastically copied by the Victorians during the 'Tudor' revival, when they would often use period panels in new framing.

Birdcage A mechanism at the top of some tripod table pedestals, enabling the top to be tilted or removed.

Block front Doors with solid wooden panels (as against glazed panes or mirrors, for example) on cabinets, bureau-bookcases and cupboards.

Bobbin-and-reel See illustration.

Bolection moulding See illustration.

Bolt and fork Brass or steel plates linked by square-pronged forks which slotted into the plates and were used to join the leaves of tables.

Bombé The term literally means 'swelling' or 'bulging' and, when applied to furniture, refers to a double-curved shape used chiefly for commodes.

Bonheur du jour A lady's elegant, small writing desk of French origin. It had a small cabinet with pigeonholes at the back, a writing surface with fitted drawers beneath, all standing on slim tapered legs.

Boorde An early term for a rudimentary table.

Boulle (boule, buhl) A marquetry technique using tortoiseshell and brass, attributed to André Charles Boulle (1642–1732). It is often loosely applied to nineteenth-century work with inlays made by pouring molten brass into machine-cut grooves.

Bow front Commodes and chests of drawers with a convex-curved front. Unlike the bombé front, the curve is horizontal only.

Boyes and crownes A carved motif depicting cherubs or putti supporting a crown. It was a favourite decoration on the crest rails and front stretcher of seventeenth-century chairs.

Bracket foot See illustration.

Bramah lock A Victorian patent lock with a barrel-shaped fitting.

Breakfront A term used to describe a piece of furniture (a bookcase, for example) with a central section jutting out beyond the side elements.

Broken pediment A pediment with a symmetrical break in the centre that leaves two 'horns'. The gap was often filled with a classical urn or an eagle motif.

Brushing slide A pull-out shelf situated between the top moulding and the top drawer (of kneehole desks, dressing tables and lowboys, for example), which prevented the powder from wigs falling on clothes and provided a convenient and retractable resting place for brushes, combs, perfumes and other toiletries.

Buffetier A dining-room piece with tiered open shelves and carved decorative uprights from which food was served. The design evolved into the sideboard.

Bun foot A slightly 'squashed' version of the ball foot, popular during the second half of the seventeenth century. See illustration.

Bureau-plat Literally a 'flat' desk, the term was used to describe an elegant writing table with drawers in the frieze, in some ways similar to the library table. It appeared first in France towards the end of the seventeenth century.

Butterfly hinge In imitation of a butterfly's wings, the plates were flared on either side. They were used particularly on the doors of corner cupboards and to replace the butt hinges of high-quality walnut furniture. See illustration.

Cabochon moulding A rounded, often egg-shaped, moulding surrounded with decoration such as symmetrical scrolls. It was used to decorate early furniture and was revived – in exaggerated form – in the mid-eighteenth century.

Cabriole leg A familiar feature of late seventeenth and eighteenth-century furniture. Although early cabriole legs were stretchered this was found to be unnecessary as the natural spring of the wood gave support enough. See illustration.

Campaign furniture Portable chest furniture originally made to be taken on the campaigns of the Napoleonic wars, and still in use during the Crimean War.

Candle slide Small, pull-out slides on which candles stood. They are most often found on eighteenth-century secretaries and bureau-bookcases.

Canted corner The corner is cut with a face at 45° to the front and side of the piece.

Canterbury A small music rack, popular with Victorians, usually mounted on castors. It is very often found these days being used as a magazine-holder.

Carcase See Construction.

Carver An open-armed chair en suite with a set of dining chairs.

Carved up When later carving has been added to the previously plain timbers of an earlier piece.

Cavetto moulding A hollow moulding commonly found as decoration on the cornicees of Queen Anne cabinets.

Cellarette A compartmented, lead-lined case with a lid, often set on legs or a stand, and used for storing wine bottles in the dining room. Principally Georgian.

Chaise longue In England known as a day bed, it refers to a simple couch-like, elongated chair.

Chamfer Similar to canted (q.v.) but applied to chair and table legs, as well as to panels cut away at the edges.

Chesterfield A button-upholstered, double-ended settee, popular in the late nineteenth century and now much reproduced in plum-coloured or 'British racing green' vinyl.

Cheval A method of construction most popularly used in the Sutherland table.

Clamps Strengthening timbers which ran at right angles and were joined with tongue-and-groove. Their purpose was to prevent the main timber of, for example, the top of a refectory table, from warping.

Cleating A cabinet-maker's term for the frame which strengthens and supports the main panel of, for example, a fall-front or brushing slide.

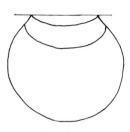

Bun foot

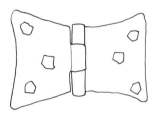

Butterfly hinge

Cabriole leg

Clout nail With a square-cut shaft and roughly rectangular head, the clout nail is similar to a farrier's nail.

Cockbeading Narrow, projecting moulding applied round drawer fronts to protect the veneer. It was used from c.1730 onwards.

Cockshead hinge Similar to a butterfly hinge, but with S-shaped plates, the cockshead hinge was made in both iron and brass during the sixteenth and seventeenth centuries. It was used particularly on cupboards.

Coffered panel A panel sunk into, rather than flush with, a frame surround.

Collar Additional moulding, usually on table or chair legs to conceal repair work.

Commode Originally French – a highly decorated chest of drawers of the eighteenth century. English cabinet-makers produced 'French commodes' from the mid-eighteenth century onwards. They were intended for use as storage furniture in the drawing room, rather than bedroom. Commodes often have bombé (q.v.) fronts, drawers or brushing slides and finely decorated doors.

Console table A version of the side table which was supported by brackets fixed to the wall and one pair of ornate – often cabriole – legs. Console tables were particularly popular during the late seventeenth and early eighteenth centuries.

Construction That pertaining to the basic framework or skeleton of a piece, as against the decorative finish. There are four basic types, as far as furniture is concerned:
Board Nailed planks with flat surfaces, such as in the board chest.
Carcase A piece of furniture is first made in cheaper timber and then veneered.
Frame A skeleton frame is made, into which panels are slotted. The panels slide in grooves between the main elements of the frame, called stiles.
Joined The piece is constructed of solid timber, each element of which is attached by mortise-and-tenon joins, dowelling and pegs.

Conversation seat A description usually applied to an early Victorian upholstered double-seat constructed in an S-shape, so that the seats face in opposite directions – thus enabling the sitters to talk more comfortably, heads turned slightly.

Cornice The moulding that sits on top of, and slightly projects from, the top of a piece such as a bookcase, secretaire or display cabinet. On top of the cornice may be a pediment (q.v.).

Counter chest An oak chest with a single drawer in the base. It was believed to have been used by merchants who not only stored their goods in one section of the chest, but also their money and documents in the drawer below.

Country furniture A term covering rural, functional furniture made in local wood (the ladder-back chair and Windsor chairs are good examples) as well as country versions of fashionable styles, often in simplified forms and cheaper woods.

Cow's horn stretcher A crescent-shaped stretcher used to strengthen the legs on Windsor chairs. Also known as the 'crinoline' stretcher (q.v.).

Credenza An Italian sideboard descended from the credence table used by priests in administering the sacraments.

Crest rail The top rail, often with carved decoration, of the back of a chair.

Cross rail A horizontal rail running across the chair back.

Crossbanding An ornamental border or veneer surrounding the main veneer panel, the banding at right angles to the main veneer grain. It was most popular from about 1695 to 1715.

Crinoline stretcher Another name for the 'cow's horn' stretcher (q.v.).

Cup and cover A leg shape typical of the William and Mary period. It is sometimes also known as 'acorn'.

Cupid's bow A wave-shaped crest rail found on mid-eighteenth century chairs – possibly the forerunner of the camel back.

Cushion drawer A convex-fronted drawer set beneath the cornice and running the full width of the piece. It is usually without pulls or handles and was used for storing important documents.

Cylinder desk The forerunner of the Victorian roll-top, it had a solid curving top that slid up inside the structure.

Cyma curve An S-shaped curve which was the blue-print for the shape of the ogee moulding, the cabriole leg and the spoon-back chair among other eighteenth-century designs.

Demi-lune Crescent shaped. For example, the semi-circular end to some tables in the late eighteenth century were demi-lune.

Dentil From the French for 'tooth', it is used to describe a regular, crenellated border – very often on the decorated cornices of the eighteenth century. See illustration.

Deuddarn A Welsh cupboard which is a cross between a buffetier and a court cupboard. It has two tiers of cupboards surmounted by an open shelf. It also had a canopy supported on balusters.

Dished When applied to card tables it denotes the slight depressions around the edge (usually at the corners) that hold the counters or chips; when applied to candleslides it describes the depression which held the candle, and when applied to chairs, it refers to the way in which the wooden seat has been scooped out to make it more comfortable.

Distressed An antiques trade term denoting a piece of furniture that has been artificially 'aged' by knocking or scratching the surface. Sometimes pieces are banged with bicycle chains to give them that well-used look.

Double height A piece of furniture made up of two separate components – each having a different function – stacked one on the other; for example, the bureau-bookcase or the display cabinet.

Dowry chest Made of oak in England and pine on the Continent, painted or carved. It sometimes had a single drawer which, according to tradition, was the 'bottom drawer' of young women before marriage.

Dovetail A technique for joining end-grain with side-grain at right-angles (for example, in drawer corners) by a system of interlocking slots and projections. Types of dovetails include:
Through dovetail the tail end of the dovetail finished flush with the outside surface.
Lapped or stopped dovetail the tail end finishes within the thickness of the piece into which it slots. It was developed from about *c*.1700 to create a surface suitable for veneering.
Mitred dovetail both pieces to be joined are cut along the edge and slotted into each other on the underside. It is sometimes called a 'secret' dovetail.

Dowel A wooden peg used commonly in early furniture where a nail would have been used in later times – hence 'dowelling', 'pegging'.

Draw table A type of extending table, where the leaves draw out

Dentil moulding

Double-height bureau-bookcase

from beneath the central section and are supported by separate bearers, so that the table remains level, whether one or two leaves are extended. It was introduced into Britain from the Netherlands during the sixteenth century.

Drawer rail That part of a chest which separates one drawer from another.

Drop handle Pear-shaped, cast-brass drawer pull, usually hollow on the underside. It often has a small rosette-shaped or rounded backplate. It was originally late seventeenth century but has been much copied.

Drop-in seat An upholstered frame with webbing underneath. It drops into the chair's seat frame and rests on the corner or 'ear' pieces.

Drop leaf A general description for any table with a fixed central section and hinged, supported, leaves.

Drum table Characterized by a circular table top on a central pedestal. The top has a deep frieze and will often be fitted with drawers, each alternate one being sham. It is sometimes also known as a 'rent table'.

Dummy drawer A decorative device of a drawer front, complete with handles, popular from the late eighteenth century.

Dust board Thin pieces of wood between drawers which were part of the carcase of a chest of drawers.

Ebonized Wood stained black to resemble ebony – a common practice in the seventeenth century and again, notably, during the William and Mary period.

Edge moulding A quarter round finish to the edges of tables and stools, with a slight 'step'.

Egg and dart moulding See illustration.

End grain The wood exposed if it is cut perpendicular to the grain. For example, and most obviously, the end of a sawn board.

Elbow hinge A brass hinge composed of two, jointed, straight pieces which can either be positioned at right-angles or folded together.

Envelope table A table with four hinged, triangular leaves which fold – like an envelope flap – over the surface of the table top. Such tables were often used as card tables.

Escutcheon The metal plate surrounding a keyhole, very often shield shaped.

Fall-front The flap of a desk escritoire or secretaire, for example, which drops down from the front of the piece and, when supported by hinges or chains or supported by wooden or metal bearers that can be pulled out, is used for writing on.

Featherbanding Used to describe a veneer that has been set on a diagonal and inlaid in narrow bands.

Fielded panel A raised and chamfered panel which stands proud of the frame that contains it.

Finial A decorative knob. For example, the small classical urns seen on the top front corners of eighteenth century bureau-bookcases of the grander sort.

Flush-edged, flushfitting A term used to describe edges that fit at right-angles. The edges are smooth and without moulding.

Flush frame Describes a chair with a completely flat side frame, without any decoration.

Fluting Decorative grooves which run down columns, legs etc. Reeding is the opposite effect in which the groove effect is achieved by convex strips. See illustration.

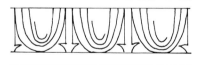

Egg and dart moulding

Fluting

Fret decoration/Greek key

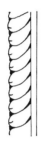

Gadrooning

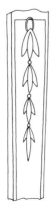

Husk motif

Fly bracket A small wooden bracket supporting the narrow flap of a table, such as a Pembroke.

Food hutch An English aumbry (q.v.).

French foot A type of bracket foot for case furniture, the outer edge of which curves outward (rather than being straight).

Fret decoration Also known as 'Greek key'. See illustration.

Fretting, fretted decoration Pierced decoration or open carving, cut out with a fine-bladed fret saw. The term is applied particularly to the chinoiserie styles favoured by Chippendale.

Frieze The border immediately below the cornice. The word is also used to describe the horizontal framework containing a drawer in a table, or broad decorative band.

Gadroon An ornamental border or carved moulding – almost like the fingers of a clenched fist.

Gallery A raised border, made either of wood or metal, that surrounds the edge of furniture – particularly Davenport tops and some small tripod tables of the late eighteenth century.

Gate leg The stretchered legs attached to the swivelling underframe of a table.

Gesso A composite plaster-of-Paris substance. It was used in place of carving to add rich and complicated decoration. Mirror and picture frames of a more ornate kind are often built up of gesso, which is then sanded and gilded.

Girandole A candle sconce (holder) incorporating mirrored glass or hanging crystals. It originally referred to wall-fittings but was used later to describe lustre-hung candlesticks.

Greek key See Fret decoration.

Harlequin A term used to describe a set of chairs which, although similar in style, do not match.

Harlequin table A variation of the Pembroke table with a concealed rising top that contains drawers and pigeonholes. The top was raised by an ingenious system of springs and weights.

Herringbone Two narrow strips of diagonal veneer, often in black and white, inlaid to resemble the rib-bones of a fish.

Husk A decorative motif, similar to bell-flowers. See illustration.

'Improved' An antiques trade term denoting furniture that has been carved and decorated at a later date to increase its market value. The Victorians were particularly fond of 'improving' oak pieces.

Incised Usually refers to decoration that has been cut into the wood, rather than attached to the surface.

Inlay Refers to decorative woods such as boxwood or holly, or to ivory, mother-of-pearl, brass or silver that have been set into the surface of a solid wood. Inlay may be combined with veneer as an additional embellishment.

Japanning A style of painting and varnishing to resemble the high-gloss finish of Oriental lacquer. It was often accompanied by gilding and, frequently, relief ornament on a gesso base applied to the carcase over stretched hessian. Japanning was particularly fashionable on early eighteenth century English secretaires, clocks, dressing mirrors, etc.

Knife box A fitted box, usually in mahogany, with a sloping top. Cutlery slid into specially designed divisions. Knife boxes were introduced during the seventeenth century.

Knife urn The development of the knife box in the shape of an urn. It had a domed lid surmounted with a decorative finial rising on a spindle. The classical shape of the knife urn was particularly favoured by Adam.

Knuckle The projecting part of a wooden hinge.

Lacquer A gum-like substance which dries as hard as varnish. When dried it was coloured, and applied in layers, particularly to papier mâché in the Oriental style, as well as to wood and metal.

Ladder back See illustration.

Laminated Thin strips of wood with alternating grain directions are glued together, rolled and clamped. Used first in the mid-eighteenth century for fretted decoration as an alternative to solid wood.

Linenfold See illustration.

Lion's mask Stylized lion's face used for bas relief decoration, particularly on the knees of cabriole legs. It was very popular c.1720–50, and was later revived during the Regency period.

Lion's paw A cast-brass foot in the shape of a lion's paw.

Lip moulding Quarter circle profile moulding used on the edges of tables and chests, and as a protective moulding on drawer fronts.

Livery cupboard It originated in the late fifteenth century as a cupboard with an open-work front. Food could be stored in a way that made it readily accessible to any member of the household as required.

Lock rail A strip of wood into which a lock fastening was set.

Loo table A table at which the card game 'loo' (popular during the Regency and early Victorian periods) was played. With its circular top and pedestal base, it

could accommodate six to eight players.

Marquetry A form of decorative veneering on furniture. Small pieces of veneer are fitted together like a jigsaw to create an elaborate pattern. They ranged from geometrical designs to leaves, birds, flowers and scrolls. Marquetry was introduced into England from the Continent, particularly the Netherlands, in the seventeenth century.

Marriage Used to describe a piece that appears to be genuine and all of a whole, but is in fact made up from two or more elements taken from different pieces of furniture, often all of about the same date. Marriages are particularly common among double-height furniture.

Monopodium A central support (which is thicker than a single column) with a single foot – usually a lion's paw.

Mortise-and-tenon A traditional jointing method used to join the end grain and side grain by means of a 'tongue' (tenon) that fitted tightly into a slot (mortise) and was then secured by dowelling, pegging or pinning. Only wooden pegs were used on old pieces, never nails or screws.

Mule chest A coffer or chest with one or two drawers in the base. It was particularly common during the seventeenth century, and can be regarded as a forerunner of the chest of drawers.

Muntin A vertical or horizontal strengthener to a panel or drawer bottom.

Ogee The slender S-shaped double curve or cyma curve. It was used particularly on classical-style moulding and on bracket feet. See illustration.

Ormolu Gilded cast brass or bronze used for decorative furniture mounts, girandoles, sconces etc.

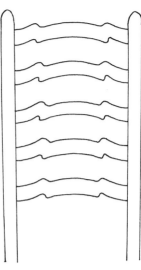

Ladder back

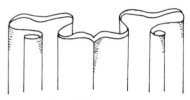

Linenfold decoration

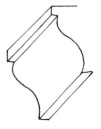

Ogee moulding

Ottoman A type of upholstered, low-backed sofa which was sometimes round with four low arms radiating from the middle. It became popular towards the end of the eighteenth century and by the 1840s had developed into an upholstered storage box.

Overhang That part of a table top or top of a chest of drawers which projects beyond the main construction.

Overstuffed A chair seat where the upholstery has been attached to the outside of the seat frame; also sometimes called 'stuffed over'.

Ovolo moulding A convex moulding in the shape of a quarter circle; it is often used on mirror frames.

Oyster veneer Veneer cut from the knotty sections of wood. The knots, when sliced in section, produce a circular figuring that resembles an oyster shell.

Pad foot A rounded foot resting on a turned circular base and often used in conjunction with cabriole legs. It is sometimes also known as a club foot. See illustration.

Parquetry A form of marquetry in which the veneers are cut in strictly geometrical shapes, as in a 'parquet' floor.

Patina, patination The colour and texture that wood acquires naturally as a consequence of years of handling, polishing and general use. This quality is extremely difficult to simulate, so it is critical in any assessment of antique furniture.

Pedestal A term applied to furniture such as desks that stand on columns which contain drawers or cupboards, rather than on legs.

Pediment Originally an architectural term which, when applied to furniture, refers to the triangular element which surmounts the cornice of a cabinet, bookcase, secretaire etc.

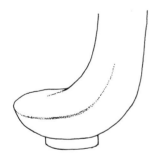

Pad foot

Pegged Early furniture, such as trestle tables and chests, were held together with wooden dowels, or pegs.

Piano top A curved, lidded top which resembles a piano's keyboard lid. It is often found on Davenports.

Pier glass A particularly tall mirror in what was often a highly decorative frame. It hung on the wall between windows, very often with a table directly beneath it.

Pin hinge The interlocking knuckles of the hinge were held together by a small rod or pin.

Plate stay Thin fillets of wood were attached towards the front of the shelves of, particularly, a dresser or display cabinet in order to hold plates vertical.

Plinth base The base of a piece that does not have feet.

Plinth moulding A built-up moulding resembling a classical plinth – in other words stepped, and usually square-sectioned.

Plumbago Fanciful eighteenth-century word for plum wood used as an inlay or veneer.

Prie-dieu An exceptionally high-backed chair with very short legs on which to kneel during prayer. The crest rail was often broad enough to take a book and for propping elbows. See also Reading chair.

Provenance The history of a piece – usually documented – that establishes its authenticity.

Pummel pin A screwbolt secured with a square nut, used on drawer mounts.

Quarter veneer Refers to a surface that has been veneered in quarters for decorative effect.

Quartetto table A nest of tables, first made in the late eighteenth century as occasional tables for parlours and drawing rooms.

Oyster veneer Carolean chest of drawers

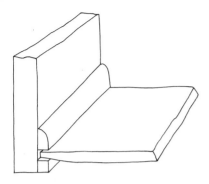

Rail The horizontal struts of a chair or the horizontal, narrow sections of chests, as in the drawer or lock rail.

Reading chair Sometimes also known as the cockfighting chair. Shaped so that a man could sit astride facing the back, using the crest rail as an arm rest – similar to the prie-dieu.

Rebate Overlapping join, often secured with nails. See illustration.

Reeding Parallel lines of small, half-circular ridges – seen, for example, running down a chair or table leg – which is the opposite of fluting.

Rising top A section of drawers and pigeonholes – often hidden – that rises, by means of an ingenious mechanism, from the back of the writing surface of Davenports and some other desks.

Riven A technical word for 'split', that is when timber is made into planks by splitting rather than sawing. It was split along the grain with a riving tool.

Rocaille A rococo decorative motif of rock and shell.

Rope twist A commemorative symbol of Nelson's victory at the battle of Trafalgar in 1805. It is found on chair backs, particularly those of Thomas Hope (1770–1831).

Rout chair, rout stool Flimsily constructed, usually with caned seat, for use at balls (routs). They were not designed to endure and, furthermore, would have taken fairly heavy use during their often brief but exuberant lives.

Rule hinge Fixed to the undersurface of tables and to the insides of cabinet doors, so that the join is scarcely visible.

Rule join A join that has one concave and one convex edge, both with a small lip, so that there is no gap between the edges. Also known as a 'Spider join'.

Saddle seat Relates particularly to Windsor chairs that have a solid wooden seat shaped to fit the body. Ridges prevent the sitter from sliding forward.

Scagiola A composite material that resembles marble. It was used particularly for the tops of pier and console tables, from the late eighteenth century onwards.

Scrutoire Obsolete word for escritoire.

Secretaire à abattant An elegant French fall-front writing desk on tall legs.

Semainier French commode with seven drawers, which were sometimes concealed by decorative doors.

Shepherd's crook arm The double curving shape of an arm rest and arm support.

Shoe A brass fitting, usually incorporating castors. Very often it was a box shape or a lion's paw. It is usually found on a pillar-and-claw type table support, particularly Regency.

Shoe-piece The wooden socket into which slotted the back splat of a chair. On pre-mass produced chairs it was made separately and attached to the seat's back rail.

Slatted The flat, parallel bars of a chair back.

Smoker's bow Low-backed version of a Windsor chair, where the back and arm rests form one continuous sweep.

Snap top Another name for a tilt-top table which fastened with a brass catch.

Spade foot See illustration.

Spider join Another name for a rule join.

Splat The central back upright of a chair back.

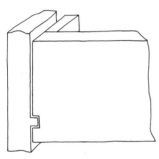

Rebate joints

Reeding

Spade foot

Squab seat A padded cushion shaped to fit a chair seat.

Strap hinge Originally on coffers and chests, with the leaf-shaped plate at either end of the hinge 'strapping' the lid to the chest. Originally in iron, and much copied by the Victorians during their romantic 'medieval' phase.

Strapwork Repetitive carved designs taken from engravers' pattern books and carpenters' design books; leaves, scrolls and arabesque border decoration in low relief are common.

Stiles A technical term for the vertical parts of a furniture frame.

Stretcher Horizontal strengthening rails between the legs of chairs and tables.

Stringing Inlaid strips of wood or metal let into a solid wood surface. It was also used in conjunction with veneer and marquetry.

String of beads Half-round moulding cut into the shape of beads.

Stump work A style of embroidery, frequently using seed pearls. Pictorial scenes were the most popular and stumpwork was used to cover seventeenth-century caskets and mirror frames, as well as being framed in its own right.

Sumpter chest Originally a cloth or leather-covered box strapped to the side of a pack-animal.

Swag A term for a decorative festoon or garland, often draped like a floral chain between supports. See illustration.

Swan necked Two facing S-curves, separate as in the swan-neck ends of a broken pediment, or joined as in a swan-necked drawer handle.

Tambour The roll-top or roll-front of a desk.

Tang A rudimentary split pin that, when hammered flat, held the pinion of a drawer handle to the inside of the drawer.

Taper turned A rounded stretcher or chairleg that tapers at either end.

Teapoy During the Georgian period it meant a small tripod table on which stood a tea caddy. During the Regency period the two elements were combined.

Tenon The tongue of a mortise-and-tenon join that fits into the slot or mortise.

Thumb moulding A simple rounded moulding to, for example, a table top, which has a thumb-like profile.

Tille An antique term for a drawer.

Torchère A single pillar, turned and fitted into a small base and topped by a circular, often dished, tray on which stood a candlestick or candleholder.

Tridarn A Welsh cupboard with three tiers of open shelves and cupboarding. See also Deuddarn.

Tunbridge ware A type of parquetry in which the woods were cut on the end grain, unlike veneer which is cut on the grain. It was used in small quantities on decorative boxes during the late eighteenth century and, more predominantly, during the nineteenth century.

Turkey work A knotted-pile woolwork which uses the same technique as rug-weaving. It was used mainly for upholstery from the sixteenth to the eighteenth century.

Tusk tenon Used mainly on refectory tables to secure the ends of the central stretcher to the end legs. See illustration.

Underframe The equivalent of a carcase when applied to tables and chairs.

Swag or festoon decoration

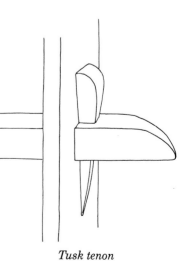

Tusk tenon

Vargueno Decorative chest on stand, often with a miniature shrine in the central recess which was surrounded with small drawers and architectural motifs such as pillars, cornices and pediments. It served as a household shrine in Portugal and Spain.

Veneer Thin slices of well-figured, decoratively grained wood which, having been cut to shape, are applied (usually glued) to the plain carcase wood. Early veneer was slice-cut with a swinging knife blade; at a later date it was cut with a fixed knife; later still, saw cut and, finally, machine cut. Early veneer was about one eighth of an inch thick, but as cutting techniques became more accurate it gradually became thinner – machine-cut veneer is almost paper-thin and can be as little as one-fiftieth of an inch thick. Veneering is a highly skilled craft, involving not only the cutting of sheets of veneer, but also cutting the small decorative pieces with a fine marquetry saw.

Welsh dresser Applied loosely to many varieties of oak dresser. The native design of true Welsh dressers is a regional variant along with many English and Irish regional variants. It is not a generic term.

Whatnot A small stand, usually on tripod legs, with several circular shelves in graduated sizes – the largest furthest down the pedestal. It was used for the display of small ornaments.

Wine cooler Less grand version of a cellarette, often brass-bound and lead or zinc lined. Bottles were stored in it in the dining room.

X-frame Carolean and Commonwealth chairs and stools often had two curved, X-shaped frames which formed the back and front legs with a slung seat, often of leather, between. The term can also be applied to the end supports of rudimentary trestle tables.

X-stretcher Typical of the William and Mary period. The stands on which stood chests as well as chairs had a sinuous, flat, curved stretcher, sometimes with a decorative finial at the crossover point.

Bibliography

Anscombe, I. and Gere C., *Arts and Crafts in Britain and America*, 1978.

Aronson, Joseph, *The Encyclopedia of Furniture*, London, 1966.

Aslin, Elizabeth, *Nineteenth Century English Furniture*, London, 1962.

Bossoglia, Rossana, *Art Nouveau: Revolution in Interior Design*, London, 1973.

Chinnery, Victor, *Oak Furniture, the British Tradition*, 1980.

Coleridge, Anthony, *Chippendale Furniture: the Work of Thomas Chippendale and his Contemporaries in the Rococo Style*, London, 1968.

Edwards, Ralph and Macquoid, Percy, *The Dictionary of English Furniture from the Middle Ages to the Georgian Period*, London, 1954, (abridged), 1979.

Edwards, Ralph, *Sheraton Furniture Designs*, London, 1962. *Hepplewhite Furniture Designs*, London, 1955. *English Chairs*, HMSO, 1978.

Fastnedge, Ralph, *English Furniture Styles from 1500–1830*, London, 1962. *Regency Furniture*, London, 1965.

Fleming, John, *The Penguin Dictionary of Decorative Arts*, London, 1977.

Field, Rachael, *The Which? Guide to Buying Antiques*, London, 1982; revised, 1983.

Fitzmaurice Mills, John, *The Genuine Article*, London, 1979. *How to Detect Fake Antiques*, London, 1972.

Gilbert, Christopher, *Late Georgian and Regency Furniture*, Feltham, 1972. *The Life & Work of Thomas Chippendale,* London, 1978.

Gloag, John, *A Shorter Dictionary of English Furniture*, London, 1964. *The Englishman's Chair*, London, 1964.

Harris, Eileen, *The Furniture of Robert Adam*, London, 1963.

Harris, John, *Regency Furniture Designs 1803–1826*, London, 1961.

Hughes, Therle, *The Country Life Collectors' Pocket Book of Furniture*, 7th edition, 1980. *Cottage Antiques*, London, 1967. *Old English Furniture*, 1963.

Jourdain, M., *Regency Furniture 1795–1830*, London, 1965.

Joel, David, *Furniture Design Set Free*, London, 1969.

Joy, Edward T., *Walnut Furniture: Connoisseur's Guide to Antique Furniture*, London, 1969. *English Furniture 1800–1851*, London, 1962. *Antique English Furniture*, London, 1981. *Pictorial History of British Nineteenth Century Furniture Designs*, London, 1980.

Kenworthy Browne, John, *Chippendale and his Contemporaries*, London, 1973.

Lucie-Smith, E., *Furniture: A Concise History*, London, 1981.

Macquoid, P., *A History of English Furniture*, reprinted 1972.

Molesworth, H. D., and Kenworthy Browne, J., *Three Centuries of Furniture in Colour*, London, 1972.

Musgrave, Clifford, *Adam and Hepplewhite and other Neo-Classical Furniture*, London, 1966.

Nickerson, David, *English Furniture of the Eighteenth Century*, London, 1963.

Page, M., *Furniture Designed by Architects*, London, 1980.

Osborne, Harold, *The Oxford Companion to the Decorative Arts*, Oxford, 1975.

Roe, F. Gordon, *English Cottage Furniture*, 1950. *Victorian Furniture*, London, 1952.

Ramsay, L. G. G., *The Complete Encyclopedia of Antiques*, London, 1962.

Sparkes, Ivan, *English Domestic Furniture 1100–1837*, 1980. *The Windsor Chair*, 1975.

Symonds, R. W., *Furniture-Making in Seventeenth and Eighteenth Century England*, London, 1965. *Veneered Walnut Furniture 1660–1760*, London, 1946.

Tomlin, Maurice, *English Furniture: an Illustrated Handbook*, 1974.

Toller, Jane, *Country Furniture*, Newton Abbot, 1973.

Ward Jackson, Peter, *English Furniture Designs of the Eighteenth Century*, HMSO, 1958.

Wills, Geoffrey, *English Furniture 1550–1760*, 1971. *English Furniture 1760–1900*, 1969.

Wolsey, S. W. and Luff, R. W. P., *Furniture in England: The Age of the Joiner*, London, 1969.

Index